CINEMA

To my friends from *L'Art du cinéma,* and to my son, André Balso-Badiou, in particular.

CINEMA

ALAIN BADIOU

Texts selected and
introduced by
Antoine de Baecque

Translated by Susan Spitzer

Polity

First published in French as *Cinéma* © Nova Editions, 2010

This English translation © Polity Press, 2013

Polity Press
65 Bridge Street
Cambridge CB2 1UR, UK

Polity Press
350 Main Street
Malden, MA 02148, USA

ISBN-13: 978-0-7456-5567-3 (hardback)
ISBN-13: 978-0-7456-5568-0 (paperback)

A catalogue record for this book is available from the British Library.

Typeset in 10.5 on 12 pt Sabon
by Toppan Best-set Premedia Limited
Printed and bound in Great Britain by MPG Books Group Limited, Bodmin, Cornwall

For permissions, please see Acknowledgments page.

The publisher has used its best endeavors to ensure that the URLs for external websites referred to in this book are correct and active at the time of going to press. However, the publisher has no responsibility for the websites and can make no guarantee that a site will remain live or that the content is or will remain appropriate.

Every effort has been made to trace all copyright holders, but if any have been inadvertently overlooked the publisher will be pleased to include any necessary credits in any subsequent reprint or edition.

For further information on Polity, visit our website: www.politybooks.com

CONTENTS

CONTENTS

CONTENTS

ACKNOWLEDGMENTS

Chapter 14 is an excerpt from Bruno Bosteels' translation "Rhapsody for the Theatre: A Short Philosophical Treatise," in *Theatre Survey*, 49: 2 (2008), pp. 187–238. Copyright American Society for Theatre Research, and reproduced with permission of Cambridge University Press.

Chapters 15 and 16, with slight modifications, are from "The False Movements of Cinema," in Alain Badiou, *Handbook of Inaesthetics*, trans. Alberto Toscano, pp. 78–88. Copyright 2005 by the Board of Trustees of the Leland Stanford Jr. University for the translation. All rights reserved. Reproduced with the permission of Stanford University Press.

Chapter 21 was translated as "Philosophy and Cinema," in Alain Badiou, *Infinite Thought: Truth and the Return to Philosophy*, eds. and trans. Oliver Feltham and Justin Clemens (London and New York: Continuum, 2005), pp. 83–95. The slightly revised translation is reprinted with the kind permission of Bloomsbury Publishing Plc.

Chapter 26, with minor revisions, is Alberto Toscano's translation "Dialectics of the Fable," in *Science Fiction Film and Television* 1: 1 (2008), pp. 15–23, Liverpool University Press.

FOREWORD

"Cinema is a Thinking Whose Products are the Real"

For Alain Badiou, cinema is an education, an art of living, and a thinking. He has written of his relationship with "the seventh art" in about thirty different texts, dating from the late 1950s to the present. This in itself amounts to a comprehensive vision and interpretation of cinema, even if most of these articles deal with individual films or groups thereof. Such an approach is in fact one of the characteristic features of Badiou's thought: thinking on a case-by-case basis, deriving a whole system from one particular work of art considered in its specificity. As a result, these texts offer a wide-ranging survey of the cinema of the past fifty years, from filmmakers of modernity (Murnau, Antonioni, Oliveira, Tati, Godard) to a few contemporary American films (*The Matrix*, *Magnolia*, *A Perfect World*), by way of a few unique experiments (Guy Debord, the cinema of '68, the militant films of the Groupe Foudre, and so on).

Like quite a few thinkers of his generation (Rancière, Genette, and Deleuze, for example), Alain Badiou was brought up from an early age on the cinema as a vector of thought. His cinephilia was boundless, and he turned to writing about it right from his student days, when he contributed to *Vin nouveau*, the journal of young leftist Catholics at the École Normale Supérieure, in 1957. Beginning with his ambitious, important first text, "Cinematic Culture," a few specific ideas emerged that would run throughout his subsequent work: cinema does justice to the human figure inscribed in the contemporary world; cinema considered in terms of its "subjugating" relationship with the other arts; cinema as an imaginary voyage and a thinking of the Other. With his turn to militant commitment and a political philosophy, Badiou pursued his critical work, contributing to *La Feuille foudre* and *L'Imparnassien* in the 1970s and early 1980s. The latter were militant journals in which a judgment was issued, the

ix

judgment of a political tribunal of sorts. The verdict would come down: such-and-such a film was "revisionist," or such-and-such films merited more respect and consideration. In the line of fire were the French leftist fiction films, while among the few filmmakers admired enough to be spared the sentence were Bresson and Godard.

In 1981, along with Natacha Michel, Badiou founded the biweekly journal *Le Perroquet*, the intellectual core of anti-Mitterrandism, and for ten years staked out an altogether remarkable critical itinerary in a number of articles he wrote about films of interest to him. Some highly stimulating analyses of the features of the French comedy film, the filmmakers of "the second modernity" (Godard time and again), and Swiss cinema as the emblem of "cinematic neutrality" are also worth noting.

These were followed by more extensive, theoretical texts, published over the past fifteen years in the journal *L'Art du cinéma* as a rule and written in clear, simple language – one of the hallmarks of Badiou's philosophical writing style – on "the dialectics of the fable," film as a "philosophical machine," and cinema as a "democratic emblem." In these essays, the philosopher develops the idea of cinema as a "producer of a truth of the contemporary world" and of film as a "sensible configuration of the truth of the world." Films think, and it is the task of the philosopher to see them and transcribe that thinking: What is the subject to which the film gives expressive form? This is the question at the root of Badiou's thinking about cinema. In many of these texts, cinema becomes an impure art cannibalizing its times, the other arts, and people – a major art precisely because it is the locus of the indiscernibility between art and non-art. It is all this, explains Alain Badiou in a clear and irrefutable way, that makes cinema the social and political art par excellence, the best indicator of a civilization, as were Greek tragedy, the *bildungsroman*, and the operetta in their respective eras. Last but not least, included in this book is the text of a seminar given by Alain Badiou in Buenos Aires in 2003, "Cinema as Philosophical Experimentation," in which he develops his thinking of cinema at length and in great detail, illustrating it with many new examples from Mizoguchi, Ozu, Rossellini, Visconti, Hitchcock, Godard, Lang, Hawks, and Anthony Mann. This text can be read as a veritable manifesto of cinema as conceived by Alain Badiou.

Antoine de Baecque

"CINEMA HAS GIVEN ME SO MUCH"

An Interview with Alain Badiou by Antoine de Baecque[1]

The first thing that struck me when I was assembling all your texts on cinema for this volume is how spread out over time they are, as if the cinema had accompanied you throughout your entire intellectual life. The last text, on Clint Eastwood, dates from 2010; the first, "Cinematic Culture," was published in June 1957 in the journal Vin nouveau, *when you were twenty years old. Cinema would seem to be a very important art in your education.*

Cinema has played an essential role in my existence and my apprenticeship of life and ideas. I'm all the more convinced of this because, even though that first published text dates from when I was twenty, I'd already been involved with cinema before then, having participated in and run that organization which was so invaluable back then, the high school cinema club. First in tenth grade and then in eleventh, I frequently took part in commenting on the film being shown. Cinema's presence in my life goes way back and has been geared for ages toward the idea that it's something other than mere entertainment. I remember a lecture I gave at age eighteen in Toulouse, when I was in my first year of the preparatory class for entrance into the École Normale Supérieure. It was a lecture on Orson Welles' *Othello* and had to do with the relationship between cinema and the other arts. I boldly argued that Welles' film was on a par with Shakespeare. I was fascinated by Welles' voice, which I thought was cinematic in and of itself. When I became a student at the École Normale Supérieure, the Cinémathèque française was only a few dozen meters away, on the rue d'Ulm, and I used to go there nearly every night. I had the feeling that, of all the arts, cinema was the one that really guided your entry into the contemporary world, and, basically, something like my own delayed entry into the century. At the

Cinémathèque I of course began seeing the films of Stroheim, Griffith, and Chaplin, which Henri Langlois[2] projected in abundance. And at the same time as I was going to see those movies I was also going to museums, concerts, and operas.

But these apprenticeship experiences are not all the same: films, even the classics of the silent era, afford an idea of the world that is always contemporary, something that's no longer provided by a Tintoretto painting or a Beethoven quartet. I still feel this difference: there's something about cinema's relationship with the world that educates and instructs in a unique way. Now I can learn about the geography of some countries I know nothing about, some languages I don't speak, some social situations that are at once very specific and completely universal, simply by watching films. Cinema captures that. Its only possible rival might be the novel, but films have a more intense availability, circulation, ability to capture the imagination. It's hard to find a Kazakh novel that has been translated only a year after its publication, whereas several times a year you have a chance to see a Kazakh, Armenian, Kurdish, Syrian, or Senegalese film, or a film from Bangladesh or Indonesia, in a Paris movie theater. As a result, since cinema is a profound art form – hybrid but profound nonetheless – we learn quickly and in depth that we're contemporaries of Kazakhstanis or Bangladeshis. This doesn't have anything to do with documentary footage; on the contrary, it's usually fictional films, which are quite complex and remote from us by definition, that are the ones we learn the most from.

So were you a cinephile?

Between 1950 and 1960 I was a passionate cinephile, but a little like everyone was back then. It wasn't anything out of the ordinary . . .

It does in fact seem as though a whole generation of intellectuals was educated at the movies. Jacques Rancière, Gilles Deleuze, Gérard Genette, and so on have all acknowledged their debt in this regard. But there were also Rivette, Truffaut, Godard, and Douchet close by – the first generation of the Cahiers du cinéma. *Did you hang around with the cinephile crowd?*

I wasn't an organic cinephile, so to speak, during those early years of my education. I was an isolated one, who didn't show up on the map of little cinephile circles or groups. It was only much later that I really became part of some cinephile groups, by way of politics, with a different perspective. Back then, I was a perpetually amazed young provincial – who'd nevertheless already been somewhat exposed to cinema – discovering, in Paris, at the Cinémathèque or in the Latin Quarter movie theaters, an abundance of films that was sufficient unto itself. In those days, you could make the cinema, its history as well as its contemporary dimension, your own with the greatest of ease by going to it often. But it was more of a solitary sort of education, even if there were, of course, the usual café discussions about the films several people had gone to see. That's an important point, though. The cinema has always been the subject of everyday conversations and that reinforces its role as a form of ongoing, informal education. In a certain way, it's a very broad-based kind of education, or at any rate it once was: lots of people go to see films and talk about them. That's why you can almost speak of popular education when it comes to cinema. It's a shared art form: we know that when we see certain films, we're seeing them along with millions of other people. But that fact doesn't tell us anything about the film's value, either positive or negative; rather, it tells us that we're dealing with a sort of school for everyone. The role of extending culture to everyone that was played by the novel, or even poetry, in the nineteenth century was taken over by cinema in the twentieth century. So I did feel that sense of amazement you get from cinema, but I wasn't involved in any organized form of cinephilia.

In Toulouse when you were young, then later in Paris when you began your studies at the École Normale Supérieure, were there any films that played a more specific role than others, in terms of helping to raise your consciousness, for example?

You have to make a distinction between what was a matter of cultural catching-up – my discovery of entire continents of cinema, the great silent films, for example – and what I used to go see, with no less passionate enthusiasm, in terms of the current films that were being shown in the nearby theaters. I was enthralled by a lot of silent films – Chaplin, of course, but it was probably Eisenstein, Murnau, and Stroheim who made the deepest impression on me. Naturally enough, it was their obvious artistic power that struck me. There's nothing at all unusual about that, but in my case it was very important. What

3

struck me was how versatile that power was. As far as the more contemporary cinema was concerned, I didn't see a lot of American films, as opposed to classical cinephilia, the *Cahiers du cinéma's* cinephilia, for example. So it was French films that left their mark on me, not the "French quality" ones that were condemned by that same cinephile school, but rather Tati, Bresson, Franju, rather oddball, pre-New Wave filmmakers. A bunch of oddballs.

At the very same time, in "A Certain Tendency of the French Cinema," *François Truffaut contrasted the French "quality" films that he denounced with the filmmakers you're talking about (adding Renoir and Becker to the list), calling them* "auteurs."

Without having read that piece at the time, and quite unconsciously, I felt the same way about that contrast. I had the same opinion as Truffaut, if you like. I experienced the beauty of Bresson's cinema very deeply. *Un condamné à mort s'est échappé* (*A Man Escaped*), *Pickpocket*, *Au Hasard Balthazar*, and so on, are genuinely moving esthetic memories for me. And I've always been a great admirer of Tati, as a comic genius but also as a researcher: there are formal propositions about space and sound in his work, particularly in *Play-time*, that fascinated me. So those were my first preferences in cinema: the vast expanse of silent films and a few French mavericks.

Did your love for the cinema go hand-in-hand with other discoveries, in other arts?

In my own personal case, I remember perfectly well how my discovery of silent film and my reading of Greek tragedies occurred simultaneously. I would argue rather paradoxically that they were mixed up together: Aeschylus' tragedies and Murnau's films, Griffith's *Intolerance* or even some of Méliès' shorts ultimately had the same effect on me. There's this extraordinary feeling that an emergent art form immediately sets a very high standard, regardless of whether it's a tragedy or a film. It's not because something's ancient that it's good but because it's truly extraordinary. The audacity of those artists, who had to deal with an elaborate apparatus – the choruses, the masks, the staging, in the case of Greek tragedy; the shots, the extras, the sets, in the case of silent film – testifies to an intensity of an art form's emergence that borders on an eruption of genius. The great silent

4

cinema, representing as it does an amazingly stubborn and concerted effort to push the art to its limits, affected me powerfully. That megalomaniacal feeling of being in control of the whole universe seemed indistinguishable to me from the birth of an art form. With that cinema, you could imagine you were controlling all the visible elements, which created an absolutely wonderful purity of dramatic violence. That's why I loved a film like Griffith's *Broken Blossoms* so much.

You weren't a "card-carrying" or an organic cinephile, so why, already at that time, did you feel the need to get into writing about cinema?

I wrote for *Vin nouveau*, a Catholic journal that was recruiting heathens, heathen mercenaries! It was a journal run by young Christian École Normale students: I was friends with them, and they asked me to write for them. What I learned from the experience was that, thanks to writing, you could present your ideas in all the different styles made available to you by the diversity of your tastes. As a philosopher, I could venture to talk about cinema not because I was an expert in it but because it was something that mattered to me. What's more, I also wrote about poetry in *Vin nouveau* (a piece on Senghor's poems), about music and opera (an account of a trip I took to Bayreuth), about song (an article about Brassens), and of course about politics. So it wasn't so much the desire to write specifically about cinema as it was the real discovery that it was possible to write about anything that interested you without, however, becoming too eclectic in the process. The truth is, behind all this can be glimpsed the silhouette of the person who was my role model at the time, Jean-Paul Sartre, Sartre and his "Situations," Sartre and his political interventions. That sort of philosophical writing about everything and anything, which was occasionally very harshly criticized, didn't bother me in the least – quite the contrary. A stimulating conception was then emerging of philosophy as an activity conditioned by tastes and interests that precede it. A career in philosophy is made up of the combination of all these various points of view and, in my case, it went from cinema to contemporary mathematics by way of music and radical political action. It's this multi-faceted dimension that creates the possibility of philosophy. So I started writing about cinema there, in *Vin nouveau*, at age twenty, and, with only a few interruptions, I have continued to do so right up until today, as a natural component, shall we say, of my philosophical temperament, with one special aspect that I felt, and still feel, particularly strongly about: cinema is associated in an intense, unique way with the contemporary.

If you analyze that first article in Vin nouveau *a little, the first thing you notice is that there's something of the manifesto about it.*

As is usual in a case like this – it's an article by a young man.

For you, cinema seems to be the manifesto of "human presence."

That was my intra-humanistic – or existentialist, truth be told – way of enhancing cinema's value back then: by saying it was a "culture." Cinema thereby becomes the witness, the vector of human experience, in its immediacy. Cinema supplies a formal power, which is put at the service of a universal value: human existence, freedom. Cinema's formal power is put at the service of the mode of presence of someone who exists, who makes a choice, even if that mode of presence is somewhat off-kilter, odd, unsettling . . . Cinema enables you, all of a sudden, to say: "Here, there's someone . . ." Even the most contemporary cinema, even Godard, if you like, is bound by this law. Ultimately, in *Passion*, for example, there's a way of filming a face that does justice to human presence. Of course, the overwhelming majority of cinematic productions don't do justice to anything at all. But, as Conrad wrote of the novel, its task is to do justice to the visible world. And that's even more the task of cinema! This notion can be defined as follows: in bad films, human presence is wasted, it's marshaled to no avail, whereas in a good film, even if it's only for a couple of seconds, that presence is made visible. That's what happens, for instance, with me in *Film Socialisme*, Godard's latest film. People have sometimes said to me: "Hey, you're in the film, but we don't see a whole lot of you!" But I don't agree, because, in just a few seconds, in the scene where I'm working at a desk, I've never before seen images of myself where I'm so much myself. So I'm pleased with the mode of presence attributed to me in that shot. The fact that it only lasts a few seconds is not the important thing, since this shot by Godard did justice to me. The article in *Vin nouveau* is after something quite similar: to be able to say about a "cinematic culture" – in other words, the films I'd seen over the course of the year – that it renders human presence visible, which testifies in no uncertain terms to human freedom.

The other important idea in the text, an idea that's very dear to your heart, is, as you expressed it back then, "the interpenetration of cinema and the other cultures."

That has to do with the fundamental impurity of cinema. Cinema's very name, "the seventh art," which defines it as having an intimate relationship with all the other arts, must be taken very seriously. It's even quite possible that cinema recapitulates the other arts and – as Hegel would say – heralds their closure. In any case, cinema is always related to the other arts, without exception. Its conflict with painting is a conflict of passion; its affinity with the theater is so obvious as to be blatant; the presence of music in it is more than essential; and the use of choreography is absolutely crucial as an intrinsic element of the *mise en scène*. All the arts flow through cinema. It doesn't just use them or intermingle with them; it defies them and presents them with challenges that are very hard to meet: to achieve by themselves, on their own, what cinema is able to do with them. Cinema uses and magnifies them, according them a distinctive emotional power. There's a power of revelation of the arts, a power of subjugation of the arts in cinema that truly makes it the seventh art. When Visconti uses a Mahler symphony, all honest people have to admit that they only remember that Mahler symphony now via Visconti. There has been a permanent leap forward in that capture by cinema: it raises music to a simultaneously impure and heightened formal power that affords it a new timelessness.

What's so striking about this first text of yours is that your ideas on cinema seem to be amazingly consistent over time: cinema as the affirmation of human presence, cinema as the transformation and magnification of the other arts. In over fifty years of doing philosophy you haven't changed at all.

As I was rereading that text I thought: Bergson's right, unfortunately; our thinking never changes! The die is cast very early on. Afterwards, you develop, you expand your ideas, you expand them some more. Those two issues – cinema doing justice to the human figure and cinema considered in terms of a subjugating relationship to the other

7

arts – amount to constants in my philosophical relationship with films; other issues have since glommed onto them, as it were. Even the idea of the cinema as an imaginary voyage, as an instrument for a thinking of the Other, was also present very early on and continues to make me feel deeply grateful to cinema. Yesterday, with Ford, the cinema did justice to American farmers; with Mizoguchi, it did justice to Japanese prostitutes. Today it does justice to Chinese factories, to little Indonesian hustlers, to history's lost men in Rumania, to the complexities of interpersonal relationships in Argentina, and so on. For each country, it provides an extraordinarily profound and illuminating center of gravity. In France, where we're under the illusion that we live without workers now, we're aware, thanks to the cinema, that workers still exist in China. A great Chinese cinema has grown up around this very question: What is becoming of our factories and our workers? Such testimony about the world is unique to cinema; no documentary-style reporting can ever be a substitute for it.

Let's leave the late 1950s now. About fifteen years later, your relationship with cinema was expressed through a relationship with the political and even more so with politics as militant practice and ideology. In the present book, that relationship is represented by all the texts you wrote for La Feuille foudre *in the mid-1970s.*

The general logic is different: those writings are texts of political intervention. In terms of the general logic of spectacle, we organized a group, *Foudre*, that would both express its opinion and, if need be, intervene concretely in certain productions, in order to create/promote them or, on the contrary, denounce/stop them, on the basis of and within the horizon of political categories.

That's the meaning of La Feuille foudre's *subtitle*, "Journal for a Marxist-Leninist Intervention in Cinema and Culture."

It was a phenomenon of the times, even in the important journals and among the influential personalities. The *Cahiers du cinéma* converted to Maoism and the Great Cultural Revolution, as did an iconic filmmaker like Godard. It was a broad trend, in which cinema played an important role because it's a mass art and one that can be put to use in a militant context. But this militant activity involving cinema is more complicated than people imagine today or even than can be gleaned from those journals, in which only a small part of the use we made of cinema appears. For one thing, we continued to do the work of criticism but by changing the standards, by introducing extremely divisive ones. For another, we used the showing of films in militant practice itself. And we pushed this logic to the point where we attempted to make, to produce films befitting that militant practice. That's why the examples from Soviet cinema took on fresh colors at that time: we realized that cinema, with its numerous complementary connections with politics, had already been of use at least once in history, in an exceptionally important way, at least in the 1920s. There were a lot of instances of such reactivating of history in the post-'68 period, and Soviet cinema lent itself wonderfully to that. Those revolutionary periods, paradoxically, are always periods of imitation of great predecessors, exactly the way the French revolutionaries constantly referred to the Romans. We referred to the earlier epics, to the Soviet, the Chinese, and even the French ones, with Year II of the Revolution and the Resistance. Cinema fit naturally into this reactivation of mythology because there were already precursors, knowledge, and references, and because the films were available, materially. *La Feuille foudre* was not really associated with any militant filmmaker collectives, even though we occasionally projected educational films in working-class locales. We were focused on the first of these activities, mentioned above: producing critical standards, a tribunal for the militant judgment of films. It was a work of evaluation involving discussions, often very long ones, which the journal did not really give an account of since only the final synthesis appeared in it. It should be pointed out that, even in the chaotic context of the moment, the question as to whether a film is progressive or reactionary is not an easy one. It's complicated. It was clear that this was the case, since, when people who shared pretty much the same values, the same books, the same references were prey, so to speak, to a film, things became complicated – and even more complicated the closer the film in question was to political subject matter. The more contemporary the politics, the more important the nuances. Two groups that appear to be similar when seen from a distance can turn out to be bitter enemies when viewed closer-up. Any given details can set them in violent opposition to each other, and real practice, in this case of cinema and criticism, always has to do with details. People always say, "Those splinter groups fought tooth and nail over ridiculous details." No, you have to put things back in the correct historical perspective: for those groups, back then, those details were not ridiculous in the least but rather the very essence of their discussions and disputes. Nowadays, it's easy to make fun of them; even I do. But when you're in the thick of it, you know very well how important details are. They're the thing itself. We're much more willing to acknowledge such a thing in a different sphere: in our love lives, tremendous violence can spring from a tiny detail. In a certain way, we were involved in politics back then the way lovers are in a lovers' quarrel.

When it came to cinema, those political disputes were very virulent. Was it basically another way of doing criticism?

There were certainly a few summary executions, with no real debate, but I mostly remember discussions that were in fact very closely argued, very exhaustive. We'd watch the films, and the nature of those arguments, in which cinema and politics were intermingled, was nothing short of critical *disputatio*.

One of your chief targets was what were then called "leftist fictions."

Yes, films like Tavernier's *The Judge and the Assassin*, Sautet's *Vincent, François, Paul and the Others*, in the same vein as Costa-Gavras' *Z*, or films by Yves Boisset. Our argument was based on the following reasoning: in our opinion, films like these need to be critiqued because their reactionary dimension is not immediately obvious. They're not horrible or trivial films, about which we would basically have nothing to say; they're "French quality" leftist films.

And it's absolutely necessary to critique that fact precisely because such critique is not self-evident. Back then, we labeled these movies "revisionist" because the stories they told placed cinema, in the manner of an ideological mask or a technical artifact, in an electoral-type consensus discourse (the right versus the left), combined with a largely academic style of production. And all of our discussions were aimed at defining that mask and labeling these films for what they were.

Which films were revisionist and which ones weren't?

Contrary to what people may think, things weren't absolutely obvious to us. And there were disputes about this – it was never a trivial

matter – between the extreme extremists and the reasonable extremists. And it forced us to come up with extraordinary, in-depth analyses, which were actually the springboard for the question that some
of us would raise a little later on, in the journal *L'Art du cinéma*,
which I'll come back to in a minute: What is the subject of a film?
In my analyses of cinema in general and certain films in particular,
that question, which arose from the critical sparring matches of post-
'68 political activism, is still absolutely relevant for me: What does
the film ultimately give expression to? Both in *La Feuille foudre* and
later on, this assumed, with regard to any film, that the true nature
of its artistic proposition had to be defined.

We often kept at it late into the night, discussing some shot or
other, some editing principle, some use of narration. I have this
memory of discussions that were totally focused on cinema issues,
that had nothing to do with a strictly political tribunal. A film's
subject is not its story, its plot, but rather what the film takes a stand
on, and in what cinematic form it does so. It's from that precise site
– its artistic organization – that it affirms its subject.

So this suggests that that's what will remain in the viewer's
mind, sometimes without his or her even being aware of it. And
the Groupe Foudre was determined to take a stand on that very
thing: what remains in the viewer's mind when s/he leaves the movie
theater.

*So your memory of that period, which was often decried as a dog-
matic one, a period that made cinema take a back seat to politics, is
positive instead. It's a sort of rehabilitation.*

There's no denying that we'd set ourselves up as a tribunal, that we
issued judgments, and often summary ones, which the journal *La
Feuille foudre* reported on. We were judges. But, for one thing, it was
a sort of tribute to cinema to want to judge it that way, an acknowledgment that it was something important to us, something essential,
in the great Soviet and Brechtian tradition. And, for another, the
arguments exchanged were a lot more nuanced and in-depth than the
judgments were. In that sense, they, too, paid tribute to the films,
even the ones we denounced, because these arguments underscored
the fact that every film was taken seriously and considered in terms
of its artistic organization and the affirmation of its subject. Everyone
knows the awful story of how Stalin called Pasternak in the middle
of the night to discuss a few lines of Mandelstam's poetry with him.

11

The dictator was frightening as hell, but in his own way he was paying tribute to poetry, by discussing it. You can hardly imagine Sarkozy waking Philippe Beck up in the middle of the night to ask him whether Michel Deguy is really a great poet or not! In a certain way, that's what we, too, were all about: cinema was important enough for us to discuss it precisely and passionately as political militants. If you read those texts from *La Feuille foudre* or *L'Imparnassien* attentively, you can see this phenomenon at work in the coexistence of brutal, summary sentences that had to do with judgment and much more sophisticated, nuanced elements of analysis. Within our political parameters – which "put politics in charge" of our lives amid the great joy occasioned by its renewal, including its intellectual renewal – these texts expressed the continuity of a true passion for cinema in the context of an era (Maoist political activism). We sort of placed our extensive passion for cinema within the framework of the era's revolutionary fervor. Nor were we the only ones to do so. Ultimately, it can be said today: assuming that during that fabulous period of time, between 1966 and 1976 or thereabouts, the "red decade," we made some mistakes, as prevailing opinion today would have everyone think, those mistakes would have to do with political judgment and wouldn't involve cinema's development. Because, in a way, we kept French cinephilia alive – and was it ever alive!

During that time, you yourself favored a few films, either militant ones or ones that rose above "revisionism" by virtue of their form. So, without disguising your admiration – even if you considered the form to be in the service of a nihilistic, depressing, almost anarchistic message – you wrote about Bresson's Le Diable probablement (The Devil Probably) *or even about Demy's* Une Chambre en ville (A Room in Town). *And then there's Godard. In* "Reference Points for Cinema's Second Modernity," *an important piece published in* L'Imparnassien *in 1983, here's how you began: "Mention Godard first."*

There were things I said about films and cinema in those texts, even the political ones, that I still stand by today. I could also have written about a film that I liked a lot back then, Van Effenterre's *Érica Minor*, especially the wonderful opening sequence featuring the woman who has decided to go to work in the factory.

Another interesting aspect of these texts is your use of pseudonyms: they're not usually signed Alain Badiou but James Strether. It's reminiscent of the way certain noms de combat *were used during the Resistance.*

Don't forget that we were often arrested by the police, after all. I don't want to play the martyr here but I was arrested sixteen times, taken into custody almost as many times, and given a suspended jail sentence of sixteen months. So it wasn't all just a question of Resistance mythology – we really *were* arrested, frisked, interrogated. We had to take certain precautions, and the pseudonyms helped us cover our tracks so that the guy sitting across from us at the police station wouldn't have a ready-made file on us with the texts we'd written and be able to say "You wrote this, this, and this . . ." We'd each made a habit of having several different pseudonyms, which were used according to the type of activity and writing we were doing. In my case, "Georges Peyrol" wrote political or literary texts (Peyrol being the name of the hero of Conrad's last novel, *The Rover)* and James Strether (an allusion to my admiration for Henry James because Strether is the name of the hero of *The Ambassadors)* dealt with cinema, theater, and music. Although the context was obviously a lot less stressful than under the Occupation, we were nevertheless living under the threat of being tracked down at any time. That was no small thing, after all.

One final legacy seems to date from that period in this collection of your texts: the importance you attach to farce and comedy film. That constitutes a major genre for you, and it's also a potent political, social, and esthetic weapon.

The idea of daring to stage a comic take on the contemporary dominant world order has always been close to my heart. And the idea that comedy in the cinema was a way of showing working-class life, its resistance to the powerful of this world, its potential victory, is an important one. That seemed to me to be lacking in the cinema, especially the French cinema, of the 1970s and 1980s, whereas it exists in silent film, in auteur cinema (Tati, obviously) but also in the theater, where there's a true French tradition of defiant laughter, of pamphlet-like laughter, of laughter as the vision of another possible world. This idea has been with me for a long time. In *Vin nouveau*, for example,

13

I wrote a piece that dealt in a farcical way with the discourse of power on the Algerian War. That mocking-the-powerful dimension, requiring as the agent of the comedy the presence of what I call a "diagonal hero," someone who embodies the positive aspect of the laughter, the force of resistance in it – that dimension was lacking in French cinema back then. There was no longer any effective, man-of-the-people character embodying laughter, a Charlie Chaplin, for example. Yet that's important: when very great art intersects with social critique via comedy.

In particular there's the text in L'Imparnassien *from 1983 entitled* "Interrupted Notes on the French Comedy Film."

In that text I tried to isolate the French comedy film from the underlying tradition of reason and seriousness in French cinema in general. But it wasn't easy to do because the French comedy film too often overlaps with another typically French traditional genre, the intimist family comedy. Louis de Funès is a fairly typical example of comedy of this sort, which, in France, never manages to free itself from the straitjacket of the family film. De Funès owes all his box-office hits to the latter, whether it be the series of *Gendarme* films, in which he's also and above all a father, or the large number of films he made that were based on boulevard comedy. There's a kind of unexploited comic potential in De Funès, probably because he never found the directors who could exploit his explosive, "nasty" side. Only Valère Novarina was able to reveal De Funès' true comic resources, but that was in a text, *Pour Louis de Funès*, and the actor had died shortly before. At that time, however, in the early 1980s, the French comedy film was given a new lease on life by a genre that I was more interested in: cabaret, café theater. A movie like *Le Père Noël est une ordure* (*Santa Claus is a Stinker*) was of interest to me because of the violence of its satire, because of its virulence. But it never went very far because there was no formal passing of the torch, as far as either directors or actors were concerned. The French cinema of that time lacked someone like a Tati or a Jerry Lewis to exploit its comic potential.

You next began another stage of your writing on cinema, of your writing in general, with the experience of Le Perroquet, *throughout the 1980s. You were more than just a contributor to it since it was*

14

you yourself who founded that biweekly journal with Natacha Michel, and you both served as its managing editors.

We started the journal in Autumn 1981 in the context of Mitterrand's election, with the stated objective of denouncing the Socialists in power. It was an anti-Mitterrand journal. We had absolutely no doubt that Mitterrand and his government were not what they claimed to be and that they had no right to claim to be on the left, if "left" meant a real desire to change the very idea of what politics was capable of.

It soon became clear that on a whole series of issues – the right of asylum, immigration policy, the control of financial speculation, France's role in Africa, the alignment with the American model – Mitterrand was instituting a very conservative politics, which was cloaked in leftist rhetoric. It was this hypocrisy that we denounced most vehemently. Right from May 1981 the conversion to a neo-liberal system, which would ultimately remain the hallmark of Mitterrand's politics, was underway. *Le Perroquet* tirelessly denounced that fraud and did so as a generalist journal of current events with a cultural orientation, combining articles of political analysis with chronicles of cultural events of a theatrical, cinematic, literary, or philosophical nature that mattered to us. But, provided they shared our defiance toward Mitterrand, the range of contributors was quite broad, and the *Conférences du Perroquet* that we organized on a regular basis at the Palais de Chaillot, thanks to Antoine Vitez's extraordinary support, included a considerable portion of the French intelligentsia. *La Feuille foudre* and *L'Imparnassien* were militant journals, but *Le Perroquet* was an open, welcoming journal that published a wide variety of people opposed to Mitterrand.

What sort of texts on the cinema did you write for Le Perroquet?

I did art criticism, in the tradition of opinion journals, a sort of "symptomal analysis." Usually it was based on a movie (Volker Schlöndorf's *Circle of Deceit* or Pierre Beuchot's *Le Temps détruit*, for example) and I would explain what the film as a subject could tell us about the state of the world. What I was interested in was: what does the film bear witness to in the debates of the moment? So it was the symptomal function of critical writing that interested me at that time, often in an attempt to understand questions of history, political issues, or problems linked to the then-current climate of public opinion. It was a way of reactivating film's witnessing role, using a style of writing that was free of militant rhetoric, a free-associative kind of writing. So I'd describe it as a sort of free-wheeling exploration of cinema, which I found very stimulating.

Your next "period" corresponded to the journal L'Art du cinéma, *for which you have been regularly supplying texts for the past fifteen years, and even most of your recent texts on cinema.*

L'Art du cinéma grew out of the activity of Denis Lévy, one of the members of the Groupe Foudre, who wrote for *La Feuille foudre* and then for *L'Imparnassien* and taught at Vincennes and later at the University of Paris-VIII at Saint-Denis with me. Denis Lévy is a very important, underappreciated theoretician. He has written some essential things about the notion of the "subject" of a film, about genres, and about classic Hollywood cinema.

In the early 1990s, after the experience of *Le Perroquet*, we had no journal to write for anymore, so Denis Lévy, Dimitra Panopoulos, and Élisabeth Boyer, in particular, and I decided to start a new group that would be completely devoted to thinking about cinema. Denis Lévy in fact had some interesting cinema and philosophy students at Saint-Denis, and it seemed important at that time to bring these forces together. At first, it was a matter of showing films, which were followed by a public debate, and then later we moved on to the journal. *L'Art du cinéma* came out of this, in a cinema context that had changed and in which a more formal analysis of films and directors was possible again, without it being either militant judgment or free-wheeling criticism. We then went into the question of the real subject of films in greater depth.

It was starting from that time that you began to develop a thinking of cinema on a continuous basis.

Right. I didn't suddenly become a theoretician of cinema; it felt more to me as though I were continuing my relationship with cinema but in a more committed, more sustained, more focused way, with the awareness that I was providing a more continuous type of thinking. I was carrying on, as it were.

16

You sometimes even enumerate the arguments, ideas, and concepts; that type of enumeration is often used in your writing, like something irrefutable, something very concrete in the argument.

That's what I call my "Chinese style": "the five modernizations, the seven stages of industrialization, etc." It's a thinking that classifies things. I saw how important and useful it was in the analyses of Lévi-Strauss, who made it a key feature of what he called "the savage mind."

While I was reading your texts, I wondered whether cinema wasn't a metaphor for thought for you, kind of like Nietzsche's expression about "choreography as the very movement of thought."

More to the point, I would say that cinema is a metaphor for *contemporary* thought. I've always been convinced that tragedy was a metaphor for Greek thought and it may very well be that the cinema is playing the same role for the contemporary world: a thinking that's grasped in the mobility of its reflections, a thinking that absorbs human presence in something that exceeds it, that takes it over and projects it all at once. A representation of the world in which human presence is affirmed over against an extremely powerful exteriority. Cinema is drawn toward a representation of exteriority whose power is so enormous that man is always on the verge of being imperiled by it. The standard plot of a terrifying exteriority, against which the hero rises up in order to confront and vanquish it, is so prevalent in cinema of any kind that we have little choice but to think that that's really what cinema is all about, that that's its very subject. Exactly like when Godard suddenly shows the beautiful indifference of the outside world: the sky in *Passion*, the sea in his latest movie, *Film Socialisme*, the better to make us feel human turmoil struggling against and with that power in the shots that follow. Cinema testifies to this in an exemplary way because it's able to show in one and the same shot, as Godard would say, the indifference of nature, the aberrations of History, the turmoil of human life, and the creative power of thought.

Would cinema be the indicator of a civilization, of our "democratic age," the way tragedy was for Greek civilization or the operetta was for bourgeois civilization?

17

Absolutely. That's what I attempt to show in a text originally published in the journal *Critique*, "On Cinema as a Democratic Emblem," one of the more recent ones in this collection, dating from 2005. The fundamental indicator of the nineteenth century was the novel, in particular the coming-of-age novel. And the cinema has been playing that essential role from at least the years following World War II. Here we're coming back to an idea we discussed at the beginning of our conversation: cinema as education, the part that cinephilia played in the lives of so many young people, whether unknown or famous, particularly in the 1950s and 1960s. An education in the contemporary: cinema introduces a certain number of young people, males more often than not – since cinephilia seems to be a toy for boys – to something having to do with their orientation in the contemporary world, the world and its exaltation, its vitality but also its difficulty, its complexity.

Is a film a producer of a truth? What do you hope to achieve when you describe and analyze a film?

What I call my "inaesthetics" in philosophy attempts to say that philosophy doesn't have to produce the thinking of the work of art because the work of art thinks all by itself and produces truth. A film is a proposition in thought, a movement of thought, a thought connected, so to speak, to its artistic disposition. How does this thought exist and get transmitted? It's transmitted through the experience of viewing the film, through its movement. It's not what's said in the film, it's not how the plot is organized that count; it's the very movement that transmits the film's thought. It's an individual element that's transmitted by every important film, but it touches on a form of the universal. Identifying it is complicated, of course, because a film, every film, is a combination of things that makes or remakes the world with an extraordinary complexity, especially since a great number of parameters are uncontrolled. The director counts a lot on chance events, which he welcomes when he's shooting a film, for example. The truth produced by cinema is influenced by all this; it's transmitted all at once through its movement and reconstitution. That's what's so stimulating and extremely complicated when you ask yourself: "Can a film be spoken about?" Of all the arts, this is certainly the one that has the ability to think, to produce the most absolutely undeniable truth. It's steeped in the infinite of the real. Which raises another question: Where is cinema – this art that originated in the strict control, both in the studio and during the editing process, of the representation of the world, and is now steeped in a sort of lava flow of images, consumed by its own infinity – heading? Godard himself works on something very similar to this: the attempt to produce a truth, not through simplification, as in the cinema of old that carefully constructed an image in black and white, but through stratification, through piling up the different layers of meaning.

In your texts as a whole, the director who appears most regularly, continually, is, as a matter of fact, Jean-Luc Godard.

I think it's undeniable that he's been the great director of contemporaneity, accepting as he does, with his legendary ill humor, to live, and to film, all the different periods of his life "as they really were," in all their diversity, even their contradictions, without repudiating or transforming them but rather changing them into such familiar cinematic forms. It's something that's almost independent of the love, the admiration or annoyance, the hatred one feels for his films: that's "just the way it is." Godard is our contemporary.

Did the fact that Godard reads you and even contacted you to play a role in his latest movie, Film Socialisme, *surprise you?*

It touched me. Because it seems to mean that I'm part of the present time, in a film that incidentally deals with all the hubbub of the world.

In a certain way, he transformed you into a truth of the world.

What struck me is that he didn't try to "blend" me into the rest of the elements of the film. I exist in myself, by myself, even if I exist very little, since in three weeks of filming he only kept a few seconds of my presence, twice. But nevertheless, that's where my place is, that's where I exist, that's where my truth is: I'm nothing at all on that tourist cruise; I work at my desk, fleetingly, and I give a lecture on Husserl and geometry to a non-existent audience, in an empty lecture hall. But it's absolutely me, irrefutably me, in a matter of only a few seconds.

19

In this collection there are a few texts on films or genres that one would not necessarily expect, coming from your pen, texts on a few Hollywood films, for example, or French-style comedies — we talked about this before. Are there good and bad objects in the cinema, as far as you're concerned?

I write about a film because it has produced some effect on me. Is that effect appropriate or not? I prefer not to ask myself a question like that, because it has to do with judgments of taste and I'm not a film critic, I don't confer legitimacy on films. But, philosophically, I ask myself why I was affected by a film and I accept the situation of being affected by a film that's not part of the pantheon of auteurs. I like Viennese waltzes and the tango. I know that those genres don't have the stamp of musical legitimacy, but I'm not going to fight it: if I talk about them, if I'm affected by them, I'll try to understand why. Their way of bearing witness to time has affected me, and I'll give back to them what they've given me.

Has the cinema given you a lot?

The cinema has given me far more than anything I've been able to give back to it by writing about it. This book that you took the initiative of putting together, something for which I'm truly grateful to you, encapsulates my counter-gift. Everyone will be able to judge how great my ongoing debt is to this incredibly generous art, the subject matter of which is our times, so torn with strife.

20

— 2 —

CINEMATIC CULTURE

"The art of the screen has been dead since its birth owing to [the] absence of man," said Alain.[1] If there is such a thing as a cinematic culture, it is this very absence that it ought to challenge, by offering us instead one of those languages thanks to which man continues to hold on to and name the highest part of himself. We are now at a particularly critical juncture of the esthetic choice: either cinema is a complete presence of man in its own way, or it is an absence; either Malraux's film *L'Espoir* (*Days of Hope*, also known as *Man's Hope*) is a collection of images assembled to the glory of a great novel, or, as something completely different from the literary work, it is also completely identical to it owing to the process whereby it occupies a same space of values.[2]

It is clear that any examination of cinematic culture must begin with a question about existence. Whether it encompasses a culture or not is tantamount to the question of "to be or not to be" when it comes to this still-disputed art. But such a question cannot in fact be resolved, because an art can no more be proved than something's existence. If, after seeing Jean Renoir's wonderful *Le Fleuve* (*The River*) – in which the cinematic language attempts to go beyond man's actions, to which it seemed to be devoted, toward the duration against which those actions unconsciously stand out – someone were to casually remark that "there were some beautiful colors in it," that person would be harboring a denial that only he himself could elimi-nate, for it is in the very truth of what he says (there really *are* beauti-ful colors) that an experiential error is concealed. My intention is therefore not to convince but to describe, to show how, *as far as I am concerned*, "the presence of man" is achieved in cinema.

To that end, I have chosen to proceed from the outside to the inside, from acquired knowledge to intuition. A "culture," in the broadest sense of the term, is in fact a having, but also a being. It is at once the possession of tools for understanding and the understanding itself. And since these two aspects are inseparable, the inner unity of the having and the being is achieved in the culture. Someone who knew the complete filmographies of Henri Pouctal[3] and Camille de Morlhon[4] as well as how many low-angle shots there are in *Lola Montès* (Max Ophuls' last film) but considered *Intolerance* (Griffith's 1916 masterpiece) to be "terribly outdated" would not necessarily be cultured, any more than would someone who was unaware that Stroheim's true glory lies in his having been a director, who wondered what a tracking shot was, but was deeply moved by Griffith's *Broken Blossoms*. We will nonetheless have to separate the having from the being, at least at the beginning, and seek in film history and technology the secret they possess yet which, once discovered, renders both of them unnecessary.

Cinematic culture, like other cultures, starts out being a form of knowledge, and, like all knowledge, constantly refers us from a technology back to the history of those who have used it. In the cinema there are devices that must be handled according to certain rules; the ongoing improvements in a technology; and the periods of great directors' creative work. "A shot in which the camera moves from a position below and points upward on an almost perpendicular axis is called a low-angle shot."[5] "Close-ups were first introduced in the work of D. W. Griffith." "René Clair's first film was *Paris qui dort* (*Paris Asleep*, 1924)." These are all sentences that leave art at a distance by imposing our own world's standards on it. This language lacking in any intuition is typical of a culture's inception. But is it really part of that culture? That is the question.

Cinema history, like literary history, suffers from the contrast between esthetic intuition, whereby the work merits its place, and that place itself, subjected to the tedium of chronology. Great directors are like happy peoples: they have no history, since what is unique about them is precisely the fact that they appear unexpectedly. The history of recent French cinema will no doubt have to classify and compare the "quality" directors: Autant-Lara, Clouzot, and Clément.[6] These three directors owe their place in film history to a certain altogether conventional formalism that affords them a common stature in the evolution of French cinema. The category in which Renoir's recent work will be placed, on the other hand, is of little consequence: *The River*, *The Golden Coach*, *French Cancan*, and *Elena and Her Men* assert nothing but a "difference." And that gap establishing the work as something different is tantamount to the ahistorical uniqueness of creative invention.

As a result, the "cultural" interest of cinema history turns out to be very limited. When it comes to establishing a system of classification, the great director, as we have just seen, is the one who gives the lie to it. Take, for instance, the "avant-garde" of the mid-1920s. The directors whose style was firmly wedded to the principles of Louis Delluc[7] (Marcel L'Herbier[8] in particular) can now only bear witness to what the endeavor once was; they have become mere historical markers. By contrast, it was in the asceticism that Jean Epstein practiced "on the basis of" those principles that he would discover his genius, as he moved from spare expressionism in *La Chute de la Maison Usher* (*The Fall of the House of Usher*) to the documentary-like rigor of *Le Tempestaire* (*The Storm-Tamer*). When it comes to defining genres, as the Collection 7^e Art systematically does, the confusion is even greater. We know for certain that Lloyd Bacon's *The French Line* from 1953 is a musical comedy (which was moreover made to show off Jane Russell) and that Cecil B. de Mille's *Samson and Delilah* is a big "historical extravaganza." But between the former and *La Symphonie des brigands* (*The Robber Symphony*),[9] which is also a musical comedy, and between the latter and all the Babylon scenes in *Intolerance* there is the same relationship as between flowers on wallpaper and Van Gogh's irises. What culture is concerned with is everything in Feher's and Griffith's films that has to do with that difference, which appears as a mockery of a certain kind of analogy. Only the extrinsic requirements of discourse can lead to establishing a system of classification in which Molière and Edmond Rostand[10] would be grouped together rather than Molière and Mazo de la Roche,[11] Charlie Chaplin's *The Gold Rush* and Laurel and Hardy's *Air Raid Wardens* rather than *The Gold Rush* and *Le Défroqué* (*The Unfrocked One*).[12] The only relationship that exists is a relationship of exclusion, one that proceeds from the work to nothingness.

Besides, "genre" hardly exists in cinema, whose flexible style, and especially its rapid transitions, allow it to disregard the "technical" problem of mixing tones. Where great directors are concerned, the film is constructed through rhythmic processes, and the versatility of the language is in fact based on the ambiguity of the situations. A musical film like *Les Grandes Manoeuvres* (*The Grand Maneuver*)[13] is an excellent example of this. René Clair's style lies in the way it moves from the "allegro" movement (the humorous symmetries of the image: the two women with the same yellow hat) to the slower movement (the long shot of the closed window, at the end of the film), depending on whether the story is imparting its spitefulness or its sparkle.

If you like, style is then nothing but the language in which the contrasting rhythms symbolizing the ambiguity of the real come together. The great work, in cinema perhaps more than anywhere else, is a paradoxical creation. And *Limelight* is without a doubt the most brilliant of such paradoxes. That is why it has remained pretty much misunderstood, a good example of nostalgia for a genre (the "comic") repudiating culture itself. And let's not forget the more conventional paradoxes: the same director, Howard Hawks, made crime films (*Scarface*, 1932), Westerns (*Red River*, 1948), comedies (*Monkey Business*, 1952), and historical "extravaganzas" (*Land of the Pharaohs*, 1955). Ultimately, the only thing the notion of genre has contributed has more to do with problems of technique than with questions of style. It is interesting, but not much more, to learn that we owe to the Western the images of the horizon that cinema has since made such extensive use of.

It could be objected that, if culture is the process whereby the unity of human presence is achieved within the multiplicity of different forms of knowledge, then it should include not only differences but also influences. No doubt we need to know in what way the "suspense" of the ending of Hitchcock's *Notorious* differs from the artificial anxiety experienced by the viewer of Clouzot's *Diabolique*, or how John Ford's *Stagecoach* differs from some *Adventures of Buffalo Bill* or other. But we also need to know, at a more mysterious level, how Hitchcock and Ford, oblivious to the conventions of the crime thriller and the Western, were able to gain access to that unique realm of creative genius that distinguishes them definitively from the mere workmen of the genre. And isn't it possible to think that the historical fabric of influences, that long, slow progression of discovery from one work to another, that succession of tributes directors pay to one another more surely by expropriating each other's discoveries than by politely acknowledging them in speech[14] – that all this constitutes the material trace, as it were, of the shared creative work that great directors have been pursuing for fifty years now? And this has been the case even though there is far more material resistance where cinema is concerned than there is with any other art.

No doubt this is the sort of research that is most fruitful for a history of cinema. But it is likely that it still remains to be done. Apart from technical apprenticeship per se, "on the set," so to speak

(Stroheim was Griffith's assistant), the notion of influence is difficult to pin down. At their inception, art forms, having no traditional language to rely on, owe that much more to human genius. The history of cinema includes many self-taught directors, for whom cinema was just a uniquely new way of expressing the world, their world. These men were perhaps the greatest ones of all, like Homer: I'm thinking, in particular, of Griffith, Stroheim,[15] and Gance.[16]

And if we keep going backward from one influence to another, we will probably always find these influences to be incontrovertible, in the same way as, going backward through the hours of dwindling daylight, we finally arrive at that miraculous moment when the sun comes up, a moment that was preceded by night. And one of the essential meanings of culture is always to remember those presences that have by now become inseparable from cinema's own existence: to forget and to sense at the same time that the eroticism of *À propos de Nice*[17] owes a lot to the eroticism of *Foolish Wives*, or that the scene of the strikers being mowed down in the modern section of *Intolerance* is almost "visible" behind the great staircase scene in *The Battleship Potemkin*. This will help us understand that, if we want to regard an influence as having an explanatory power, it always moves from the indeterminate to the determinate, hence from greater to lesser. If the new work is truly a work of art, what concerns culture is once again that difference the work maintains between its irreducible originality and the whole fabric of influences that went into its development.

Thus, Griffith invented the close-up, which was used over and over by Dreyer in *The Passion of Joan of Arc*. But what matters is actually the dramatized spiritual significance that Dreyer imparted to faces, "on the basis of" Griffith's discovery, a significance that in turn became the starting point for Bresson's quest to achieve a completely inner expressiveness. In this case, influence in no way explains the creative work: it is anti-cultural. By contrast, if the work is a minor one, the influences may become overbearing and make it possible to explain the meaning of the film and to reveal a conflict among the influences to which it attests. A test like this could be applied to *Calle Mayor* (*Main Street*/US title *The Lovemaker*), the latest film by Bardem.[18] There is a scene in the film where the couple is positioned, so to speak, against the sky owing to the very deep focus of the shot (a horizon seen from the hill on which the characters are standing). This technique was borrowed from Orson Welles. But where Welles was concerned, it acquired a very precise meaning: the hero is overwhelmed by the forces of the world with which he is struggling (a meaning that is particularly evident in the scene in *Mr. Arkadin* that takes place at the foot of the hideous castle where Van Stratten's enemy lives). Bardem adds nothing to that dramatic tension of the image; rather, he strips it of its signifying importance by attempting to make it illustrate a conflict that it exceeds. The upshot is that his film is not an object of culture but the work of a cultured man instead. We thus come back to the principle that there is no history except that of minor works.

The long negative path I have taken up to this point has already enabled me to situate the world of references of a cinematic culture. An analysis of technical issues would probably show that, as regards them, too, the basic notion is that of difference. My competence in this area is rather limited. But it was Renoir who said, in the short that preceded *Elena and Her Men*, that technique had ceased to interest him. Should at least an elementary familiarity with cinema techniques be part of culture, given that the creative work is everything that is "after" these techniques?

I think a distinction needs to be made between two things here: the immediate intuition of a scene's merit and the justification of that intuition. It is on this border between emotion and judgment that the importance of technical knowledge lies. Let's take as an example the famous sequence of the murder in *Strangers on a Train*, one of Hitchcock's most brilliant films. The stranger strangles a girl whose glasses have fallen into the grass. The murder will only be shown in the reflection in the glasses. The emotional impact of this technique lies entirely in the strange elongation of the image on the convex surface of the improvised mirror; the act takes on a sort of fluidity, of terrible, mute slowness, and we are struck by the contrast between the violence of the act and the almost poetic grace of its reflection: death is easy. But we don't think about the very deliberate origin of the contrast; it is only later that we find the language to express our emotion in the analysis of the technique. There are many films that first impose a sort of commentary of their own techniques on us, but these are "eloquent" films, in which the figure of style, encountering so little emotion, takes on an exaggerated importance "all by itself." I am thinking in particular of the close-ups of objects in Clouzot's films (truck wheels in *The Wages of Fear*, bottles, faucets, and typewriters in *Diabolique*). These close-ups might be justified if they conferred the value of a tragic sign upon the object. But if their only purpose – as is the case – is to elicit a "fleeting" feeling of fear in the viewer, then the object's enhancement by the technique, even if it is remarkable, is no better than the feeling it supports.

In other words, technical excellence is not primary, since it must always be related to the taste governing it. But its importance should not be underestimated in the limited sphere of criticism, where intuition has to find as accurate a language as possible. Yet it is still only a language, even if it is part of culture. If it were true that *The Art of the Fugue* could only be appreciated by professional musicians, it is likely that only film technicians could appreciate *Les Mauvaises Rencontres*, which seems to have exhausted all the rigorous subtleties of black and white. But I don't think it is true for either one. Naturally, knowledge of the rules of counterpoint or of the value of *découpage* enriches our intuition, but it cannot elicit it.

As an objection, the case of films that have remained unappreciated because insufficient attention was paid to their technical achievements could possibly be mentioned. In particular, frame composition – that way of cutting from the world the portion of space that possesses the richest significance at a given moment of the action – is an expressive value that is difficult to grasp. Thus, some people have claimed that the difference between Hawks' *Land of the Pharaohs* and any Cecil B. de Mille film was to be found in the very high quality of the frame composition of the former. I admit that this is something I was unaware of, and I continue to think that *Land of the Pharaohs* isn't a great film. Rather than being a constraint, being cultured should mean having reasoned judgment, sustained by taste. A technique is first and foremost a meaning. The sequence in *The Gold Rush* in which Charlie is looking through the window of the dance hall, for instance, is an excellent example of the expressive necessity of shot composition: Charlie in close-up, in the corner of the screen, outside, dark and sad-looking, and the window as a luminous opening, a symbol of the joy from which he is excluded. Knowledge of frame composition techniques should not be something that forces my admiration; rather, I should be able to account in part for the emotion I feel by talking about the composition of the frames. This is not a subtle difference: it is in this shift from intuition to language, and not the other way around, that the real importance of technical knowledge, like that of the knowledge of film history, lies.

I have arrived at the extreme point where the notion of culture, stripped of everything derivative in it, boils down to that intuition preceding all language: taste. I will now have to define what a cinematic sensibility might be. This is the crux of the matter, but it is at the same time something that can hardly be spoken about since it involves everyone's secret preferences. I am now sure that the notion of difference eliminates from the cultural field a certain number of hacks, from René Clément to William Wyler, directors whom history has passed by. But when taste traverses and names that mysterious place where Chaplin and Bresson, Malraux and Tati, Vigo and Aldrich all come together, it plays a positive role that is very hard to define inasmuch as it varies according to each director's own originality. Taste is a fragmented intuition, especially since cinema is perhaps the most versatile art there is. Do a cartoon from the school of Bosustow[19] and a documentary by Franju inhabit the same esthetic sphere? And yet, aren't the whimsical appearance of a flower-eating unicorn in the garden of a sedate middle-class couple (*The Unicorn in the Garden*, directed by William T. Hurtz and produced by Stephen Bosustow) and that way of changing a salmon fishing expedition into a strange, poetic spectacle (Franju's *À propos d'une rivière* [About a River]) reflective of the same virtue of the image: dreaming up the world that it should represent?

At any rate, taste, even if fragmented, still corresponds to an attitude, the attitude of the cultured spectator, without which he would suffer the consequences of a fundamental error that is typical of cinema. There is a certain laziness associated with film-going that must be guarded against: the notion that it only exists to fill up the empty moments of a day, like a kind of gratification requiring scarcely any co-operation on our part. But if we regard cinema as an art, then we need to be convinced that watching a film is a sort of activity not unlike reading a book. There is a "decision of interest" that governs true cinematic culture. And, in fact, observing the complex, rigorous way in which *Lola Montès* is constructed, understanding the reason behind those glittering scraps that the actress wrests nightly from her past, requires an effort of sympathy, itself linked to that initial decision, the basis of any culture. Cinema is an art, that is, a presence of man and the meanings that man ascribes to the world. (In the example I just gave it is the relationship between life and theater, the endless exchange between what matters to oneself in one's own acts and what matters to others in those same acts. The camera is particularly apt at embodying this dialectic of the gaze.) But where does the laziness end and the effort begin? Every culture encompasses the problem of its own birth, cinema more than any other since "everyone" goes to the movies. There comes a moment when the object of attention changes, and it is important to identify the signs of that conversion to art.

These signs are, as usual, essentially negative ones. The most important one is probably the fading away of interest in the plot. A film is not a story first and foremost, and the best proof of this is provided us by Orson Welles, who said of his masterpiece, *The Lady from Shanghai*, that "he hadn't understood its plot yet." Once the threshold has been crossed, you can more easily sense the weakness of films constructed around an excellent script, "British humor" films, for instance: *Passport to Pimlico*, *Whisky Galore!* or even the best of them, *Kind Hearts and Coronets*.

On the other hand, we appreciate the genius of Rossellini, for example, who does away with the story, strictly speaking, to such a point that the image itself, right down to the last detail, becomes "narrative." In *Journey to Italy*, the scene on the ruins of Pompeii where Ingrid Bergman and George Sanders witness the discovery of two corpses locked in an embrace is the very story of the drama the couple is living out, of their fear. This ability to abolish the simple linear presence of the story goes hand in hand with the discovery of all the fake tricks that account for the success of a "literary" or "big issue" cinema. The quality (a bit suspect, incidentally) of Jacques Prévert's dialogues can't redeem Marcel Carné's *Quai des Brumes* (*Port of Shadows*). On the contrary, the overwhelming importance of the text brings to light the pretentiousness of the image, because we have the feeling that we are watching two parallel works. The fog, the glistening paving stones, Michel Simon's pitiful, demonic face – none of that is the text but instead reinforces the original facts of the text or, rather, reinforces its suspect romanticism. Conversely, the mediocre dialogues of *Mauvaises Rencontres* don't spoil the purity of Astruc's style, because they are reduced to their essential function: to be the outward signs of the relationships forming between the characters, relationships whose hidden truth can be found only in our apprehension of a visual syntax. In the scene of the party at the doctor's, all the relationships among at least five characters are elucidated by the position they each occupy in the great hall of the house.

In the same way, so-called "social issue" films stir up controversies that are completely out of proportion to their real importance. Cayatte is a pretty awful filmmaker on account of his overblown style and his taste for artificial antitheses. It is not *Justice est faite* (*Justice Is Done*) but Kurosawa's *Rashomon*, with its incident recounted by four witnesses in four different ways, in an absolutely spare style (two sets and five characters), which affords the problem of guilt a properly cinematic ambiguous meaning, because we "see" the scene of the rape and murder four times, and the issue is the truth of the gaze. Finally, we should not be taken in by a certain conventional kind of beauty that in fact produces the absence of man Alain was talking about. The "perfection" of its colors does not make Kinugasa's *The*

Gate of Hell a masterpiece, and, conversely, the apparent dullness of the windows "across the way" in Hitchcock's *Rear Window* is indispensable to the stark, distant light that illuminates them.

But if we manage to resist the easy temptations of language, color, or discussion, what should the focus of our interest be? Here, we are at the very crux of the famous problem of cinema's uniqueness, and all we come face to face with is an absence. This is because an art form's uniqueness is inseparable from its existence, and "what is unique about cinema" is nothing but all of its different manifestations. We have seen everything cinema probably is *not*; I won't say what it *is* in general. Those who have studied the problem have always ended up saying merely that "such and such a thing was cinematic." In Claude Mauriac's case, for example, it is scenes viewed through windows or the play of reflections. (As a matter of fact, a whole book could be written about cinema and water to extend Bachelard's analyses in that domain.[20] Just think of Jean Renoir's *The River*, Jean Epstein's *Le Tempestaire*, Jean Vigo's *L'Atalante*, Orson Welles' *The Lady from Shanghai*, Flaherty's *Louisiana Story*, and so on.) I, too, will take a specific example, seeking more in it than just a definition – rather, a presence.

No issue is more controversial than the relationship between cinema and psychological time. Alain said that "the object proper to the screen would seem to be the eternal present rather than real time." In Vittorio De Sica's *Umberto D.*, for instance, the long, repeated scene of the coffee grinder aims to dissolve cinematic time in the pure present of an ordinary, forgettable gesture. But is there any more truthful time than that of *Les Vacances de M. Hulot* (*Mr. Hulot's Holiday*), in which we scroll through the succession of days and nights? And by the end of the film, the character has lost that impatience for living, which, at the beginning, he had dissolved in a solitude he understood only poorly: these holidays first and foremost measure the slow progress of disillusionment. Where is the truth of cinema? In the crystallization of an arrested time, in the intuition of an ordinary time, on a par with the people it changes?

I don't think the problem is located at that level. Cinema's specific function, its most original contribution, lies instead in the description of temporalized psychological states. Starting from a present that its movement, albeit rapid and continuous, has trouble overtaking, cinema, more than any other art, is able to uncover the temporal roots of that state, the way in which the shimmering of the present captures its own past like a reflection. It is an art of memory, and the growing importance of flashbacks amply demonstrates this. The latter technique, as opposed to superimposition, for example, maintained its expressive value even after the birth of talking pictures. Of course, there have been some wonderful superimpositions in the history of cinema. Take, for example, the giant Iron Man appearing against the nocturnal background of apple trees in bloom in Stroheim's *The Wedding March*. But we can't fail to note that that technique is hardly used anymore except in "quality" films (the king's nightmares in Laurence Olivier's *Richard III*, for example).

By contrast, a number of great recent films – Cavalcanti's *Dead of Night*, Ophuls' *Lola Montès*, Kurosawa's *Rashomon*, Mankiewicz's *The Barefoot Contessa*, Astruc's *Les Mauvaises Rencontres* – are built entirely on flashbacks. Just think of the extraordinary scene in Sjöberg's *Miss Julie* when the protagonist, at the height of the psychological crisis he is going through, "sees himself appear" before himself as he was several years before. At that moment the image brings about that organic synthesis of present and past that could be called Proustian. The role of the psychological state can moreover be played by an idea. The theme of "the conflict between the forces of love and intolerance" in *Intolerance*, for instance, subdivides into four simultaneous actions (the fall of Babylon, Christ's Passion, the Saint Bartholomew's Day Massacre, and a modern judicial error) throughout the story, and this temporal dispersion of the four interwoven stories serves only to call attention to the constantly present force of the idea underlying them. So, to an even greater extent than the novel, the cinema enables the present to be detachable from all the richness of the past. It can even propel the present toward a future that gives it its meaning and literally become an art of fore-seeing. For instance, in Mozzhukhin's *The Blazing Inferno* (1923), a woman has a strange dream that will be completely explained by the next day's events; the visual present of the dream is thus the symbolic equivalent not of a character's desire (as in Bunuel's *Mexican Bus Ride*) but of her real future. The effect is even more striking than the effect of a dream occurring in tragedy.

This preliminary comparison with the novel and tragedy will allow me to introduce a final set of remarks. The surest "proof" that a cinematic culture exists can be found in the interpenetration of other styles of culture and cinema itself. There are films that cannot be understood without our having a sort of familiarity with some other art – literature, painting, or music – not because cinema is a pale reflection of the other arts but because there is nothing more fruitful for a mode of expression for which they weren't intended than the use of distinctive features of style or exposition. Thus, Roger

Leenhardt wanted to "punctuate" his film *Les Dernières Vacances* (*The Last Vacation*) in the manner of a novel, by using short, successive movements, without any continuous, dramatic progress in the crisis that the adolescents in the film are going through. Doesn't Malraux say that "ultimately, the sequence is the equivalent of the chapter"?

Likewise, the American director Mankiewicz's *The Barefoot Contessa* is inspired by the expository techniques of the modern novel when it presents the same event seen by two of the "parties" involved in it. It is no longer a matter, as in *Rashomon*, of dissolving the objectivity of the action in the ambiguity of the gaze but rather of showing how the same objective (and in this case, known) fact, a slap, is divided up differently depending on the psychology of the person doing the seeing, and the way the framing changes is in a sense more revealing than the difficult changing of the language depending on which of the characters is speaking, in a novel. Similarly, everyone knows how Jacques Feyder's *La Kermesse héroïque* (*Carnival in Flanders*) or Renoir's *French Cancan* each in its own way attempts to rediscover the vision of the world that the Flemish or Impressionist painters offer us.

While Feyder's rather lifeless images are unconvincing, Renoir succeeds to the extent that, in the painters he is inspired by, he rediscovers a principle of movement that will become the subject matter of his cinematic work. In particular, the scenes involving the old dancer display an "extension" of Degas in terms of movement, evincing both fidelity to the painter and an original work of art. Finally, Eisenstein's somewhat narrow theory of "audiovisual counterpoint" was nevertheless responsible for a masterpiece, *Alexander Nevsky*. The painstaking collaboration between the director and Prokofiev can at times seem childish (as when a descending line on the screen necessarily has to correspond to a descending musical phrase) but it obtains striking results, for example, from the big final chorus, which is at once tumultuous and united, like the enthusiastic crowd. What's more, as an art of movement and rhythm, cinema in general owes much to musical constructions. I have already mentioned the melodic aspect of *Les Grandes manoeuvres*, but it would also be safe to mention the "symphonism" of Gance, for example, and especially of his *Napoleon*. In any case, cinema justifies its place among the arts not just by its uniqueness but because at every moment it refers us to other styles of culture, joining with them in occupying the same space of values and offering man the mask of his own power and solitude.

There is a little-known film by Michael Powell called *A Matter of Life and Death* (also known as *Stairway to Heaven*). In it, a flyer, evading the "controllers" of the great beyond, survives an accident that could only have been fatal. He is thus alive sheerly by chance and makes the most of it to fall in love. But the officialdom of Heaven (an automated, boring place, in black and white, whereas the rest of the film is in color) puts him on trial, arguing that he no longer has the right to be alive, that he must return to Heaven's sterile grayness. He will nevertheless win not only the trial but also the colors of the world by proving that he is "really" alive because he is loved.

Isn't this allegory really the allegory of cinema? Born by accident from a mechanical invention (Lumière didn't think his industry had any future), it struggles each and every day against the black and white world of producers, of the commercial industry that it is "in any case," as Malraux said, which challenges its right to be creative and free. It triumphs by proving that it is "really" alive since it has its own masterpieces and knows the language of the other arts. And having to prove this over and over is indeed a "matter of life and death" for it. Cinema is a precious part of the riches of this world that must really be called the world of culture, since we have no other word for it. Born fortuitously, and only a short time ago, it is perhaps still occasionally astonished at being alive. And, as far as I am concerned, granting it that friendship or love will prove once and for all that it really does exist. Cinematic culture is still – and this is perhaps its strength – a trial to be won.

Vin nouveau, May–June 1957

— 3 —

REVISIONIST CINEMA

A Synthesis for Evaluating Such Films as 1900, L'Affiche
Rouge (The Red Poster), Mado, Le Voyage des comédiens
(The Traveling Players), Le Juge et l'Assassin (The Judge
and the Assassin), *and Other Films, Either Existing or
Yet to be Made*

A revisionist film can be immediately recognized by the following: its
ostensible subject is the people; its obvious doctrine, the existence of
two opposing camps; and its purpose, to rally people to a vision of
history and politics.

So how in the world is it bourgeois?

The foundations and discourse of the new bourgeoisie lie in
the idea of popular unity. The only things it excludes from its consideration, it claims, are the "big monopolies" – and the Maoist
revolutionaries. So what is the "popular" in this "unity?" It's what
revisionist cinema is responsible for showing images of.

What does the old bourgeoisie show?

In the process, rivalry has come into full play. Solely because "the
people" are now present, the new revisionist bourgeoisie is establishing its esthetic difference from the classical bourgeoisie. In its current
state of decay, the classical bourgeoisie couldn't care less about claiming to be allied with the people. The time of Balzacs and Zolas is
long past. It's all about the soul now. And as for the soul, it's all about
sex.

This gloomy take on things is indicative of an ending. All we get
now are faces of anxiety, games of death, obscure forces of desire,
and mysteries of madness. Bergman is the representative filmmaker
of such people. Even though the traditional bourgeois cinema may
leap into the breach of History to fend off the attacks, it brings its
whole arsenal with it. Executioners and victims can't be told apart
in the mirrors of desire and death, chance equates betrayal and resistance, and "investigation" testifies to the fact that spinelessness,

uncertainty, submission, and moral ambiguity make up the law of such a world.[1]

All is vanity. This is also the moral of Stanley Kubrick,[2] who is adulated much more here in France than anywhere else: the upstart's vitality is itself excessive. Trying to change your class is lunacy. Hence, the pretentious, slick image, in which vapid little men are constantly sent back, by a reverse tracking shot, to the pretty immutability of hills, gardens, and castles. Nothing ever happens.

Whereby it can be understood that the classical bourgeoisie has nothing left to show, in terms of progress, but the principle of decomposition.

When a popular typology does emerge in this twilight world of neurosis, it is so as to perform the limited functions of French comedy, which is moreover permeated with provincial nostalgia for the old France of the Third Republic. Bistro owners, concierges, street sweepers, drunks, little office girls, ridiculous vacationers, junior managers, cunning farmers, heckled teachers, chirpy cartoonists, wine deliverymen, and gas station attendants make up a bland operetta set for the imbroglios of adultery, treasure hunts, preposterous, grotesque murders, and witty one-liners reminiscent of boulevard theater. This backward, shabby wholesomeness, "mass" art par excellence, meshes perfectly with the nihilistic pronouncements whose pernicious profundity is offered up for snobs.

The new bourgeoisie at work

The new bourgeoisie, believing it is on the rise, sets itself up as the heir and legislator of the people's natural goodness. Our concern, it boldly proclaims, is the farmers, the workers, the resisters. Class struggle, basically. We are this enormous mass of ordinary working people, standing up once and for all to a handful of monopolistic lunatics on the decline.

The revisionist films' line of attack can be found in this protest of "the people," which is adept at concealing the new bourgeois' political project (bureaucratic State capitalism) the better to highlight its sheer wholesomeness and thus to flaunt its power as an alternative to the corrupt backing down of its Giscardian rivals.

This is what the Groupe Foudre, owing to its history, had trouble understanding. Organized in opposition to the murky, crypto-fascist psychological unanimity of films about the Nazi period, the Groupe Foudre had established three rules of progressivism in cinema:

1. Show the people as the real creators of history, not as the libido of subjects.
2. Show the confrontation between two camps as the driving force behind the movement and do not avoid taking sides.
3. Start from the perspective of resistance, not oppression. Stick to a logic of the victory of peoples.

These rules were fine for direct anti-fascist action. They were democratic rules of our time. Note that they took a stand on History, not politics. But now that the new bourgeoisie have mounted the stage of the artistic infrastructure, our rules only have incidental power. The "artists" of the PCF [French Communist Party]:

1. pride themselves on showing the people, including farmers and workers;
2. declare that there are two camps (the Common Program[3] and everyone else);
3. are candidates for victory and spread propaganda to hasten it.

Direct democracy is no longer sufficient to turn petit-bourgeois opinion, mesmerized by this image of the people onscreen, against these "artists." We have to become politicians, Maoists.

The revisionists' "people"

I am putting forward three theses here to serve as a guide for the mass critique of revisionist productions.[4]

(a) In the cinema, the revisionists' "people" are an apolitical aggregate, a grab-bag of customs and wholesome characters, essentially innocuous in terms of the question of the State, and about which nothing is said other than that they deserve different masters from today's corrupt ones.
(b) The revisionists' two camps do not involve class antagonism, which is always political, but rather the conflicted coexistence of an overwhelming majority of good, decent working people and a tiny (sometimes even invisible) handful of big crooks lacking any morality.
(c) The vision of history and politics the revisionists advocate carefully distinguishes between:

36

 – concrete popular unity, the ordinary mode of which is the family meal, boozing it up with buddies, male bonding, "normal," happy sexuality, the Fête de l'Humanité,[5] and the full-scale mode of which is the big, colorful street demonstration with all its red flags, displayed in the pseudo-epic expansion of the wide screen and leading to a massacre whereby it is demonstrated that the people united can die silently and admirably; and

 – politics as such, which is supposedly suitable for concrete popular unity but which actually gets played out elsewhere, regardless of what happens, since the Party, History with a capital H, ideology, the real enemy, and victorious action are all relegated to the wings.

The current essence of revisionist cinema seems to me to be summed up in the notion that party politics is purely and simply the *external custodian* of concrete popular unity as it presents itself (in the revisionists' eyes), and that, thanks to us, "the people" are able to preserve their ancient virtues, which are endangered today by the putrid stench of their old masters. That is the constant refrain.

Revisionist cinema is thus subject to an odd function of duplication. Radically removed from the people, revisionist politics only want to *stage* the "popular unity" it prides itself on.[6] For the people of the PCF, a revisionist demonstration, even one that turns violent, is only ever a strategic reserve put out there not for its own sake but only to serve the rivalry between the new bourgeois and the old ones. "The people" in this case are the extras in a play they have no hand in writing, playing a role that is in no way their own. They are involved through the unions in rivalry rather than being involved politically in class antagonism. The revisionists expect their "people" to show off their virtues in opposition to the old world so that the new bourgeois political class can rise to power through a coup.

In its presentation of the people, revisionist cinema is *the staging of this staging*. It creates images of the people as they *should be* so that their sole function is to be subject to the supervision and exhibition intended for them by those whom the Portuguese farmers in revolt called "the new masters."

Hence, this cinema's "people," inordinately enlarged, are merely a figuration of the extra [*une figuration de figurant*]. In my opinion, this is what is at the root of the revisionist filmmakers' fondness for meta-fiction: films depicting actors who are depicting the people's action. It is here that the crucial secret is revealed, namely that, for our new bourgeois, the masses are the subject matter of their project rather than its source – a mere role, a subjugated force, rather than a creative thought.

Should that thought happen to emerge (and that is what Maoism, the revolutionary politics of the people, is all about), it would have to be ruthlessly repressed, because for the revisionists, in the rivalry between the old bourgeois and the new, between the fascists and the social-fascists, the "people united" are and must remain a *politically neutral* element.

Such neutrality explains the strictly anthropological, perfectly contemptuous gaze that revisionist cinema casts on the people it pretends to set such great store by. It is all about customs, considerable hard work, old-fashioned speech, songs, short-sighted wisdom and bone-headed stubbornness. Courage itself is a sort of absurd monolithic block. There is no thinking at all. Food, sex, and death epitomize life eternally.

Celebrations are the colorful allegories of that insurmountable distance between the revisionist political eye and the object of its gaze: the wholesome unity of the people. The Party's anthropologist shows us what life on the reservation is like: sinister celebrations, as far as our taste as revolutionaries of the people is concerned, about as truthful and charged with as much meaning and progress as the description of an Amazonian ritual by a Spanish mercenary flanked by a Jesuit priest.

As for the enemies, regardless of whether they are the main attraction or only absurd absences, the only thing we'll learn about them is that, through their own doing, not the proletariat's, they have lapsed into madness and vice and, as opposed to the hearty celebrations of popular unity, *they* have only sadistic, baleful black rites.

What direction of attack?

To crystallize public opinion and a mass critique of these arch-reactionary films, we cannot just be satisfied, as we were for a while, with seeing false Marxism at work in them: for example, the idea that the classes are depicted in their being rather than in their struggle.

What we need to take a stand against is not just the false-Marxist perspective on history but the new bourgeois perspective on politics. This is because the purpose of these films is to propagate the view that the people, even if involved in struggle, may be a historical substance (who could deny that?) but never direct political actors; that they may struggle (who doesn't know that?) but never, by themselves, be able to change the reality of the state and society; that they feature on the stage of history but, in politics, are only mere pawns for outside forces.

This moreover explains the formal style of cinema like this. It goes from (ethnological, folkloric, or sung) reportage, or from the filmic re-creation of society, to the gestural and figurative appearance of the epic, but radically forecloses the very essence of revolutionary politics today, which could only be filmed from up close: the gestation, in terms of a political program and organization, of the class perspective among the politically active people.

The revolutionary art of our times is not free to choose its subject. In its heart it must have the image of disciplined self-work, of the progress of practical consciousness, of the people and the proletariat, in the political struggle on two fronts, the struggle against both the bourgeoisies.

And this immediately identifies revisionist cinema for what it is: a form of counter-revolutionary populism.

La Feuille foudre, Winter 1977

— 4 —

ART AND ITS CRITICISM

The Criteria of Progressivism

The proletariat, a barbaric class

Art can never transcend the power relations to which it bears witness. There is an irreducible historicity about this. "Proletarian art" is of course something we want, something we hope for. But it can (will) only exist to the extent that the proletariat itself exists, not as the objective masses, as the exploited working class, but as a historical and political agent, as a subject concentrating and purifying its force, as a direct agent, leading all the people, in the general open attack on imperialist society.

Art is at the far limit of a class's subjective existence. It requires the strongest achievable world view. It rewards battles and encourages the efforts to begin them anew. In France today, the proletariat is scarcely a politically constituted entity. It is emerging laboriously from decades of painful collusion with imperialist society. Part of its objective strength has been co-opted by the counter-revolutionary project of the new bourgeois of the PCF [French Communist Party] and the unions. Given such conditions, the notion of a "proletarian art" surging forth from the whole web of vulnerabilities, triumphantly arising from the barely begun efforts to ensure that the class can simply *exist* in its priority space – politics and combative organization – smacks of excessive idealism.

And even afterward the road is not easy, because, throughout its revolutionary history, the proletariat has been a destructive class, wholly defined by its opposition to both the old and the new bourgeoisie, and whose entire program provides for no stable order of domination but rather the destruction of any such orders in line with what constitutes the only true political *theory*, for which this class is a vehicle: communism, a society without any classes or State. And so, especially at the beginning of its venture, when it is constantly engaged in the unprecedented task of clearing away the old and ensuring its withering away, the proletariat continues to have an admittedly barbaric dimension. The concern for unifying the enormous active masses of the people and overcoming obstacles constantly takes precedence over the elitist refinements on which art has fed for ages, quite frankly making the vast sea of excluded people the condition of its elevated status and the oppression of the overwhelming majority of humanity the hidden source of the delights of art collecting available to only a handful of wealthy people. It must be acknowledged that there are serious reasons for art to be constantly regarded with suspicion and subjected to very harsh imperatives by revolutionary proletarians.

The proletariat, a universal class

But we can also say that, in the final analysis, like everything vital and new, the art of the exploitative classes themselves, at least during the period of their revolutionary ascent, captures something of the historical energy of the masses, of the progress of the general movement, which keeps on growing because, as Marx said, "The class making a revolution appears from the very start, if only because it is opposed to a class, not as a class but as the representative of the whole of society; it appears as the whole mass of society confronting the one ruling class. It can do this because, to start with, its interest really is more connected with the common interest of all other non-ruling classes [. . .]" (*The German Ideology*, International Publishers [1970], p. 66).

This makes the artistic heritage of the doomed classes – at least their "great art," that of the period when they promoted the interests of humanity as a whole and had not yet adopted the irreversibly conservative stance that ushered in the time of their decline – a legacy that the people, the only true agents, ultimately, of the progress of world history, can rightly claim as their own, even though they have long been deprived of it.

Class art, mass art. Art wedded to surrenders, art open to transformations. A reflection, yes, but of what? A double reflection: of the contradictions of an era and of a perspective on those contradictions. And so, all powerful – "classical" – art, even if it subjects the fabric of History's contradictions to intentions of order, allows us to glimpse it, torn and folded, thereby testifying for the real, hence for the people.

41

The present times

Of course, the bourgeois art/proletarian art pair is not without its virtues. It reminds us that, here as everywhere, it is important, above all, "not to forget class struggle." But, in itself, it is only a kind of static algebra that says nothing if it is not plunged back into the current context of contradictions, of which there are always two facets, namely that:

1. the bourgeoisie/proletariat contradiction is at work within it in varying operative terms. Today, for example: a revolutionary people against an imperialist society; and
2. everything is relative to the subject (that is, the proletariat as effective agent) who sets up and makes use of this distinction, to whatever degree of consistency it has attained.

Since I am speaking about a proletariat and a people rising up, a people in the process of constituting themselves, the main criterion for evaluating artworks, as far as I am concerned, cannot be Zhdanov's knife. Based on the Russian people's tremendous efforts to overcome their handicaps, that doctrine led, in terms of criticism, to nothing but the (justified) exaltation of great classical bourgeois art and, in terms of artistic production, opened the way for nothing but those pure, powerful epics in cement, the great Soviet novels of the 1930s, a genre that was new, distinctive, and barbaric in the good sense of the term, but cannot be imitated and is of no use *here and now*.

We are working – although this could change in a flash – in every domain, with needle and scalpel. Critical discernment must be able to enlist the very carefully considered alliance of everything that stands up against imperialist society and for an opposite hope, everything that refuses to give in to either the old bourgeoisie's nihilism or the new bourgeoisie's populist arrogance.

I need to define what I call *progressive* works (or a progressive movement), bearing in mind that it is more often than not a matter of a *prevailing trend*, countered from within by passive or even patently reactionary aspects. Because pure progressivism is nothing but the non-existent phantom of the raw proletarian. A progressive work is something that, by showing how imperialist society is neither a natural order nor a closed metaphysical figure and that there are forces at work to challenge and overcome it, strikes a difference with the propaganda of the bourgeoisies.

The key issue is an open popular political space, somehow apart from all the complicities with imperialism and whose possible existence, if not real content, is at least suggested by the progressive work of art.

The six criteria of progressivism

A progressive work is a work that is not only compatible with Maoist politics but preparatory for understanding and practicing it.

It is in this spirit that, bearing in mind the state of the world and its peoples, I am formulating six criteria of progressivism that are applicable here and now.

1. The basic principle: to have the intention of showing the people not just as an objective reality but as subjects. Therefore, to show the people not as maintainers of the old (the people of Constancy) but as agents of the new. To show this in terms of the whole of the people as well as in terms of the different social classes and forces they are made up of, not in terms of a closed (historical or geographical) exception but as a universal trend.
2. The principle of progress: to show the real – whether objective situations or forms of consciousness – as being subject not to a law of repetition but to one of real transformation, entailing not only evolutions but ruptures.
3. The principle of strategic optimism: to convey the conviction that the transformation of the real is strategically positive for the people-subject.
4. The principle of division: to show that, with respect to any given problem, there are always two opposing camps and that, in the people-subject's camp, unity is always achieved by resolving secondary contradictions. Two camps, then, but also two ways.
5. The principle of non-compromise with the new bourgeoisie.
6. The principle of respect: not to launch any hostile attacks on existing revolutionary movements.

The key feature of these six principles is that they are about content. The reader can analyze them critically and will quickly see that Principle 1 ultimately dictates all the others. Of course, "the people" must be taken in the sense of artistic description, not necessarily in its collective meaning. "The people" – in a given historical context – signifies everything that has no distinctive interest in maintaining oppression and exploitation, because it endures these things rather than practicing them itself. Better yet, "the people" signifies that which is *not reducible to* imperialist society. This is obviously a relative notion and, in art, usually finds expression in the notion of a character and even more so in the notion (when operative) of a main character.

It is therefore very important, with respect to a given situation, that the main character(s) represent(s) the people or some component thereof. This principle has been rightly emphasized by the Chinese.

This notwithstanding, the organizing principle, in the art we are familiar with, might not be a character who is a subject in the strict sense of the word. In Natacha Michel's novel *La Chine européenne* the organizing principle is the revolutionary movement per se, expressed through metaphors and with the various main characters hitching on to it, so to speak. In a particular famous scene of Berg's opera *Wozzeck* it is a single note, a B-natural, around which everything coalesces. In Straub's film *Fortini/Cani* it is a text. In Rohmer's *La Marquise d'O* it is First Empire painting. In Wenders' films it is Germany. On the reactionary side, it is parts of bodies in pornography; the flag in many war movies; and the Devil in horror films.

So my first principle could be reformulated in the following way, which breaks it down into two:

1. To have an organizing principle that, in one way or another, designates the people or a part of the people (not necessarily in a figurative or representational way: it can be symbolically, through a metaphor, or "implicitly," or through quotations, and so forth).
2. The people so designated should be a subject rather than an object.[1] They should convey historical novelty, not just oppressive repetition.

Progressive art always bears witness to a principle of *creative disorder*, to positive resistance whose political (Maoist) consequence, even if not explicit – something that cannot be required of a progressive art form today – can be extrapolated without any major conflict through the development of trends internal to the work.

The precautionary principles, 5 and 6, endeavor to ensure that no such conflict arises. Explicit attacks on socialist China, Cambodia, or the Sahrawi people inevitably become the main political feature of a work of art today and dramatically alter the potential progressivism of the rest. Likewise, even though a class *attack* on two fronts – which would equate progressivism with revolutionary art – cannot be demanded of it, it must nevertheless be required that the new bourgeois' project should in no way be endorsed in progressive art.

The constraints of the subject

Two final remarks now. First of all, the strictness of the first four principles paradoxically increases the closer a work's subject comes to having explicit political content. Far from making progressivism "easier," a historico-political subject (a workers' revolt, the Paris Commune, a national liberation struggle, and so on) makes it that much more difficult, since simply remaining faithful to the principles will in this case inevitably lead into the vicinity of *Maoist political consciousness*. If you depict a popular revolt, you can only make the people a subject by identifying what is expressed from a class perspective in the masses. Otherwise, the revolt will lapse back into the objectivity of courage, into the *nature* of the people. Similarly, strategic optimism (Principle 3) will then directly concern issues of communism, and the resolution of contradictions among the people will concern the issue of organization and the party (Principle 5).

Tackling the "big subjects" in the history of the people is fine, but, far from being a guarantee, it exposes you more than anything to bourgeois deviation if the subject matter is not imbued with Marxist integrity. Hence, the majority of progressive works (in the big imperialist cities) come at things obliquely, with characters who embody revolutionary revolt less than they do the people's *implacable opposition* to the law of Empires. These films are more about class instinct than class consciousness, more about rupture than organization.

And now for my second remark, which will be explained more fully later. These six principles have an impact on form; they *restrict* freedom in this regard. This is obvious when it comes to the work's subject, in the sense that Mao says that, to be progressive, it is preferable to talk about workers and peasants rather than about landlords. Or, where we are concerned, to talk about the people rather than about business executives' moods. But it must be clear, too, that the formal organization of optimism or division does not stem from the same origins as that of nihilism or vague unanimity. These are difficult issues, but they can be dealt with, negatively at first: the calculated emptiness of Bresson's images serves to bring out the religious signs of grace. Such a visual dialectic of the sacred cannot, as such, be of any use to us.

The seventh principle: The law of forms

Arising from these issues, the seventh principle of progressivism is connected to what Mao says, namely that if a work with acceptable subject matter is "ugly," it will change (in terms of the propaganda for its subject matter) into its opposite. So, at the risk of sounding ridiculous, I might then claim that the progressive work must be beautiful. Because they disregarded this rule, the pathetic flops that the militant films of the 1960s often amounted to helped the revolution only marginally and only for a very short time.

If the problem is examined more closely, it could be said that, at the very least, progressivism in art must really be art. It could be said that there must be an *artistic credibility* of progressivism.

The notion of credibility is itself a historical one: form, let us remember, consists of all the means used to generate enthusiasm for the content. It is clear that at any given moment enthusiasm is only generated by specific techniques, *which are therefore located in the history of forms*: the history of the great systems of representation (figurative painting, tonal music, the novelistic narrative in the era of the bourgeoisie), the history of their dissolution-reconstitution (non-figurative painting, serial music, fractured prose), the history of movements (in poetry, for example: Romanticism, Symbolism, Surrealism, Ontologism), the history of trends and schools, and so on.

But this history does not just reflect the curve of rise, apogee, and decline of a class. Owing to its innovative versatility, it also expresses the *entire* evolution of contradictions; art's mass basis can be seen in it. However petit-bourgeois its explicit philosophy may have been, the Surrealist movement, thanks to its poetic force, also gave expression to the overall effects, the worldwide ideological effects, of the October Revolution, in the face of the reactionary academies. The history of forms is an ideological product, a resultant. Hence the fact that it is *one* (there are no "popular forms" opposed to "bourgeois forms" or "reactionary forms").

So the problem is as follows. With regard to the history of form, a credible progressive art (but a revolutionary art as well) must be an art *of its time* (but the revolution *changes time*). It must take a stand on current art forms so as to be viewed as being internal to the unbroken progress of art, while putting that topicality to use in the service of mobilization for progressive subject matter.

I will therefore formulate my seventh principle as follows:

7. The principle of artistic credibility: a progressive work must take a stand within the current history of forms and be able to justify that position from the twofold perspective of serving the subject matter and effectively mobilizing both individual and collective contemporary awareness.

This is how my seven principles link art to historical effectivity and define what, within this effectivity, makes ideology at once a sign of and the support for the political struggle of the people.

La Feuille foudre, Spring–Summer 1978

— 5 —

THE SUICIDE OF GRACE

Robert Bresson, *Le Diable Probablement*
(*The Devil Probably*)

The screen depicts what a Catholic writer, Pierre Jean Jouve, called "the desert world," but it is the world of the cities of imperialism: elevators, staircases, the bourgeois' doors and locks, maid's room doors, bus doors, the neon lights of the night, hotels, more staircases. The city – dark beige, gray, midnight blue, made up of blind spots and wet surfaces – dissolves in the loss of meaning. Man in this city is nothing but an aimless wandering, without direction or purpose, to which the strange shots of legs at ground level, with no identity other than the indifferent regularity of their steps, are well suited.

The green splendor of the forest may offer the eye an unexpected oasis, but the scene is one in which trees are being cut down and cleared away and in which the thud of the trunks hitting the ground heralds the spread of the desert. Bresson overlays this with a very solemn monotony, with that uniform, uninflected tone of voice everyone uses, mouthing ordinary ecology's litany of nonsense, according to which the world's misery, we are told, culminates in the plight of baby seals.

In these dead spaces of the night, the young people are sleek, remote, living indolently on the quais of the Seine as though in some primitive monastery: recorders and drugs, silences, blank faces, and stupid remarks.

Naturally, the *gauchiste* bookseller, a lecherous manipulator, goes around prophesying absolute destruction in the crypts, while a labor activist priest is bitterly attacked by his congregation, who hunger for hope and the mass performed in Latin.

After all this, there is the ritual suicide of the angel-faced adolescent, the external light of the gaze drained of all expression except for an opaque certainty, in the quintessence of death that is symbolized in the heart of the darkened city by a Père-Lachaise cemetery with broad, dead-end avenues.

But unlike other nihilists, Bresson only empties everything out the better to pick up God's trace. In a bare room, a bowl of oranges glows with the splendor of Dutch still lifes. Bent over the suicidal young man is the dense curve of the nape of a woman's neck. The tribal gathering of the quasi-derelict dissidents on their embankment is reminiscent of the very first Christians of the Roman Empire, poor wretches symbolizing the marginality of the Holy Spirit at its birth. Within the high walls of the church – it, too, inhabited, contrary to its official function, by two young strays in their sleeping bags – the swelling music, the esthete's typical gimmick, stirs up the emotion needed for preparing to receive the Lord's anointing.

Bresson – and this is his strength – is saying that this world so full of comforts is actually a dreary twilight. He is saying that youth is tempted by a sort of radical absence, which is exactly right. Having come to this point, as the meticulous promoter of theological reactionism that he is, he creates a cinema of signs, of appeals, of milestones, leveling everything into austere nothingness in order to make God's unchanging watchfulness shine forth, far in the distance.

As regards the content, Bresson represents the path of the far right, in terms of a certain reality of young people in the cities of imperialism after 1972: the path of prophetic suicide. As regards the form, it is quite lofty; it is dialectics in its purely structural version. In the night of negativity there rises a pale star so old that, in actual fact, its light won't reach us, however empty and dark Bresson may make his screen, ever again.

La Feuille foudre, Spring–Summer 1978

— 6 —

A MAN WHO NEVER GIVES IN

It is unlikely that you could arm the revolution with nostalgia for the old world and incite people to resistance when you hold, with Ecclesiastes, that "unto the place from whence the rivers come, thither they return again."[1]

It is unlikely that you could achieve the status of a cinema auteur when your only principle is to use images that are "all trivial or false."[2]

Yet Guy Debord's film *In girum imus nocte et consumimur igni* (*We turn in the night, consumed by fire*) is made up of just such unlikelihoods.

It is even more unlikely that you will be able to speak about a film that intentionally precludes all commentary. Debord warned us: "Those who claim to like this film have liked too many other things to be capable of liking it."[3]

Have I liked too many things to be capable of liking *In girum*? It is true that this film comes so close to the real that, to impart its virtue, you have to forget a few other films.

The image functions here as an allegory of a ruined world, our world. It works against the text, whose burden of meaning, loftily arranged in the purest syntax, epitomizes the legacy bequeathed us by an adventurous, undaunted Debord. Thus, the Situationist, at the conclusion of his project of solitude, affirms the ultimate superiority of the written word over the image, a superiority that is also that of the Revolution over careerism and of the proletarian over his own alienation. Everything is interrelated.

Through the figure of the film viewer's abjection, the first part of the film describes the general abjection of the ordinary citizens of our big cities, who are methodically compared to slaves, serfs, and proletarians. This prologue leads to the film's true subject matter, when

Debord announces his intention to "replace the frivolous adventures typically recounted by the cinema with the examination of an important subject: myself."

This "myself'" is a fifty-year-old man who "from the very beginning thought it fit to devote [him]self to overthrowing society, and acted accordingly." As a result, the story of his life, however self-satisfied that remark may seem, is tantamount to the evaluation of thirty years of his own personal political action under the constant banner of the proletarian and communist revolution.

I acknowledge everything Debord speaks about as being precisely what really matters, the rest, practically all the rest, being only irrelevant debris. And I acknowledge this all the more since, with the exception of cities – Paris, which Debord says no longer exists; Florence, from which he was banned, like Dante; Venice, where everything ends and begins again – there is no mention in the film of any of the major events or places of the period. We thus go right to the temporal heart of things owing to their lack of a surface. In this respect, Debord is the anti-journalist par excellence.

Debord is a communist, with enough imperious certainty to say as much in an offhand, elegant aside. His film "does [the spectator] the bitter favor of revealing to him that his problems aren't as mysterious as he thinks, nor even perhaps as incurable, provided we manage to abolish classes and the State someday." Debord knows how worthless the labor-union vision of the world is and who its lackeys are: "the flourishing union and political officials, always ready to prolong the proletarian's grievances for another thousand years with the sole aim of preserving their own role as his defender."

Debord knows how to treat with the requisite detachment the reversals and desertions that we have witnessed on such a wide scale in recent years: "Unlike so many others, I have not changed my opinion once or several times with the changing of the times; it is rather the times that have changed as my opinions have changed."

It is so rare to come out of a film, as we do from Debord's, feeling fortified, light-hearted, and intelligent! Because the man we have seen giving an account of his personal transparency, at a magnificently slow pace, is someone who never gives in.

Debord knows that longstanding commitment is the tribunal of truth and that theories, however correct or ingenious their workings, "are military units of varying strength that must be sent into battle at the right moment." Nor is Debord's own theory, the society of the spectacle, an exception to this rule. Generalizing as it did the Hegelian theme of alienation, it had no more than a rudimentary or descriptive force, it must be said, and the watered-down form of the theory – the polemic against the "society of consumption" – never helped anyone to avoid surrendering.

If Debord is this savvy, it is because, very early on, he asked the question that all the others are explained by, because he wondered "whether the proletariat actually exists, and if so, what it might be."

The course of that existence is basically the story of the truth to which his whole life was devoted, and the story of everything opposed to it as well. Paris glorified by the incipient movement of youth in revolt, Paris destroyed by Pompidou; May '68, followed by the renegades; communism, followed by anti-Marxism; the Situationists, the Maoists, followed by Mitterrand . . .

We've kept a cool head and haven't let go of the guiding thread of truth. Debord helps us say: no, we, the stubbornly unbowed revolutionaries of these past few decades, did not go astray. Not that we didn't make enormous mistakes. But because the main thing is not to have given up, and thus to have the subjective resource of truth, and therefore of its progress, always at our disposal.

Has the time come to challenge this unscathed interlocutor? I could do so, inasmuch as his nostalgia blinds him, in spite of himself, to the current context of what all his perseverance derives from. You can't just have thirty years of history end on a shot of the high waters of the Venice lagoon and expect to get away with it. The final words of the film, "Wisdom will never come," reveal that too much solitude can end up being dangerous to you. To put an end to defensive poetry you must also bear in mind that the people are working on themselves, here and now, in a new alliance with a politics that would keep Debord, were he to be part of it, from regarding himself as the stoic survivor of a defeated avant-garde.

But we also need to understand poetry's protective function. Why was it in the resource of art that twice – first with the Surrealists after October 1917 and then with the Situationists in the early 1960s – new historical circumstances produced, in France, a true break, unprecedented intensity, tremendous repercussions with regard to an ossified political Marxism? Marxism should learn from such amazing cunning! We won't miss the opportunity this time.

This Marxism – of which Debord, in terms of the ethics of the subject, would be the interlocutor and, in his own way, the equal – I could call a living Marxism.

In this respect, rather than being a mere fellow traveler of such a Marxism he could be considered its true friend, because Debord rightly says – this is the theme of the film of his that is most permeated with nobility of feeling – that friendship boils down to the equality of friends.

Le Perroquet, November 11, 1981

— 7 —

IS THE ORIENT AN OBJECT FOR THE WESTERN CONSCIENCE?

Volker Schlöndorff, *Circle of Deceit*
(*Die Fälschung*)

Volker Schlöndorff's *Circle of Deceit* is a film that I intend to show is pernicious. A campaign needs to be mounted here against a perverse treatment of everything that is in fact convoluted about the paths of truth. The title of this film,[1] referring though it does to a character, refers more fundamentally to its *director*, who claims to be expressing the truth about deceit while what he is actually doing is exploiting it, exacerbating it, and immersing us in it.

Of course, this is hardly the first time an artist has prided himself on being a master of illusion and fakery. Should we make a big deal about it? I say yes, we should, given that he is concerned with the intricate workings of the truth of an era and of a place where everything comes at the cost of deaths, wars, or famines.

Of the five possible subjects of this very devious film there is not a one that isn't distorted by the contemptuous angle of the gaze. This is an even greater tragedy in that I had really liked the same director's *The Lost Honor of Katherina Blum*, and his *Coup de grâce* even more so. Could it be that those two films owed a lot to Margaretha von Trotta? At any rate, attrition and disavowal are often the order of the day.

– I –

War. We know that dealing with that threat today requires commitment and the keenness of the political eye. Not everyone can be a committed pacifist. *Circle of Deceit* plunges us into in a situation of counter-revolutionary civil war: Lebanon, where a people are constantly enduring the bloody machinations of the powers involved: pro-Soviet Syria and pro-American Israel. And yet we don't encounter a single Lebanese in the film. Not one of the people directly con-

54

cerned, only warmongering puppets spouting absurd or violent remarks, or a few non-entities who enter the camera's field of view only to be massacred. No one lays out the basic facts of the situation, making it all the more easy to chalk the whole thing up to universal absurdity, to the nightmare of history, inasmuch as the filmmaker, right from the start, has refused to provide the slightest explanation. This proves once again how those who are always decrying pure horror start by crippling people's minds. In this respect, the film is obscurantist, against the Lebanese people and in favor of intellectual helplessness in the face of the threat of war.

– II –

The Western intellectual's relationship to "peripheral" situations. Let's call a spade a spade: the perspective here is one of imperialism, intellectual arrogance, racism. The Lebanese horror is merely the raw material, the means for the only thing that really matters: the torments of the Westerner's conscience. The German character holds the monopoly on the thought process, for which the Lebanese and Palestinian puppets are merely the pretext. The excruciating spiritual crisis of the tiresome Bruno Ganz (the main character) focuses dubious attention on someone who has never seriously considered that an Arab might have a soul. The radical negation of the idea "The Lebanese people are thinking and changing" is what the film promotes. The only positive, thoughtful interlocutor of our tormented hero is moreover another German, a woman, smack in the middle of Lebanon, who couldn't care less about Lebanese politics since she is only there on account of her desire to be a mother, a desire quickly fulfilled by the children put on the adoption market by the civil war. The little Cambodian or Arab child has always delighted the criminals of Empire.

The only character who utters any political thoughts about Lebanon is an alcoholic colonialist, a purveyor of weapons and photos of mutilated bodies, who is overcome with nostalgia for the Orient of old.

The Orient in this film is the object of reflection for the West, and the horribleness of that object is what makes the German journalist's dubious redemption possible.

– III –

Journalism. Let's talk about that. *Circle of Deceit* is a symptom of the slow but sure mounting of universal criticism of the journalist, the "neutral" figure of aging empires, the taboo subject of Western freedoms, along with his crony, the union activist. The film gets out ahead on this, in a certain way, by doing an about-face in the guise of a fake pose of self-criticism: "Yes, the journalistic perspective is part and parcel of the horror it bears witness to." The great moment of lucidity of the journalist struggling with the conflicts of authenticity occurs when he stabs a Palestinian, in a gratuitous, sordid act. This is how he learns that he can and must leave his newspaper . . .

But we couldn't care less, actually, because nothing in *Circle of Deceit* ever goes beyond the mindless voyeurism of the patrons of big hotels, with their loyalty cards and their drunken telexes. As a viewer of this film, I am myself forced into, shackled, so to speak, to the position of the dazed journalist counting the murders and splashing the dead bodies all over the front page.

A breed of journalists who will traffic in the charming cynicism of their own disgrace is in store for us. Big-city journalism, like the Jesuit fathers before it, has spread all over the world – apart from a few bold exceptions like John Reed – in the train of imperialist domination. The gloom and doom of a few clever people will hardly fool anyone, especially when it is embedded in the very images it inflicts on us, all the while claiming that they are only basely commercial.

– IV –

Bruno Ganz shuttles between two women the way he does between civilization and barbarism. Some might think that, after the turmoil of feminism, he is seeking or asserting some sort of stable contemporary masculinity. I don't envy him if, to assist him in his rainy return home to the little guerrilla war of his love life he needs a detached, criminal sojourn among a suffering people, plus the dubious jealousy he feels toward a compatriot in exile, which all of Hanna Schygulla's talent can't keep us from seeing is just an irrelevant fantasy. This account of recent complications in the history of couples is at once overblown and unseemly.

– V –

It was the German national question that gave the early films of Wenders, Fassbinder, and Syberberg all their vitality. Its quasi-implicit nature produced their poetry and gave life and purpose to their formal ingenuity. The same question is becoming clear and relevant today. It requires political commitment since, as the German pacifist movement shows, it has entered into broad popular consciousness. The forward-looking role of artists has come to an end. Every German film now drones on about the Wall, Hitler, the East, Bismarck, and Prussian art, without convincing anyone to move forward.

Follow-up addendum

Schlöndorff's film – as was already apparent in *The Tin Drum* – is a sign of the rightward shift of the German question. We are inevitably shown the border with the other Germany, the Germany of the East. But it is certain that no clarity will come out of this, no fraternal feelings for what will then be shown of the Lebanese and Palestinian national questions. Here, too, the primitive Orient is only the means for the return, in the worst sense of German nostalgia, to a national question that is in fact pursued as the most important one.

The oppressed peoples of the earth are not objects for the exquisite inner turmoil of European consciences. They are subjects from which to learn how to exercise political intelligence and action.

Obviously, colonial arrogance is a long time dying.

Le Perroquet, December 17, 1981

— 8 —

REFERENCE POINTS FOR CINEMA'S SECOND MODERNITY[1]

- Mention Godard first. He was also part of our historical frame of reference: the New Wave. The line of demarcation, the difference between the New Wave and what we are attempting to call cinema's second modernity, passes through him.
- Note that, inasmuch as it is not a movement, a genre, or a school, it is a cinema that is not measurable. It is not a region of cinema but rather its furthermost tip.
- Can we say: a cinema of subjectivity? Rather, a cinema of the encounter with the question of the real, as an elusive term denoting the capture of subjective processes. A cinema of the question of the real, as such, in an opening made solely by its representation.
- Therefore, a cinema of modernity, as the generic identity of a cinema of truth [*un cinéma de la vérité*]; that deals with the question of truth. This is different from *cinéma vérité* (the latter enabled neorealism to be assimilated): it is its negative, in fact.
- For the record: Prior to Orson Welles, classical cinema experimented with the whole repertoire of its technical resources until mastery was achieved, in an atmosphere of ideological harmony; transparent propaganda, actually. Orson Welles introduced a reversal of perspective whereby cinematic processes would have to account for the production of images as specific ideological forms. Cinema refracts the worldview through its own prism: the scene in the hall of mirrors at the end of *The Lady from Shanghai* is the most spectacular metaphor of this.

  Since the way the image was organized could be perceived, Orson Welles invented a cinema that exposed this organization to view and asked the spectator what the basis of the story was.

– At the heart of modernity is anxiety about the death of classical cinema returning in the form of its failure: that of messages.
– The cinema has nothing left to give. With its repeated divorces from synchronization has come a lack of self-confidence, as the breakdown of communication. While for many directors this means adapting literary texts as the only way around the problem, doing so is sometimes accompanied by a simple recourse to the book of the Law (each having his or her own one).
– In Duras' case, after the destruction of the codes of representation came the time of the prohibition on images as the supreme law of the impossibility of representation.
– Included in the question of that impossibility: the issue of a *partition* of the real – what, of the real, might make cinema possible? No longer in the dimension of refusal, subject to the laws of the imaginary categorical imperative (Duras, Debord), nor in the stance of a permanent guarantee either (Straub), but in the wager on the present.
– Straub, again. We said that the guarantee, where he is concerned, is permanent. His is a Leninist cinema. As opposed to Godard (see below), what it is important to choose has already been established. Truth does not circulate; it insists, even in distanciation.
– Godard, again, the only one who really takes on the question of what a truth for today might be: his willingness to be truth's traffic cop [*agent de la circulation de la vérité*], not by putting the causes of a crisis on trial but through an encounter with present conditions.
– Even though the stakes are clearly defined, the confrontation with the real in his two latest films nonetheless amounts to an esthetics of subjective indecision. What is left unresolved is whether taking sides is such a small part of the real. Thus, there is an oscillation (reminiscent of the blinking light in *Alphaville)* in which indecision prevails as a maximum subjective surface area for a limited real.

   A repetition, in fact, of the questions raised in *Sauve qui peut (la vie) (Every Man for Himself)*, serving, moreover, the interests of the truth of cinema's current challenge: courage – as the political name of its transmission – versus anxiety – as the law of its guaranteed paralysis.
– The cinema of modernity: the emerging cinema of this dialectic.
– Therefore, something that cannot be represented, a real that slips away through the point of obscurity of its capture: the decision

to take sides. The first approach consisted in saying that it is a cinema of the off-screen (its encounter with the real cannot be shown).

The question raised by these problems is: What acts as an obstacle to such an extent that it is something unintelligible?

– And yet, the profoundly heterogeneous nature of all this. Under the name of "modernity" it is difficult to bring about any synthesis. This is moreover why modernity is itself part of the crisis; it is itself in crisis. It does not ensure a second foundation of cinema. It manipulates the suspense regarding cinema's existence as art to the point of denying it, as does Debord, for the greater glory of the text. Duras' temptation.

– Digression: Are there any ways for art to exist today other than in the spectacular epic mode (as is my case in *L'Écharpe rouge*[2] and Natacha Michel's in *Le Repos de Penthésilée*)? Because, in that case, by creating something out of what is not, art can operate in the context of its failure vis-à-vis the real.

– Modernity – its obstacle: space. After all, space is the support of representation. Modernity could be said to be suspicious of space. In the past, there was a meticulous, creative, theatrical method of fabrication (the studio), but there was also wide open space (adventure). After Welles' breaking of the frame and after the Godard of the 1960s – who took the image apart, used collages, subverted signifiers, pinned a character against a wall, with no distance, in a two-dimensional frame – modernity foundered on space. As though in order to gain more of the real, to get truth going, the frame had to be restricted. Reduce the resources to increase the gains.

– In *Every Man for Himself* the slowing down of the action already suggests that speed (the traversal of space) needs to be redefined. In *Passion*, the blue sky is a tribute to openness, saturated with religious music. It is a tribute to the bygone days of light. The rest, in terms of clutter, is tightly packed, jammed together: stairs, balconies, doors, kitchen, and then the implausibly frozen disarray of the paintings. Modern cinema, the film is saying, is an enigmatic sort of graphic design.

– Space, 2. In Duras' work, space is a nowhere place, an exile in non-being, which is refracted in the mirror: dizziness for the spectator, directly faced with the disappearance of the real from the image.

– Space, 3. Wenders' itinerary, which was a deep, fresh breath of air until its abrupt curtailment in *The State of Things*. An almost breathless cinema. Whereas *Kings of the Road* invents a modern kind of breathing, at once full and problematic.

- Space, 4. Straub. Space signifies forcefully. But all representation of space is like concrete. There is a huge system of constraints, an extreme ponderousness. The prime example of this is the complete closed circuit in the camera's great pan over the countryside in *Fortini/Cani*: there's where the dead are, there's nothing but stillness there, but the filmic mass of space forces the meaning, forcefully.

- Space, 5. There is a certain strangeness about Dindo[3] that comes from his self-confidence. His approach may quite often precede his own formulation of the categories that would explain it. As a rule, there is no indecision where he is concerned, since he is only too happy to follow the process of montage. In Dindo's work there are "felicities of montage style," the way we say there are "felicities of writing style."

  In *Max Frisch*, only the lighthouse really signifies a space, because there is a sort of lack of formal resolution in it. All the rest of the system of places is generated by the text. The lighthouse comes back as the return of a certain real, the emblem of chance.

- Space, 6. Allio. An extraordinary clarity in his work. A depth, a colorful substance. In *Retour à Marseille (Return to Marseilles)* there is the same breadth of field as in Straub, but the depth is different.

- Space, 7. Space, then, as the designated place of the real, resists any sensible representation. Captured in the figures of absence, of enigma, of fragmentation, the real tends to be subject to accounting operations, as a proof of its certainty. Yet we are very well aware that the real can't be measured, that we can't be certain about it: we can only choose to be a part of it. And what is unconsciously brought about in this way by the ultimately invariable pitfalls of "the impression of reality" (accounting) is the avoidance of that truth.

- Space, 8. The representation of space. Follow Denis Lévy's approach in *L'École de mai* and *Mémoire en blanc:* the deconstruction of the urban landscape's frame of representation so as to prevent any figurative repercussions. An opening that reconstitutes space as a poetics of the sensible real.

- Modernity: The elements of dignity of this cinema in their confusion. To put an end to the influence of the other arts and the misconception of the image, which is obliged to be the ultimate, eternal guarantee of the reality effect.

Thus, the coherence of this jumble of investigations, or even contradictions: the foundations of an art of the future.

- Modernity: The issue of cinema's survival is not a matter of the future or the present, since, once the image has been shown to be nothing but a media entity subservient above all to its market, as merchandise, the image, that which is linked to its fetishistic status, is in the process of dying from an overdose: inflation as the rule of every market.
- Modernity: We will say, on the contrary, that cinema exists in the order of rarity today. Rarity as the only possible exception to the general rule, inflation. To say that cinema is rare today, even very rare, is a truth that proves that *Les Cahiers du cinéma* (the standard of cinema criticism) is lying. Gauging cinema's existence as broadly as possible may be in line with the journal's obsessive management of its readership numbers, but it amounts to betraying the essential truth of art: that it is always exceptional.
- The text, again. Modern cinema subdues the text in order to inject subjectivity into it. In French cinema, this runs up against the obstacle of the biographical, of personal sentimentality, the junkyard of which is so-called "French intimism." Even in Marguerite Duras' work, the voice, her famous voice, allows sentimentality in.
- The actor, 1: Arbitrarily place the actor, as the unnamed stakes, at the heart of modernity's problematic issues of representation.
- The actor, 2: At the beginning, and for a long time thereafter, the actor was the support of theatricality, imported into the cinema. The theater has always had its actors; painting, its models; literature, its characters. Cinema incorporated all three of these to turn them into a whole: by creating the star, it afforded itself the quintessence of the actor (performance), the model (reality), and the character (identification), for the greater glory of a lifelike cinema.
- The actor, 3: In the interests of its own particular esthetic, modernity adopted the lessons of the New Wave to some extent – using the actor as the negative of his function in order to disrupt the process of identification – but it also removed the actor from the screen in all the versions of the relationship to this absence: from the way his quest was organized to his elimination, as being impossible.
- The actor, 4: Temporarily, the actor, the instability of perplexity, circulates in modernity as the place where truth is obfuscated.
- The actor, 5: In the meantime, pay attention to the productive processes of this perplexity: the attempts to eliminate the figura-

tive effects connected with the body, as the removal of a first layer of obscurity. With *Max Frisch*, Dindo succeeded in making a film with characters but without actors, or the opposite case with Godard: the actors as non-representation of characters. And again the actors in Straub's or Duras' work as radical impossibility.

L'Imparnassien, May 1983

— 9 —

THE DEMY AFFAIR

It is not often that you see critics becoming politically militant and trying to mobilize public opinion. As regards Jacques Demy's film *Une Chambre en ville* (*A Room in Town*), there have been no fewer than two full-page petitions in the newspapers signed by a group of critics who joined together to urge everyone to go en masse to see the film.[1] This is obviously a political symptom. One of the petitions came directly from the Left: the critics of the PCF [French Communist Party] and PS [Socialist Party] newspapers. The other was organized around the *Cahiers du cinéma*. That's politically committed criticism all right.

But committed to what? In actual fact, *Une Chambre en ville* celebrates, at the very moment of their death, "*le peuple de gauche*" rallied around a dynamic, good-natured working class singing its demands before stolid CRS [riot control police] troops. The colorful effect is substantial: the film is based on a people representable in all its fullness, a nostalgia for the 1950s (it is about the Saint-Nazaire and Nantes strikes) that the critics, in their allegiance to Mitterrand, to May 10,[2] have sought to emphasize. This film reduces Gaullism to a mere parenthesis. It activates – and deactivates – the myth of the continuity between the workers' movement of 1936 (or 1947) and the Left's current legitimacy.

The verdict of the public, unmoved by the critics' appeals, reflected, no doubt unconsciously, the futility of such a subject. The labor union movement, connected through its visible song to the leftwing parties (SFIO[3] posters on the walls in the film), is actually a corpse that is only just able to lend its symbols to some outmoded fable. Film critics are the only ones who are still capable of imagining that such a thing could be a possible referent for a "great popular leftist film." In their challenge to Belmondo and *L'As des as* our petition signers were defeated before they even began. The Right seems to be way ahead of the Left when it comes to promoting turkeys to a gullible public today.

Cutting across the film's creaky workerism, the love story presents the ecumenical theme of a cross-class alliance in the guise of Surrealist mythology (the woman naked under her fur coat): the aristocratic bourgeoisie embraces the young proletarian. The only villain is the shopkeeper, the man of the PME-PMI:[4] a cheerfully gruesome Michel Piccoli cuts his throat in his shop. Serves the people who elected Chirac right.

As compared with the stuttering factory girl in Godard's *Passion*, the moral of Demy's film, well suited to lifting the Left's spirits, is that the proletariat doesn't stutter; it sings. When we see the union representative (Where's this guy from? A cautious Demy indicates neither the CGT[5] nor the PCF) singing on the table in the café: "We didn't get anything we asked for, we've been laid off, so come on, guys!", the refrain is not so cheerful, however. Demy is unwittingly telling us that the approach, the politics, and the leaders have definitely got to be changed. It all has to be done over.

The *Cahiers du cinéma* has had to completely abandon its former high standards in order to endorse such a product. It is here that politics, as soon as it becomes parliamentarian, leads to a rush to abandon modern reason and the sense of the avant-garde.

Implicitly, of course, any symptom is of its times. Demy is after all combining the desire for a "social" representation and the infiltration of theatrical, or operatic, modes into cinema. This cross between the political as such and formal excess (or arbitrariness) is a problem of the times. Bonitzer[6] pointed this out, noting with satisfaction the conjunction of a realism and a formalism, that of musical comedy.

The trouble, in this instance, is that the film's politics is representation (yet politics' real cannot be represented) and its formalism is as spiffy as can be because it's backed by the good news: the Left is here!

The task is to establish in a void the limited subject matter of what it is that preserves the hypothesis and the trajectory of working-class force. The only thing appropriate for this is an art split between the sense of a lack and the utopia of the montage. Demy would have us believe that there is no crisis, either of the people or of cinema. This is what accounts for the critics signing petitions. But it is by inscribing, through formal transformation, the crisis of the people that the crisis of cinema will perhaps be assessed. This is the time when we need the Marxist art of the period of the crisis of Marxism. Forced to do everything when it is impossible to do so, Demy has only one solution, a Christian one: with the cathedral basically serving as its backdrop, the demonstration he depicts is a religious procession.

Where an ethics is attempting to define itself, Demy instead praises virtue. A belief like that is harmful, because it weakens the toughness required by confidence.

L'Imparnassien, May 1983

—10—

SWITZERLAND: CINEMA AS
INTERPRETATION

What does Swiss art say? That Switzerland is a burden to itself. There is a too-muchness about the old and empty nation insofar as it has never been involved in history on account of tradition and preservation. Swiss "neutrality" is a blank form of national surfeit. And, on top of all that, there is a thinness about the people: no single language of their own but three (German, Italian, and French) that pull them toward the great cultures of Europe; no more of those *montagnards* who liberated them from the Austrians and who are now either prosperous farmers or residents of banking cities; and workers who have come there from other places (the great wave of Italian immigration). Affluent and freshly painted, Switzerland stands under its powerful symbol: the Swiss franc.

In his autobiographical book about cancer (*Mars*), Zorn showed just how far the artist's hatred of the Swiss bourgeoisie can go in such circumstances. He unhesitatingly imputed the origin of the disease to it. He had been "educated to death" by the Swiss family. This chilling, virulent book's argument can be easily summed up: Switzerland is a cancer. Nor was this disputed by Ziegler's sociological and political essay, *Switzerland Above All Suspicion*, which caused a scandal in the Swiss Parliament.

Swiss art, and especially the country's brilliant cinema of the past twenty years, is therefore the art of that suspicion, which must be sought somewhere below the surface. Over the smooth surface of overwhelming Swiss conformity the country's cinema hunts around for a stigma, the stigma of History.

Remember that Jean-Luc Godard is Swiss. His own perspective has a touch of provincialism about it that sets Switzerland apart from France through a sort of calmness of its cities, which are modern in a heavy way – a bit like German cities, although the latter have the excuse of post-war reconstruction – but dull, and through the green and blue of its countryside. Switzerland is the midpoint from which Godard observes the world, and where the problem he is concerned with – can the image be derived from the real? – is undisturbed by any excess. Godard the man is therefore not an exception to anything. He is clearly enmeshed in the language of the times. Switzerland is itself too exceptional in Europe for any Swiss to be an exception.

There is a special kind of Swiss perspicacity in an art that reflects on what it is possible to communicate. Godard is thoroughly involved in this since he asks: What am I communicating through cinema? Since Switzerland has never had any wars or revolutions or colonies but only the importing and exporting of watches and capital, what can the identical generations of Swiss, coming one after another in an unbroken line of national certainty, possibly have to communicate? Since William Tell, has there ever been anything in Switzerland's experience that needs to be assessed?

Patricia Moraz's film *Le Chemin perdu* (*The Lost Way*) made the labor movement a metaphor for this issue. The old Leninist, the grandfather of the main character (a little girl), was at least able to teach her what the red flag had once meant. He was nothing but a veteran now, taking part in shabby May Day celebrations, and in danger of becoming a skeptic. But this failing was not insignificant. The film – Swiss, as a result – was concerned, for the first time perhaps, with the question of the demise of the old labor movement and with the fact that communicating this issue, making it possible to think about it, is the basis on which the younger generation can become organized (the parents, for their part, locked into their unhappy love-life and their petty business concerns, have nothing to report).

This is proof that Swiss cinema, although stripped of any reference to current experience, through a kind of elimination of history, manages to allow truths – including political ones – that go unnoticed elsewhere to circulate. After all, it is also Godard who, in *Passion*, articulates the most radical questions about the possibility of cinema (What is light? Is there any light in art other than that in Christian art?) and the political silence of the proletariat, embodied in the character of a factory girl who stutters. Thus, the Swiss Godard wonders whether, after Christian art – its light, its music, which are ever-present in the film – there shouldn't be an art, a Marxist one, let's say, whose condition of possibility, if not its very subject, would be working-class political force.

And this reminds us that at the very moment when tribute was being paid to and stock taken of the greatest ideological movement of the past few decades – the decision made by thousands of young intellectuals between 1966 and 1973 to go to work in factories – it was in the Swiss film *Érica Minor* by Van Effenterre that the most sensitive, powerful portrait by far of one such person, played by Brigitte Fossey, could be found, and in the usual dull, provincial setting at that: a village, a very small factory of women. This seemed to make it possible, by eliminating the big objective realities, to focus on the subjective truth to which the film intended to bear witness.

Even the properly petit-bourgeois aspect of the 1960s – that Baudelairian version in which personal moods, the sense of instability, and inner changes are erroneously placed at the heart of the movement of the times – found its most affectionate chronicler in Alain Tanner. It is a cinema as limited as his vision but in which he gets the flavor of things exactly right. His latest, totally shallow film, *Dans la ville blanche* (*In the White City*), in the abstract guise of a "Swiss sailor" fictionalizes the South by using Lisbon, where the hero wanders around and a powerful young female Portuguese character reveals the enigmatic place of truth. There is the charm of nothingness about this; Switzerland's dreamy South is relieved of all allegory. Compare this with the dense power of the Portuguese sequence in Margarethe von Trotta's *The Second Awakening of Christa Klages*. Lisbon, whose sprawl or whose monumental spaces are never captured, passes through the Swiss filter of diminishment, of visual metonymy, and that wonderful city (a whole Empire flaking away, like some capital city in the desert region of the Syrtes) is reduced to the pure point of its light.

When it is focused on the enigma of a nation that is a product of totally happy accident, Swiss cinema can be the greatest one of all. Richard Dindo, for example, is a real expert, who crafts an extremely complex art in order to pursue the combined themes of communication, writing, and nationality. Take *Max Frisch*, adapted from that writer's autobiographical texts. (Incidentally, Frisch is another amazing product of Switzerland, who starts out with parables à la Brecht – *The Firebugs* – and ends with offbeat diaries, emptied out by self-absence, in which America is the experimental protocol of Switzerland, and who, as we see in the film, becomes, accepts to be, a renowned Swiss dignitary defending humanism at black-tie ceremonies.) A cinema in which an art of montage is reinvented in such a way that the subtlety of the subject surpasses the whole combination of means used. A cinema that maintains the paradox of introducing

69

undecidability between documentary and fiction and creating characters without there being anything acted by actors. At its heart is Max Frisch's aphorism about a homeland: "A homeland is a sum of memories to which dates can hardly be attached."

In that homeland – Switzerland – Marcus Imhoof's film *The Boat is Full* exposes the flaw whereby it is attached, if only by default, to History. "The boat is full" is what a Swiss official said during World War II when the government decided to almost routinely turn away people who were fleeing Nazism. A special ordinance stipulated that people persecuted on account of their race could not be considered political refugees. It was a way of saving the signifier "political refugee" and therefore the Swiss tradition of asylum – the tradition that allowed the fleeing Bolsheviks, Lenin first and foremost, to pass through Zurich and Geneva – at the price of the death of tens of thousands of Jews.

The film has nothing in the way of formal innovation. It is a German–Swiss production, which is admittedly symptomatic. It studies with precision a type of conscience that could legitimately be called Swiss Pétainism. Many of the inhabitants of this village on the Swiss border, who aren't bad people (except for a few, almost all of whom have a social status connecting them to a greater or lesser degree to the state: the pastor, the police officer, and so on), would accept to take in the group of Jewish refugees. Some of them will go pretty far (to prison, even) to try to save the refugees. And in each instance the film intelligently points out what their particular motives are (a woman's or a child's wish, a wish to live together, even if only for a few days, and so on). However, although the administrative wheels turn slowly, they turn surely and are surely internalized, in the end, by everyone. One must be reasonable, after all. The film shows how, through the people's being divided, the general consensus of abjectness and political servility, of ordinary fear, seeping as it does into their individual, diverse concerns, ultimately leads to crime (the expulsion of the Jews to the camps and death), something that is allowed to happen as though it were coming from somewhere else. So there is no need to be a rabid anti-Semite (here, too, the film shows many different shadings) or a police officer for self-concern to turn out to be on a continuum with the worst. What is so powerful about the film is the way it ramifies and clarifies this obvious fact: as opposed to the stupid theory that there is a "beast slumbering in every one of us," Pétainism has to be explained as a rational subjective state of affairs in which each person's refusal to declare the exception, the urgency, the courage of an ethical choice is more than adequate for the State's reasonableness ("too many refugees" or, still today, "too many immigrants") to shape everyone's conscience. There are circumstances in history when accepting to be an ordinary citizen means that you are an ordinary criminal. These circumstances foreground the radical critique of a Statist conscience. The film rightly distinguishes it from the complex forms of popular conscience. And it documents the ways the latter submits to the former.

It is all contained in the scene, whose unbearable intensity stems from its absurdity, in which some people from the village, moved by the Jews' plight, accompany them to a truck that will deliver them to the Nazis, and give them Swiss chocolate.

The Swiss franc and chocolate are the general equivalents of the nation. The honor of Swiss cinema is to interpret them. Beneath the surface of capital, in the most stable and negligible corner of Europe, this cinema thus constitutes that without which no truth is conceivable: a Swiss event.

Le Perroquet, May 7, 1983

—11—

INTERRUPTED NOTES ON THE
FRENCH COMEDY FILM

– I –

The French comedy film: a staple, for internal use only, which, during its first period, featured an unvarying urban sociology. The concierge, the café owner, the tramp, the domineering grandma, the lousy husband, the parish priest, the former sergeant, the prostitute, the street peddler, the hairdresser's assistant, the heckled schoolteacher, the snobbish woman from the 16th Arrondissement. Stereotypes that were invariably played by the same bunch of second-tier actors: Noël Roquevert, Pauline Carton, Raymond Bussières, et al. A pre-industrial-age France of convivial neighborhoods, a bit on the lascivious side, addicted to red wine, far-removed from any general idea, full of cheating spouses, colonialist, and unproductive. Boulevard theater-type screenplays, less slapstick in nature (slapstick is not a French phenomenon) than "Heavens-it's-my-husband!"[1] Labiche[2] transplanted and trivialized among the "little people" of rear-courtyard-dwelling mavericks. A sort of corny, old-fashioned eternity. The humorous intrigues of your good, decent folks.

– II –

Some well-defined sub-genres nevertheless. The military comedy, which is still going strong today (cf. all the *bidasse*[3] films), having begun, like everything else, in the nineteenth century, in the theater or in the novel, with *Les Gaîtés de l'escadron* (*The High Spirits of the Squadron*) (after Labiche everything derives from Courteline).[4] A very subtle difference: military comedy is not to be confused with *gendarme* comedy (which is just as bulletproof, as witness De Funès' *gendarme* franchise, and springs from the same roots: *Le gendarme*

72

est sans pitié [*The Pitiless Policeman*], a Courteline play). The Southern/Marseille-type comedy, perfected in the cinema by Pagnol but originally descended from Alphonse Daudet's *Tartarin de Tarascon*. Pimp-whore comedy, whose template is "La Maison Tellier," a short story by Maupassant. Teacher-pupil comedy, whose source is the novel *La Guerre des Boutons*[5] (*War of the Buttons*) and the refined form of which is Truffaut's *Les quatre cents coups* (*The 400 Blows*). And still other sub-genres.

– III –

There are no "diagonal" characters in this cinema, no roles combining the popular generic element with the network of situations. No Charlie Chaplin, Buster Keaton, or even Laurel and Hardy. Tati's Mr. Hulot will already be an exception for this reason alone (and on account of so many other things!). Social types are combined and connected in relationships that nothing can ever undermine. Instead of diagonal characters there are the stars of French comedy, who represent unchanging performances, faces, and trademark gimmicks rather than organic functions or formal principles in the work. There are Fernandel ("there lies whitening now the jawbone of an ass"),[6] Rellys, the indestructible sergeant or crude peasant, and Bourvil and De Funès. The film is theirs; we look forward to seeing them play their typical roles, and the rest is just filmic rubbish.

– IV –

Today, let's face it, there's no one. What about Belmondo, it could be objected. But that's something else again. The line of descent in his case is from Arsène Lupin,[7] the typical overgrown Parisian street kid, the brawny little French stud, a fun-loving wiseguy, ladies' man, and high wire acrobat who, with only his somersault, saves France from mortal danger. Arsène Lupin was duly anti-Kraut and played the traditional English enemy for a fool (cf. *Arsène Lupin contre Herlock Sholmès*). Belmondo, as befits a more decadent age, is more restrained, but ultimately, in *L'As des as* (*Ace of Aces*), he protects the widow and the orphan from the Nazis. The typical Belmondo film aims less at comedy than pure entertainment. Historical fantasy has taken over from the sociology of concierges, who have incidentally all become Portuguese in the meantime, something that creates big problems in terms of preserving the old nationalistic connections between the crudeness of the comedy and Parisian realism.

– V –

Just as every parliamentary politician has to have the church steeple of his native village, from which he can declare his deep love for his country – Pinay from Saint-Chamond, Giscard from Chamalières, Mitterrand from Château-Chinon and Latché, Chirac from the Corrèze, and so on – the stars of French comedy for a long time had to put their provincial roots on display: Fernandel was from Marseille, Bourvil from Normandy.

– VI –

The comedic situations of this cinema are extremely limited in number. This is a crucial point: the art (if you can call it that!) of French comedy cinema is in no way an art of the gag. This is because novelty and urgency are the soul of the gag, whereas in the French comedy film, the more obvious and ordinary something is, the slower and more predictable it is, the better. It is always about fulfilling expectations. The aim of the French comedy is fulfillment (and to that extent it may unwittingly induce anxiety). So the cuckolded French husband comes in the door while the lover climbs out the window. The old battle-axe hits the policeman with her umbrella. The wino rants on his park bench. The retired sergeant brags about his war exploits. The soldier sneaks out of the barracks for a roll in the hay with the girls. The concierge yaks away. The postman rings several times. The corporal gets into trouble with his superior. The plumber walks in on the bourgeois woman in her bath. And so on and so forth.

The same rule applies to the stars as well. We expect Fernandel to bare his horse-like teeth, Bourvil to utter some hilarious Freudian slips, De Funès to throw a fit, Belmondo to jump from a plane onto a delivery bike "without a stunt double." French national sentiment of this period can be summed up in the slogan: "Nothing new!" A cinema of the eternity of the social order.

– VII –

The First World War is a taboo subject in comedy: too many deaths, too much nationalistic consensus. The Second World War, on the other hand, is one of its favorite subjects. What a riot it was, actually, this cinema suggests: just think, the defeat, the drubbing, the cowardice, the black market! It's all so good. Especially the black market: the resourceful person was the high-wire artist of daily life. The

German occupiers were perfect targets for farce because of their having dodged combat. Three dates stand out in this account, which should be interpreted as nostalgia for an era when the general historical irresponsibility empowered singular individuals. France in these films appears as what some bewildered resourceful guy makes of it. Hence, *La traversée de Paris* (*Four Bags Full*, 1956), *La Grande Vadrouille* (*Don't Look Now: We're Being Shot At*, 1966), and *Papy fait de la résistance* (*Gramps Is in the Resistance*, 1983).

– VIII –

Papy is a synthetic symptom.

– For the (prevailing) idea that everyone was more or less a Pétainist and a collaborator during the war, *Papy* substitutes the notion that everyone – except Jugnot,[8] who is consigned to being the bad guy – was a Resistance fighter. This is the fashionable Socialist Party line of the moment. The effect, however, is exactly the same: unreality and total meltdown.

– *Papy* brings together the boulevard theater generation (Jacqueline Maillan in the role of the nice grandma) and the post-'68 generation of the Café de la Gare and Le Spendid.[9] Thus, the film shows how '68 is dead and buried and there is, was, and will be only one French comedy cinema. The effect is reinforced by the fleeting presence in the film of all those actors who are as French as they come. *Papy* reconciles the nation.

– *Papy* incorporates the Arsène Lupin-Belmondo-type film, with the half-"poetic," half-pathetic character of "Super-Resistance Fighter," who, in top hat and black cape, singlehandedly plunges his little tricolor dart into the German general's forehead.

– *Papy* juxtaposes historical violence (the Resistance fighter Carmet's car blowing up, all the people rounded up to be shot) and broad cabaret humor (Villeret in his role as a Nazi officer singing a Julio Iglesias song) in a truly vulgar mishmash that completes the transmutation of national sentiment into a mere backdrop. *Papy* is (unwittingly) contemporary with a time when, the old models of French national sentiment all being foreclosed, suturing them to comedy no longer makes any sense. *Papy* is a rag-film as a result of wanting to be a flag-film.

– *Papy* is truly, inconceivably atrocious. It stipulates that "national reconciliation" within the orbit of comedy can and must take place *from below*. It is a useful index of current conditions.

– IX –

Let's take a look at the following list of recent film titles:

- *Je sais rien, mais je dirai tout* (*! Don't Know Anything But I'll Tell All*, 1973), by Pierre Richard.
- *Comment réussir quand on est con et pleurnichard* (*How to Make Good When One Is a Jerk and a Crybaby*, 1974), by Michel Audiard.
- *Plus ça va, moins ça va* (*The More It Goes, The Less It Goes*, 1977), by Michel Vianey.
- *Arrête ton char . . . bidasse!* (*Gimme a Break, Rookie!*, 1977), by Michel Gérard.
- *C'est pas moi, c'est lui* (*It's Not Me, It's Him*, 1980), by Pierre Richard and Alain Godard.
- *Courage fuyons* (*Courage–Let's Run*, 1979), by Yves Robert.
- *Les Sous-doués* (*The Under-Gifted*, 1980), by Claude Zidi.
- *En cas de guerre mondiale, je file à l'étranger* (*If There's a World War, I'm Going Abroad*, 1982), by Jacques Ardouin.

Doesn't this list say it all? Wouldn't it make Bazaine and Trochu (past participle of the verb *trop choir* [*to fall too much*], as Hugo said), Weygand and Pétain[10] laugh their heads off? Comedy would appear to have no respect for anything. No kidding! In any case, this is a cinema of the under-gifted, which you hardly need any courage to run away from and about which, whatever image you may personally have of French identity, you're happy to be able to say that if that's me, it's not that.

– X –

I had intended to cover seven other phenomenological points regarding these products, because, contrary to what the classical philosophers maintained, nothingness is far from having no properties.

I know all but I won't tell anything.

L'Imparnassien, Fall 1983

——12——

Y A TELLEMENT DE PAYS POUR ALLER

(*There's So Many Countries To Go To*)
Jean Bigiaoui, Claude Hagège, Jacques Sansoulh[1]

– *I* –

The Jews in the Arabs' place

The Jews, who parted from the Arabs when they left Tunisia, have come and taken their place here in Sarcelles. What I mean is that, within our multi-ethnic country, these Jews constitute a sort of ethnic national minority, which is in the story of their origins but now has no other task than that of transforming or generating the contemporary, multi-faceted, infinitely divided and reconciled-to-fate way of being and becoming French. The calm, composed artistry of this film lies in the way it replaces the theme of the "Jewish question" with the story of individual people wherein the old issue of "assimilation or particularism" breaks down. No, it is not a film about the Jews because, by virtue of being a film about these particular Jews, it is also a film about the Arabs, or the Africans, or the Portuguese – in short, a film about France. Not the France nostalgic for its harmonious, rural past but the France of today, where everyone, in the voice of an Other, has to give their views on how a people is created. The filmmakers' direct frontal style, the framing of a truth that is utterly unlike the random seizing upon false facts, is well suited to the subject, because it is a question of fictionalizing what we are, not of "sharing" our inner exoticism.

   In this film there is an ethics of cinema whose rule is: "If you want to avoid turning the people you are showing into a picturesque spectacle, then make sure you compose your shot carefully and have a clear understanding of it at all times."

77

– II –

The lovers of the place

When in the film we see a TV film that the characters in the film are watching, we can clearly see that the television actors are bad actors. Loulou and his family are the real actors. The fake actors are the ones on TV, while the real ones are those watching them. Performing well is what makes real actors. Charlie Chaplin, Buster Keaton, and Toto,[2] in their native state, have all been gathered together in the city by this film: Loulou and his family are great comic actors. Comic no doubt because that is one of the ways they can perform their tragedy: with quiet misadventures, when a whole slew of events is crashing down around them. The image also performs, through the same process as that of the "actors," composing and disposing itself before us in each shot, such as in the one where a few children sitting haphazardly on some steps change place and, with no miracle other than that of the filmmakers' vision causing them to do so, form a graceful figure. The image also performs: a ship sails by on the horizon as a man gazes at it from the shore. Incongruous, familiar, in the brightness of the film and the light coming from the wide open spaces, the ship, painted in vivid colors that don't bleed outside the lines, sails by and fills the screen. Slow-moving, stately, and colorful, the ship sails by in the frame, a real ship that is like a ship in the theater being pushed from the wings by 20,000 extras, an anti-*Exodus* at once melancholy and light-hearted. Not exotic because it's joyful. You have to see the film of *this* diaspora: it only occurs once every thousand years.

– III –

Mouths from the South[3]

Loulou and his family are going to leave Tunis. Tunis near La Goulette,[4] La Goulette near Tunis, the native peninsula, the luminous place at the end of the world. They are the last Jews, the last family to leave the country they love, which is their own. (The last of the Jews, the last of the Just?[5] It is not as simple as all that.) Some of them dream in color. They and the filmmakers who accompany them see things in color. In color and in their true distance.

The exact distance of the real is its proximity. When Loulou and his relatives "move," a team of filmmakers follow them, turning their exodus into a film and Loulou and his family into actors. *Y a telle-ment de pays pour aller* is a diaspora captured on film. Both a document and a comedy by the grace of the people who are in it. Never a documentary or a farce. To the "I was there" effect of newsreel films, to the portable cameras that steal images and film people without their knowledge, the directors' desire for cinema responds with a fixed camera, carefully composed shots, and the full knowledge of the protagonists. With the decision to make a real film out of a true story. A documentary is a glut of images mounted on a given subject. Having wanted first and foremost to make a film means having been able to reconnect with something that is beginning, to capture things "at their mouth" (the way we say "at their source"), the mouths from the South, and the cinema of Méliès, and/or its extrapresent (the way we say extraterrestrial) image.

Here, the film is right in front of us. There is no mounting of anything, no collage, no looking down from above. Everything takes place within the frame, within the organization of depth, within a pure image, a distributed substance full of colorful clues. Real distance requires that what Loulou and his family say and do must take place within this frame, within this scene, and not go beyond it. Loulou and his relatives leave and arrive. From Tunis near La Goulette to Sarcelles near Paris. The frame of their life, the frame of the film. A formal constraint, a real constraint. Why did they leave?

To this question an old sage – they themselves – replies: dashed hopes for a certain kind of modern Muslim state, the former closeness with the French occupiers who separated the Tunisian Jews from their Arab neighbors . . . They mention dates, events, wars. Anti-Semitism, grievances are never brought up, but rather a chilling of the neighborly relations that, together with family life, constitute happiness in life. Where should they go? What does it mean to leave?

In Sarcelles, the big bright window that they are washing for Passover shatters like a bottle breaking against a ship at its launching. The apartment, divided in half by light and shadow, and the splash of red of the bowls in the middle of it are not stage decor, mere esthetic props, let alone sociological markers, but rather the very plot, the story, the suspense that these consummate actors are performing. Their dialogues, their monologues, the wonderful text they invent owe their funniness not just to improvisation, to their gentle rather than affectionate humor, but to their brilliant way of performing this comedy of places against the backdrop of a possible historical tragedy. "With my heavy build," says Loulou, who is in fact overweight, "me with my heavy build . . . Always having to go up and down a spiral staircase . . . " Loulou is a remarkable character. He has a kind of low-key volubility; he makes you laugh not at his misfortunes but at his little pleasures. A sort of born talker, Loulou is not a storyteller or a show-off or a smooth operator but someone for whom talking has always been a physical act; someone for whom giving a performance is a way of giving birth to himself (with all that entails in terms of the presence of the mother and the family), a manner of being constantly reborn to a precise, funny way of recounting things, which fills up the screen.

Between the Tunis of the search for lost time and the Sarcelles of time regained; between the Friday nights when "it was wonderful, there was the jasmine, the *jebbas*,[6] the cured meats, a woman selling *briks*[7] and home remedies; that's the only thing that stays with you forever," and the Sarcelles of cafés, of betting, of the *kippah*-wearing grandfather walking in a landscape of Black joggers dressed in blue, the Sarcelles of kosher and *glatt*-kosher grocery stores, too, there is the enormous gap of a life played out. And the way all the immigrants have, not of adapting their customs with a kind of folkloric fatalism or of turning daily life into nostalgic exoticism, but of turning life in France into a new life in which the *boukha*[8]-baguette-of-French-bread replaces the béret in the cliché.

"To have a home of your own," says Loulou's wife. In France, in New York, in Sarcelles, or in Israel, which will be mentioned only to be rejected? Reasons, good reasons, either to leave or to stay . . . We are told what they are, but what we are shown, whether there in Tunis or in this new "there" that is here and is Sarcelles, in the beauty of its colors, in the surrounding objects (the old-fashioned tripod for holding peppers, the children's white stepstool) is a way of remaining, an anti-diaspora of feeling. The exilee of this sort is someone who is a lover of places. Of the place he or she leaves, of the place he or she finds again. Lying in bed in Sarcelles, Loulou talks about the things he enjoys: "I like it a lot here in Sarcelles. But there aren't enough leisure activities." The reasons, whether good or bad, are muddled, as are the explanations accepted for them; the ways of explaining things are muddled, in the face of the clarity of the place these people are able to inhabit. The question of the causes of their exile, of why they are leaving or have left, of when they should have done so is simultaneously present, buried, and elusive. Departicularized.

This film is no more a film about the Jews than it is a documentary. That is no doubt why a truth about them slips obstinately into the film. Those who left for a potential America that is located in Sarcelles. La Goulette, Sarcelles. Habit: "Will you be able to find peppers in Paris?" "Aren't there peppers and tomatoes," the grandmother replies, "in Paris?" Ah, habit!

Habit is the art of those who change. Not the habit of changing, of resigned wandering, but the habit of remaining, the habit of inhabiting.

Surrounding Loulou Ben Aïs are his wife, brothers, parents, sister-in-law, and children. The characters of a family who are those of a story. A story of the love of places, and of amazing people. A blue arched doorway, a yellow fly sprayer, the bottom of a door, a shadow, a curtain, the triumphant buzzing of flies . . . Who has seen these things? The filmmakers have, because the actors have.

When the blue door of the house in Tunis closes for good, there is a shot of its occupants with the shadow of the bamboo curtains streaking across them.

Le Perroquet, December 9, 1983

—13—

RESTORING MEANING TO DEATH AND CHANCE

Pierre Beuchot, *Le Temps Détruit (Time Destroyed)*

Dying as a conscript in war is, for the living who loved the deceased person, testimony to everything prehistoric and barbaric about the state of humanity. The epics of those savage civilizations in which all the young men of good family were trained for such a death were well aware of this when they allowed the protestations of women or friends to be heard in opposition to the glorification of strife and blood, without deciding in favor of either one. The fact that Andromache is as worthy as Hector, that Achilles is more deeply wounded by Patrocles' death than he is glorious on account of his own valor, tells us, in songs with clashing tones, that if fighting for the survival of one's country, a politics, or freedom is necessary, that does not automatically imply that dying for one's native land is the most beautiful fate of all. War – the just war – is a form of coercion that has come down to us from the barbarians, let's not forget, and it is certainly to the credit of the invention of politics that we are able to imagine a country where the most beautiful fate for young men would be to be able to live and to think, even if necessary wars might have to be fought in order for such a thing to be achieved.

But what can be said when, in addition, someone dies as a result of a war that never took place? And which didn't take place even though, from the point of view of the person who had to fight, it was an especially justifiable war and so he had reluctantly accepted to be conscripted for it?

This is the pivotal point of our history that Pierre Beuchot's fine film *Le Temps détruit* deals with. It is about the "phony war" when, between Autumn 1939 and May 1940, the French divisions – which were every bit as armed as the German ones, despite the myths that have been bandied about since then – were in a state of morbid stagnation behind the Maginot Line, with time dragging endlessly on, the bitter-cold winter, the spectacular incompetence of the high command, and the government's hypocrisy. After this, with a mere cavalcade of tanks, the situation was destroyed by the Nazi military machine, and the old criminal Pétain emerged from the utter shambles as the man in charge of making sure any politically valid national identity would cease to exist.

Pierre Beuchot's method is that of contemporary cinema, a cinema beneath whose rigor – as we know since the works of Straub, Dindo (*Max Frisch*), Oliveira, Godard on occasion, Syberberg, and a few others – the return of the realistic repressed leads to banal images. This cinema's principles, which are in other respects flexible, necessarily include the primacy of the text, the deliberately artificial nature of the locations, the de-centering of the actor, the historical significance of the subject, and the alignment of all the material with a conception of cinema as a process of Ideas, an act of thought, not representation.

The text chosen by Pierre Beuchot is a collection of letters written by three mobilized soldiers to the women they loved. The first of these men was Paul Nizan,[1] right after his break with the French Communist Party, a break occasioned by his refusal to accept the Party's servility with regard to the Hitler–Stalin Pact. The second was the composer Maurice Jaubert, known for his film music. The third was the director's father, a worker who died when his son was two years old. The film is thus an admirable filial tribute as well, a quest for the father, and therefore for meaning, in the very place of non-meaning. The letters, read by practically indistinguishable voices that make equals of the intellectuals and the worker, are the voice of men in the non-place of war. The letters speak, very simply, of the most important connections of life: war and love, distance and waiting, matter and thought.

On the basis of these letters, which punctuate the passage of time and in which the ultimate tragedy is almost indiscernible, Beuchot shows archive footage in which the bustle of military life is seen as a sort of camp-out in the country; in which war is not captured in the changeless, ever-identical act it is – men running and falling amid the horrifying racket and smoke of the battlefield – but rather in its food, the tedium of its duties, its overwhelming inconvenience; or else in its effects, namely the destruction it causes, rendered all the more real in that it is viewed from close up, and very calmly: walls blown to bits, bridges broken in half, precarious roads. From time to time, the grotesque, mustachioed generals, their action narrated by the stirring voices of newsreel commentators of the time, hand out sandwiches paternalistically to the soldiers covered in mud and snow. The three men and their wives – who were all very beautiful – will be seen only in some old photos.

It is not true that these three poorly informed, idle men have no desire to fight. Each of them directly connects the meaning of his life and his love to the need to fight against Nazi barbarism. The worker is plagued by serious money worries where his pregnant young wife and two children are concerned, yet he is the one who complains about their not being able to do much of anything with only two twin machine guns to shoot at the Nazi planes. Jaubert, a man of tradition, is imbued with his role as an officer and conceives of his duty as being the person who will be in charge when his men attack. Nizan broke with the French Communist Party on account of this war, and when he sees the pathetic forms of entertainment cooked up by the high command to boost "the soldier's morale" he asks them to be concerned instead with "the soldier's metaphysics."

So it was really the politicians, the film claims, who decided on surrender. A bleak period it was, when the right did not want to fight because it admired the Nazi order nor did the left since, having made no genuine assessment of World War I, half were pacifists and the other half – the PCF – went along submissively with Stalin's tactics, the only real concern of which was the fate of the Russian nation.

The calmness of the film thus delivers a harsh, painful lesson. When men are uprooted from their normal lives like this, when they consent to it, and when the hidden agenda behind this uprooting is the elimination, at the cost of defeat, of every connection between politics and national identity, you've hit the bottom of the abyss. The death of these three men, all of them good people, all of them torn between life and principles, testifies to nothing, alas, but this abyss.

For there may not have been a war, but there was nevertheless a true massacre: a hundred thousand French soldiers were killed, in a random rout, in silence and meaninglessness. Among them were Nizan, Jaubert, and Beuchot. These dead are captured in the film by the place where they died – a bridge, a forest – seen from today's perspective, in color, as if a hundred thousand men were buried in black and white within a colored memory that has forgotten them forever.

But not quite. Beuchot's film is timely: everyone knows that we need to rethink France and that such thinking founders, as though on the point of its real, which is also a point of departure, on the monstrosity of the year 1940. The film's intentional tenderness, which moves one to tears, should encourage us to examine what

happened to us there and how to prevent its being constantly reproduced in the body of the nation. The film will then have succeeded
in restoring a real meaning to these three deaths, precisely because
they died completely by chance and, by all appearances, for no reason
at all.

Le Perroquet, December 31, 1985

—14—

A PRIVATE INDUSTRY, CINEMA IS ALSO A PRIVATE SPECTACLE

If cinema is everywhere, it is no doubt because it requires no spectator, only the walls surrounding a viewing public. Let's say that a spectator is real, whereas a viewing public is merely a reality, the lack of which is as full as a full house, since it is only a matter of counting. Cinema counts the viewers, whereas theater counts on the spectator, and it is in the absence of either one or the other that critics, in a disastrous paradox, invent the spectator of a film and the viewer of a play. François Regnault discerns the spectator in the chandelier; but this chandelier is the opposite of the movie projector.

I once saw Guy Debord's complete cinematographic *oeuvre* (which, significantly, had been published in book form) projected without a break, at its heart the superb *In girum imus nocte et consumimur igni* (1978), indifferent to the emptiness as much as to the fullness (not of the chandelier but of the seat) in a movie theater in Paris. This was made possible by the grace of the friendship of Gérard Lebovici, whom some killers have since thought it would be a great idea to murder (the man behind such an idea of friendship in art, it must be said regardless of all other considerations, is immediately a bit suspect for those who traffic in shadows). This pure temporal moment speaks to the glory of cinema, which may very well survive us humans. It is utterly foreign to theater, which does not take place without spectators, since in this last case the representation (a word that we will put to the test at length) turns into an additional rehearsal – unlike those "dress rehearsals" and other "final run-throughs" that, through a bit too much of the spectator's real, change from rehearsals into the show's premature having-taken-place.

In the middle of the "red years," around 1971–2, the Groupe Foudre, a group dedicated to cultural intervention, set out to raise a racket against the first eruptions of the "revisionist" malady in the reassessment of World War II. Movies such as *Lacombe Lucien*[1] or *Night Porter*[2] turned the confusion between victim and executioner into fiction and absolved criminal choices. Since then we have seen where all this led. The Groupe Foudre thus readily went to shout down and interrupt those disturbing pieces of trash. Ah, the charming light-heartedness, the polemical wholesomeness of that era! The watchword invented at the time was: "Down with the dark obscurantism of dark movie theaters!" The mistake consisted in ignoring the fact that obscurantism can only be public and that cinema, unlike theater, is by no means a public place, even if it appears to be one. What is shrouded in obscurity is the private individual, to whom, after all, we cannot deny the right to obscurity just like that. It is pointless to intervene in cinema, because there is no spectator to be found, and, consequently, no public. Being a private industry, cinema is *also* a private spectacle. The time during which the film is being projected is that of an inconsistent gathering, a serial collection of people. Cinema, disconnected from the State, proposes no collective signification. The Groupe Foudre was justified in its polemic, full of joy in its action (ah, the splashes of ink against the screen on which the colonial paratroopers were strutting, all worked up by the awful John Wayne, in that abomination entitled *The Green Berets*!), but it was mistaken in the choice of its site: theater alone is tied to the State, cinema belongs only to Capital. The former oversees the Crowd, the latter disperses individuals. Cultural-political intervention, which was what the Groupe Foudre dreamed of, has only one possible destination: the theater. In any case, even there it risks being more theatricalized than politicized.

So theater is an affair of the State, which is morally suspect, and requires a spectator. That much we know.

Excerpt from *Rhapsodie pour le théâtre: Court traité philosophique* (Paris: Imprimerie nationale, 1990)

—15—

THE FALSE MOVEMENTS
OF CINEMA

A film operates through what it withdraws from the visible. The image is first cut from the visible. Movement is held up, suspended, inverted, arrested. Cutting is more essential than presence – not only through the effect of editing, but already, from the start, both by framing and by the controlled purge of the visible. It is of absolute importance that the flowers cinema displays (as in one of Visconti's sequences) be Mallarmean flowers, that they be absent from every bouquet. I have seen them, these flowers, but the precise modality of their captivity to the cut brings forth, indivisibly, both their singularity and their ideality.

However, it is not by *seeing* these flowers that the Idea is grounded in thought, but rather by *having seen* them. Here lies the entire difference between cinema and painting. Cinema is an art of the perpetual past, in the sense that it institutes the past of the pass [*la passe*]. Cinema is visitation: The idea of what I will have seen or heard lingers on to the very extent that it passes. To organize within the visible the caress proffered by the passage of the idea, this is the operation of cinema. Each and every time, the possibility of cinema is reinvented by the operations proper to a particular artist.

In cinema, movement must therefore be thought in three different ways. First, it relates the idea to the paradoxical eternity of a passage, of a visitation. There is a street in Paris called the "Passage of the Visitation" – it could be called "Cinema Street." What is at stake here is cinema as a global movement. Second, movement is what, by means of complex operations, subtracts the image from itself. It is what makes it so that, albeit inscribed, the image is unpresented. It is in movement that the effects of the cut become incarnate. Even if, and, as we can see with Straub, especially, when it is the apparent arrest of local movement that exhibits the emptying out of the visible.

Or, like in Murnau, when the progress of a tram organizes the segmented topology of a shady suburb. We could say that what we have here are the acts of local movement. Third and finally, movement is the impure circulation that obtains within the totality that comprises the other artistic practices. Movement installs the idea within a contrasting allusion (which is itself subtractive) to arts that are wrested from their proper destination.

It is effectively impossible to think cinema outside of something like a general space in which we could grasp its connection to the other arts. Cinema is the seventh art in a very particular sense. It does not add itself to the other six, while remaining on the same level as them. Rather, it implies them – cinema is the "plus-one" of the arts. It operates on the other arts, using them as its starting point, in a movement that subtracts them from themselves.

Let us ask ourselves, for example, what Wim Wenders' *False Movement* owes to Goethe's *Wilhelm Meister*. We are dealing here with a film and a novel. We must indeed agree that the film would not exist, or would not have existed, without the novel. But what is the meaning of this condition? More precisely: Under what conditions pertaining to the cinema is this novelistic conditioning of a film possible? This is a difficult, even torturous question. It is clear that two operators are called for: that there be a story, or the shadow of a story, and that there be characters, or the allusions of characters. For example, something in Wenders' film operates a cinematic echo of the character of Mignon. However, the freedom of novelistic prose lies in not having to put bodies on display, bodies whose visible infinity evades even the finest of descriptions. Here instead, the actress offers us the body, but "actress" is a word of the theater, a word of representation. Here the film is already in the process of separating the novelistic from itself by something that we could refer to as a procedure of theatrical sampling. It is evident that the filmic idea of Mignon is installed, in part, precisely through this extraction. The idea is placed between the theater and the novel, but also in a zone that is "neither the one nor the other." All of Wenders' art lies in being able to maintain this passage.

If I now ask what Visconti's *Death in Venice* owes to Thomas Mann's, I am suddenly transported in the direction of music. The temporality of the passage is dictated far less by Mann's prosodic rhythm than by the adagio of Mahler's *Fifth Symphony*. We need only recall the opening sequence. Let us suppose that, in this instance, the idea is the link between amorous melancholy, the genius of the place, and death. Visconti arranges (or "edits") the visitation of this idea in the space within the visible that is opened up by melody. This takes place to the detriment of prose, since here nothing will be said, nothing textual. Movement subtracts the novelistic from language, keeping it on the moving edge between music and place. But music and place exchange their own values in turn, so that the music is annulled by pictorial allusions, while every pictorial stability is conversely dissolved into music. These transferences and dissolutions are the very thing that will have ultimately constituted the Real of the idea's passage.

We could call the link between these three acceptations of the word "movement" the "poetics of cinema." The entire effect of this poetics is to allow the Idea to visit the sensible. I insist on the fact that the Idea is not incarnated in the sensible. Cinema belies the classical thesis according to which art is the sensible form of the Idea. The visitation of the sensible by the Idea does not endow the latter with a body. The Idea is not separable – it exists only for cinema in its passage. The Idea itself is visitation.

Let us provide an example. It regards what happens in *False Movement* when a prominent character at long last reads his poem, a poem whose existence he had announced time and time again.

If we refer to the global movement, we will say that this reading is something like a section or a cut of the anarchic paths, the wanderings of the entire group. The poem is established as the idea of the poem by a margin effect, an effect of interruption. This is how the idea passes according to which every poem is an interruption of language, conceived as a mere tool for communication. The poem is an arrest of language upon itself. Save that in this instance, of course, language is cinematically nothing but the race, the pursuit, a kind of wild breathlessness.

If we refer instead to the local movement, we will observe that the bewilderment and visibility of the reader show that he is prey to his self-abolition in the text, to the anonymity that he becomes. Poem and poet reciprocally suppress one another. What remains is a sort of wonder at existing; a wonder at existing that is perhaps the true subject of this film.

Finally, if we turn to the impure movement of the arts, we see that the poetics of the film is really to be sought in the manner that the poetics supposed to underlie the poem is wrested from itself. What counts is precisely that an actor – himself an "impurification" of the novelistic aspect – reads a poem that is not a poem, so that the passage of an entirely other idea may be set up (or "edited"): the idea that, in spite of his boundless desire, this character will not, will never, be able to attach himself to the others and constitute, on the basis of this attachment, a stability within his own being. As is often the case in the first Wenders – before the angels, if I may put it this way – the wonder at existing is the solipsistic element, the one that, be it from a great distance, declares that a German cannot, in all tranquility, agree and link up with other Germans – for want of the (political) possibility that, today, one can speak of "being German" in an entirely transparent manner. Therefore, in the linkage of the three movements, the poetics of film is the passage of an idea that is not itself simple. At the cinema, as in Plato, genuine ideas are mixtures. Every attempt at univocity signals the defeat of the poetic. In our example, this reading of the poem allows the appearance or passage of the idea of a link among ideas: There is a (properly German) link between the being of the poem, the wonder at existing, and national uncertainty. This is the idea that visits the sequence in question. The linkage of the three movements is needed so that the mixed and complex nature of the idea may turn into what will have summoned us to thought. The three movements are: (1) the global movement, whereby the idea is never anything but its passage; (2) the local movement, whereby the idea is also other than what it is, other than its image; and (3) the impure movement, whereby the idea installs itself in the moving borders between deserted artistic suppositions.

Just as poetry is an arrest upon language, an effect of the coded artifice of linguistic manipulation, so the movements woven by the poetics of cinema are indeed false movements.

Global movement is false because no measure is adequate for it. The technical infrastructure governs a discrete and uniform unwinding, the entire art of which lies in never keeping count. The units of cutting, like the shots or the sequences, are ultimately composed not through a time measurement, but in accordance with a principle of proximity, recall, insistence, or rupture. The real thinking of this principle is in a topology rather than in a movement. As though filtered by the compositional space that is present as soon as filming begins, false movement, in which the idea is given only as passage, imposes itself. We could say that there is an idea because there is a compositional space, and that there is passage because this space offers or exposes itself as a global time. In *False Movement*, for instance, we can think of the sequence where the trains graze each other and grow distant as a metonymy for the entire space of composition. The movement of this sequence is the pure exposition of a site in which subjective proximity and distancing are indiscernible – this is effectively the idea of love in Wenders. The global movement is nothing but the pseudo-narrative distension of this site.

The local movement is false because it is nothing but the effect that follows upon the subtraction of an image (or equally of speech) from itself. Here, too, there is no original movement, no movement in itself. What there is instead is a constrained visibility that, not being the reproduction of anything at all (let it be said in passing that cinema is the least mimetic of the arts), creates the temporal effect of a journey. On this basis, visibility may in turn be attested to "off-screen" [*hors image*], as it were, attested to by thought. I am thinking, for example, of the scene from Orson Welles' *Touch of Evil* in which the fat and crepuscular cop pays a visit to Marlene Dietrich. The local time is elicited here only because it really is Marlene Dietrich that Welles is visiting and because this idea does not at all coincide with the image, which should be that of a cop being entertained by an aging whore. The slow, almost ceremonial pace of the meeting derives from the fact that this apparent image must be traversed by thought up to the point at which, through an inversion of fictional values, we are dealing with Marlene Dietrich and Orson Welles, and not with a cop and a whore. The image is thereby wrested from itself so as to be restored to the Real of cinema. Besides, local movement is oriented here toward impure movement. The idea, that of a generation of artists coming to an end, establishes itself here at the border between film *as* film, on the one hand, and film as a configuration or art, on the other – at the border between cinema and itself or between cinema as effectiveness and cinema as a thing of the past.

Finally, the impure movement is the falsest of them all, for there really is no way of operating the movement from one art to another. The arts are closed. No painting will ever become music, no dance will ever turn into poem. All direct attempts of this sort are in vain. Nevertheless, cinema is effectively the organization of these impossible movements. Yet this is, once again, nothing but a subtraction. The allusive quotation of the other arts, which is constitutive of cinema, wrests these arts away from themselves. What remains is precisely the breached frontier where an idea will have passed, an idea whose visitation the cinema, and it alone, allows.

This is why cinema, as it exists in films, is like a knot that ties together three false movements. It is through this triplicate figure that cinema delivers the ideal impurity and admixture that seize us as pure passage.

92

Cinema is an impure art. Indeed, it is the "plus-one" of the arts, both parasitic and inconsistent. But its force as a contemporary art lies precisely in turning – for the duration of a passage [*passe*] – the impurity of every idea into an idea in its own right.

L'Art du cinéma, March 1994. Reprinted in
Petit Manuel d'inesthétique (Paris: Le Seuil, 1998)

—16—

CAN A FILM BE SPOKEN ABOUT?

There is a first way of talking about a film that consists in saying things like "I liked it" or "It didn't grab me." This stance is indistinct, since the rule of "liking" leaves its norm hidden. With reference to what expectation is judgment passed? A crime novel can be liked or not liked. It can be good or bad. These questions do not turn that crime novel into a masterpiece of the art of literature. They simply designate the quality or tonality of the short time spent in its company. Afterward, we are overtaken by an indifferent loss of memory. Let us call this first phase of speech "the indistinct judgment." It concerns the indispensable exchange of opinions, which, like talk of the weather, is most often about what life promises or withdraws by way of pleasant or precarious moments.

There is a second way of talking about a film, which is precisely to defend it against the indistinct judgment. To show – which already requires the existence of some arguments – that the film in question cannot simply be placed in the space between pleasure and forgetting. It is not just that it's a good film – good in its genre – but that some Idea can be fixed, or at least foreseen, in its regard. One of the superficial signs of this change of register is that the author of the film is mentioned, as an author. On the contrary, indistinct judgment gives priority to mentions of the actors, of the effects, of a striking scene, or of the narrated plot. The second species of judgment aims to designate a singularity whose emblem is the author. This singularity is what resists the indistinct judgment. It tries to separate itself from what is said of the film within the general movement of opinion. This separation is also the one that isolates a spectator, who has both perceived and named the singularity, from the mass of the public. Let us call this judgment "the diacritical judgment." It argues for the consideration of film as style. Style is what stands opposed to the indistinct. Linking the style to the author, the diacritical judgment proposes that something be salvaged from cinema, that cinema not be consigned to the forgetfulness of pleasures. That some names, some figures of the cinema, be noted in time.

The diacritical judgment is really nothing other than the fragile negation of the indistinct judgment. Experience demonstrates that it salvages the films less than the proper names of the authors, the art of cinema less than some dispersed stylistic elements. I am tempted to say that the diacritical judgment stands to authors in the same relation that the indistinct judgment stands to actors: as the index of a temporary remembrance. When all is said and done, the diacritical judgment defines a sophistical or differential form of opinion. It designates or constitutes "quality" cinema. But in the long run, the history of "quality" cinema does not trace the contours of any artistic configuration. Rather, it outlines the (consistently surprising) history of film criticism. This is because, in all epochs, it is criticism that provides the reference points for diacritical judgment. But in so doing, it remains far too indistinct. Art is infinitely rarer than even the best criticism could ever suspect. This is already obvious if we read some bygone literary critics today, say Saint-Beuve. The vision of their century offered by their undeniable sense of quality and by their diacritical vigor is artistically absurd.

In actual fact, a second forgetting envelops the effects of diacritical judgment, in a duration that is certainly different from that of the forgetting provoked by indistinct judgment, but is ultimately just as peremptory. "Quality," that authors' graveyard, designates less the art of an epoch than its artistic ideology. Ideology, which is what true art has always pierced holes in.

It is therefore necessary to imagine a third way of talking about a film, neither indistinct nor diacritical. I see it as possessing two external traits.

First of all, it is indifferent to judgment. Every defensive position has been forsaken. That the film is good, that it was liked, that it should not be commensurable to the objects of indistinct judgment, that it must be set apart . . . all of this is tacitly presumed by the very fact that we are talking about it. In no way does it represent the sought-after goal. Is this not precisely the rule that we apply to the established artistic works of the past? Are we brazen enough to think that the fact that Aeschylus' *Oresteia* or Balzac's *Human Comedy* were "well liked" is at all significant? That "frankly, they're not bad"? In these instances, indistinct judgment becomes ridiculous. But the diacritical judgment fares no better. We are certainly not obliged to bend over backward to prove that the style of Mallarmé is superior to that of Sully Prudhomme – who in his day, incidentally, passed for a writer of the highest quality. We will therefore speak of film on the basis of an unconditional commitment, of an artistic conviction, not in order to establish its status as art, but to draw out all of its consequences. We could say that we thereby pass from the normative judgment – whether indistinct ("it's good") or diacritical ("it's superior") – to an axiomatic attitude that asks what are the effects for thought of such and such a film.

Let us then speak of axiomatic judgment.

The second feature of the judgment about a film is that no element of the film can be mentioned without its connection to the passage of an impure idea being established. I have already said two things with respect to the art of cinema, namely:

– that it treated the idea in the guise of a visitation, of a passage;
– that it referred to all the other arts, that it was their "plus-one." And therefore that its treatment of the Idea captured its impurity in a unique way.

To speak about a film comes down to examining the consequences of the proper mode in which an Idea is treated thus by *this* particular film. Formal considerations – of cutting, shot, global or local movement, color, corporeal agents, sound, and so on – must be referred to only inasmuch as they contribute to the "touch" of the Idea and to the capture of its native impurity.

As an example, take the succession of shots in Murnau's *Nosferatu* that mark the approach to the site of the prince of the undead. Overexposure of the meadows, panicking horses, thunderous cuts, together unfold the Idea of a touch of imminence, of an anticipated visitation of the day by the night, of a no man's land between life and death. But there is also something mixed and impure in this visitation, something too manifestly poetic, a suspense that carries vision off toward waiting and disquiet, instead of allowing us to see the visitation in its definitive contours. Our thinking is not contemplative here, it is itself transported, traveling in the company of the Idea, rather than being able to take possession of it. The consequence that we draw from this is precisely that it is possible to think the thought-poem that traverses an Idea – less as a cut than as an apprehension through loss.

Speaking of a film will often mean showing how it summons us to such and such an Idea through the force of its loss, as opposed to painting, for example, which is *par excellence* the art of the Idea as meticulously and integrally given.

This contrast brings me to what I regard as the main difficulty facing any axiomatic discussion of a film. This difficulty is that of speaking about it *qua film*. When the film really does organize the visitation of an Idea – which is what we presuppose when we talk about it – it is always in a subtractive (or defective) relation to one or several among the other arts. To maintain the movement of defection, rather than the plenitude of its support, is the most delicate matter. Especially when the formalist path, which leads to supposedly "pure" filmic operations, presents us with an impasse. In cinema, nothing is pure. Cinema is internally and integrally contaminated by its situation as the "plus-one" of arts.

For example, consider once again the long crossing of the canals at the beginning of Visconti's *Death in Venice*. The idea that passes here – and that the rest of the film both saturates and cancels – is that of a man who did what he had to do in his existence and who is consequently in suspense, awaiting either an end or another life. This idea is organized through the disparate convergence of a number of ingredients: There is the face of the actor Dirk Bogarde, the particular quality of opacity and interrogation carried by this face, a factor that really does belong to the art of the actor, whether we like it or not. There are the innumerable artistic echoes of the Venetian style, all of which are in fact connected to the theme of what is finished, settled, retired from history – pictorial themes already present in Guardi or Canaletto, literary themes from Rousseau to Proust. For us, in this type of visitor to the great European palaces there are echoes of the subtle uncertainty that is woven into the heroes of Henry James, for example. Finally, in Mahler's music there is also the distended and exasperated achievement, marked by an all-encompassing melancholy, that belongs to the tonal symphony and its use of timbre (here represented by the strings alone). Moreover, one can easily show how these ingredients both amplify and corrode one another in a sort of decomposition by excess that precisely serves to present the idea as both passage and impurity. But what here is, strictly speaking, the film?

After all, cinema is nothing but takes and editing. There is nothing else. What I mean is this: There is nothing else that would constitute "the film." It is therefore necessary to argue that, viewed from the vantage point of the axiomatic judgment, a film is what exposes the passage of the idea in accordance with the take and the editing. How does the idea come to its take [*prise*], how is it overtaken [*sur-prise*]?

And how is it edited, assembled? But, above all, the question is the following: What singularity is revealed in the fact of being taken and edited in the disparate "plus-one" of the arts that we could not previously think or know about the idea?

In the example of Visconti's film it is clear that take and editing conspire to establish a duration. An excessive duration that is homogeneous with the empty perpetuation of Venice and the stagnation of Mahler's adagio, as well as with the performance of an immobile and inactive actor of whom only the face is, interminably, required. Consequently, in terms of the idea of a man whose being (or desire) is in a state of suspension, what this captures is that on his own, such a man is indeed immobile. The ancient resources have dried up. The new possibilities are absent. The filmic duration – composed from an assortment of several arts consigned to their shortcomings – is the visitation of a subjective immobility. This is what a man is when he is given over to the whim of an encounter. A man, as Samuel Beckett would say, "immobile in the dark," until the incalculable delight of his torturer, of his new desire, comes upon him – if indeed it does come.

Now, the fact that it is the immobile side of the idea that is brought forward here is precisely what makes for a passage. One could show that the other arts either deliver their idea as a donation (at the summit of these arts stands painting) or invent a pure time of the Idea, exploring the configurations that the influence of thinking may adopt (at the summit of these arts stands music). By means of the possibility that is proper to it – of amalgamating the other arts, through takes and montage, without presenting them – cinema can, and must, organize the passage of the immobile.

But cinema must also organize the immobility of passage. We could easily show this through the relation that some of Straub's shots entertain with the literary text, with its scansion and its progression. Alternatively, we could turn to the dialectic established at the beginning of Tati's *Playtime* between the movement of a crowd and the vacuity of what could be termed its atomic composition. That is how Tati treats space as a condition for the passage of the immobile. Speaking of a film axiomatically will always be potentially disappointing, since it will always be exposed to the risk of turning the film in question into nothing more than a chaotic rival of the primordial arts. But we can still hold on to the thread of our argument. The imperative remains that of demonstrating how a particular film lets us travel with a particular idea in such a way that we might discover what nothing else could lead us to discover: that, as Plato already thought, the impurity of the Idea is always tied to the passing of an immobility or to the immobility of a passage. Which is why we forget ideas.

Against forgetting, Plato invokes the myth of a first vision and a reminiscence. To speak of a film is always to speak of a reminiscence: What occurrence – what reminiscence – is a given idea capable of, capable of for us? This is the point treated by every true film, one idea at a time. Cinema treats the ties that bind together movement and rest, forgetting and reminiscence, the impure. Not so much what we know as what we can know. To speak of a film is less to speak of the resources of thought than of its possibilities – that is, once its resources, in the guise of the other arts, are guaranteed. To indicate what there could be, beyond what there is. Or again: How the "impurification" of the pure clears the path for other purities.

L'Art du cinéma, November 1994. Reprinted in
Petit Manuel d'inesthétique

—17—

NOTES ON *THE LAST LAUGH*
(DER LETZE MANN)

F. W. Murnau

There is no better proof of Murnau's genius than the use he made of the codes of the time. His unparalleled mastery did not lie in breaking them, owing to some arrogant tendency of the desire for experimentation. Rather, he brought them under his control and, through the indirect use, at once deliberate and surprising, that he made of them, he forced them into the service of a coherent poetics in which those codes were not so much subverted as *accentuated*.

Murnau always gives the impression of having invented one technique or another that we know very well was quite common in the cinema of the 1920s. So, as with Aeschylus or Sophocles, there is a *higher classicism*, something as fresh as the dawn, in his art, which transforms the seen-before into the never-seen-before.

Let us consider three of these codes of the time: the recognition of the class nature of society, the technical virtuosities of silent film, and the Expressionist acting style.

The class issue, particularly in the German and Russian cinema of those years, was pervasive in cinematic impurity, on the model of the novel and the theater in this regard. It took two main forms: a populist, pessimistic cinema and a didactic, revolutionary one. In *The Last Laugh*, at any rate, Murnau might seem to be part of the former trend. Reduced to its plot alone, the film is a social melodrama. But when you *see* it, you realize that what Murnau has preserved of the classist framework is the pure form of the Two. What might have been merely the grim story of a fall in social station is in fact the filmic exploration of the resources of duality. There are two spaces in the film, the Hotel Atlantic and the working-class neighborhood where the main character lives. And a good deal of the film is devoted to the area between them. This is the constantly varying leitmotif of the trip that takes the hero from one to the other of these two spaces.

Furthermore, the Two is incessantly reduplicated, as though it were the underlying law of the visible world as a whole. Thus, the Hotel Atlantic is itself divided into two strata – the clientele and management, on the one hand, and the hotel employees, on the other – whose places only coincide when it is a matter of incidents in which no genuine *encounter* ever occurs.

But the employee stratum is also divided in two. Between the status of doorman, which fills the protagonist with such pride, and the status of washroom attendant there is a physical gulf, depicted by the sinister staircase that descends into the washroom as though into hell. Finally, this recurrence of the Two is captured by something that is its true filmic symbol: the two uniforms, the doorman's, with its fake braids that make the protagonist feel like a colonel when he wears it, and the washroom man's white jacket. Just as with the trip between the hotel and the working-class neighborhood, the theme of the two uniforms is the basis for a number of subtle variations.

The reason for this is that Murnau's art, in this as in his other films, very often consists in extracting from spatial or social differences the pure opposition between two material symbols. Thus, the Two is ultimately condensed in the change of uniform, which transforms the visible sociology of places and roles into signs. Murnau thereby manages simultaneously to preserve descriptive accuracy (the infinite materiality of social classes is never abandoned) and to place the film in a context of overall polarization, esthetically transcendent to its classist material, which allows for a formal, and ultimately conceptual, treatment of space, signs, and everything exchanged between them.

If we turn now to the techniques of "avant-garde" film – superimpositions, distortions, and so forth – they usually lead, as we know, to a cinema hystericized by the obvious desire for effect. What is unique about Murnau is that, while none of these techniques are absent from the film, a major feature of his art is its complete dishystericization. Murnau's personal myth (and *Tabu* is the culmination of this desire) is actually a totally placid world, in which the essential, quasi-timeless serenity of the visible in its entirety is on display.

In the film under consideration here, a number of less important shots of the city, its streets, and its pedestrians have no purpose other than to counteract the story's tension by presenting a vision of the world around us that is detached, eternal, and *unconcerned about* what is happening. As a result, the use of superimpositions or distortions is intended solely to inscribe the different modes of excess: intoxication or dream. These forms are not reflective of the arrogant assertion of a style. Rather, they flow naturally from the fact that the character, no longer moving about in the serenity of the world, invents a different kind of visibility. Superimposition is first of all within Being itself, as it presents itself at a given particular moment to the character. That is also why these techniques are almost like *references*: they are invoked as something available for an obvious switch to another world. Thus, the great scene where the hero juggles with the trunk is not just treated by technically virtuosic means but also clearly refers to the conventions of the circus spectacle.

The acting style of the time, without benefit of words, was deliberately expressionistic; it featured an over-emphasis on the gestural or the mimetic, which theatricalized the actor. Jannings might seem to fit in with this trend, as might the close-ups of the neighborhood busybodies. But in actual fact the carefully controlled, highly personal use Murnau made of this very analytical acting style is part of an ambitious project concerning the question of the near and the distant.

It is important to understand that, in Murnau's metaphysical relationship to the visible as serene and timeless givenness, the poetics is expressed primarily through distance: for example, the umbrellas behind the door in the film, the traffic in the city, the play of windows and shadows . . . Man, for Murnau, is merely a sign in a world which alone is truly real. The shot of Jannings sitting on the bench in the washroom shows in exemplary fashion what is involved: the place, the wall, the light all turn the actor, as though he were incorporated in the visible, into a pure sign of desolation, so pure that this desolation itself is ultimately part and parcel of the beauty of all that is. For this reason, close-ups – and the expressionistic acting style they magnify – are only ever a process of isolating the sign, whenever a temporary disjunction between that sign and the meaning of the world needs to be shown. The main figure then is bewilderment: the human sign, incorporated yet not fitting in, is clearly separated from its worldly condition in such a way that it is inwardly seized by a sense of unreality, the feel of which is conveyed by the acting in close-up.

Murnau demonstrates just as much freedom when it comes to the question of genres. Is *The Last Laugh* a comedy or a melodrama? In the universal serenity that constitutes the foundation of being, we shift from one to the other simultaneously. This is how the doorman's trips, with their identical ritual and pace, can connote either joy in the extreme or infinite grief. The scenes that take place in the working-class neighborhood, resembling Tati in their slow, multi-faceted filling of space, occupy an ambiguous border zone between breezy comedy and persecutory tragedy. All the scenes involving the suitcases and trunks (fundamental object-signs, as are the two uniforms) can be either ecstatic or agonizing. This is because the world unequivocally allows for an object, a place, or a trip to have opposite meanings: its own particular being is still *prior to* these oppositions. We could thus say that Murnau's passion is to film the trunk, or the uniforms, or the neighborhood in such a way that they are ultimately expressed "really," thus beneath (or beyond) the variations of meaning or genre that they support.

This is how the ostensible mystery of the film must be explained: the great divide running through it near the end, which, right after a shot of absolute exile and subjective death, introduces a sequence that might have been borrowed from Chaplin's funniest scenes, from *City Lights* in particular. This divide suggests that fiction, and its diverse genres, are merely devices for capturing a truth of the world, a truth that can be split at one and the same time (for the same character, in this particular case) between opposite genres. *Truth has no genre.* It is neutral because it is like a light inherent in the world itself, and because what matters to Murnau is making that light come into his films, putting the superficial diversity of images, techniques, and genres at the service of its advent.

So Murnau can freely combine materials of the time, on the basis of a claim that only cinema can make: The world is constantly redeemed by a grace of existing that encompasses the terror it breeds. Why cinema? Because the encompassing involved is that of mobility through light. *Nosferatu* can serve as a guide for us here. The terror in the film is truly subverted, from within its own escalation, by a luminous *aura* that begins right with the gloomy shots of meadows and wild horses and ends with that radiantly sunny morning in which death and love coincide.

Murnau's cinema is a cinema of the *time of light*. Indeed, this is what is epitomized in the film by the great establishing shot of the working-class neighborhood, which is simply the capture of being-light's passage over the wall, the roofs, and the windows. But in terms of the Hotel Atlantic as well, it is the play between the doors – at once transparency and closure – and the ever-enchanting outside. As for the doorman, he is the go-between, the sign circulating between transparency and the outside.

The most splendid transcription of this capturing of movement and the closed by the serene indifference of the open was no doubt given us by Murnau in *Sunrise*, in the scene, once again altogether independent of the plot, in which there is nothing but the trolley descending into town, and in which movement itself and the slow gyrations of what it enables us to see are swept away to immobility, to eternity.

For Murnau, the contrast between black and white, which places the visible in its diversity, is not the filmic construction of matter. Rather, it is through that contrast that every thing is given only insofar as it is the visible advent of its own immateriality.

L'Art du cinéma, Summer 1997

—18—

"THINKING THE EMERGENCE OF THE EVENT"[1]

What role has '68 played in your life and intellectual career?

'68, or rather the years immediately following it, has played an essential role in my life. And I think this is so for three reasons. '68 erupted during a period of intense intellectual ferment, during the period of what was termed structuralism, of Althusser's great contributions, of Lacan's seminars, and so on. At the same time, it was a period of significant political inertia. Gaullism was firmly entrenched, the economy was going through a so-called expansionary phase, and the forces of opposition were in a pretty dismal state. And this contrast between intellectual effervescence and relative political inertia was difficult, or strange, for me since I'd always been committed, on an almost ongoing basis, to one political cause after another, the Algerian War being the one that came immediately before this. '68 erupted in the slack period that had set in politically between the end of the war in Algeria and the great "red years." It came like a godsend or a moment of historical and political grace at a time when we were threatened with a rupture between intellectual construction and the figure of politics.

There was also something I call a delocalization or a displacement. Up until then, where the intellectuals, even the politically engaged ones, were concerned, political issues were dealt with in their own sphere or in terms of being a fellow-traveler of the Communist Party. But the Communist Party fellow-traveler stayed in his place and dealt with the issues in his own sphere. May '68 provided a delocalization or a trajectory, that is, it made political intervention possible in other places, with other models, other interlocutors, whether they were workers, markets, the common people, and so forth.

The third reason is that May '68 was linked to significant crises, oppositions, and controversies having to do with the Socialist bloc as a whole, with the appearance of fierce politico-ideological tension between China and the USSR. That was the beginning of a shift, of the transformation of what the Socialist states meant. It was a very long story that continued right up to their collapse in the 1980s. I was involved in these three phenomena in such a way that I think that those years constituted a radical transformation. In my own terms, and at least for me, the '68 period really played the role of an event, that is, of something that arrives as a supplement, beyond all calculation; that displaces people and places; and that provides a new situation for thought.

How did you personally participate in everything you've just described?

At the time that the events of May '68 erupted I was a teacher in Reims. So my participation was a bit peripheral. I only experienced the reflected, or delayed, glow from the events that you get in the provinces. I took part in and organized student demonstrations and meetings between the students and the striking workers in the Reims factories of the time: Chausson, Citroën, and so forth. I went to Paris a few times to find out what was going on or to take part in a large demonstration. I wasn't connected with any of the new political groups, either Communist or Trotskyist. I was in the PSU [Unified Socialist Party] and I'd been part of the group that founded it. As is well known, from May '68 on, the PSU was something of a grab-bag; all the different factions were in it. My participation in May '68 per se was tantamount to the participation of a militant of the movement and not much more. This wasn't the case later on, however, since in 1969 I was appointed to a teaching position at the University of Vincennes. So from 1969 on I was in Paris. Vincennes was a place where all the different political groups were extremely active. It was there that I broke with the PSU (which was in any case falling apart), and then, with some friends, started a distinct Maoist group, the UCFML, the Union of Marxist–Leninist Communists of France. I then embarked on years of radical militant activity that lasted for a very long time. I was involved in politics almost to the exclusion of anything else. We thought of ourselves, if not as professional revolutionaries in Lenin's sense of the term, at least as full-time political militants. Our days were spent in meetings, interventions, and con-

106

stant moving around, not just in Paris but in the provinces as well. My life was literally transformed, as compared to the life I'd led as a teacher and intellectual during my time in Reims.

Why is there an almost systematic connection between the events of '68 and the turn to Maoism?

The turn to Maoism or the adoption of the Maoist model was one of the consequences of that period for many of us. That said, you have to remember that all of this actually occurred a little before then. The two big schisms, of the Communist students and of a small fraction of the Communist Party, which resulted in the UJCML [Union of Marxist-Leninist Communist Youth] and the PCMLF [Marxist-Leninist Communist Party of France], two Maoist organizations that were very different from and even opposed to each other, dated from 1966–7 and came about as a direct result of the Sino-Soviet schism and the Cultural Revolution, on the one hand, and of a more militant point of view, on the other, especially as regards the UJCML, which was based on forms of commitment regarding support for Vietnam. The *comités Vietnam de base* can be considered as the first militant organization of a new type, practicing delocalization, in fact, and a political style that was completely at odds with tradition. These committees, which brought together people who were determined to intervene in support of the Vietnamese people but to do so in working-class neighborhoods, dated from before '68. The establishment of Maoism in France got a kick start from '68, but its roots are really elsewhere and date from a little before then. There were leaders prepared for such developments, leaders who'd learned a certain number of lessons from the Sino-Soviet schism and from the Cultural Revolution, which had begun in 1965.

To what extent did '68 act as an event and therefore as a break?

'68 is an event in the sense that absolutely nothing could have predicted it and, what's more, the course it took was very odd. It all took off from a minor incident at the University of Nanterre which, owing to a series of developments in which government blunders and brutality played their contingent role, ignited the whole student world, even in artistically very epic ways: the barricades, the paving stones, all the echoes of nineteenth-century Parisian insurrectionalism, a whole very intense historical imaginary that contributed to the movement's expansion. Onto this was then grafted a workers' movement that was double-edged in that it allowed the Communist Party, the unions, and the traditional popular and working-class forces to come onto the scene, and that's what created an unprecedented situation.

Can't the evental nature of '68 also be seen in the fact that, for a whole month, there was an unprecedented kind of creativity that the movement possessed, a capacity for reinventing itself on a daily basis?

That's one of the basic features of all true events. On the one hand, artistic activity, in its traditional forms and genres, sort of came to a halt. On the other hand, though, a kind of general creativity had free rein and spread to all the different forms of militant activity, affecting the new style of posters, which were inspired by the *dazibaos*, the great Chinese wall posters, but found their own particular forms here. The ability to transform even the form of demonstrations – their slogans, their innovations, their decorative features – corresponds to the inevitable creativity that bubbles up when, once you're seized by an event, you have to rise to the level of its novelty if you don't want to be working against it.

Did people realize that '68 was an event at the time?

Everyone experienced something absolutely clear and absolutely unclear at one and the same time. That's why those were years of great subjective tension, which were even tinged with a little anxiety. Sometimes you stretched yourself to your limits. That's because the event is only understood as such gradually, and the question of its significance, of finding out what it means to be faithful to it is an effort that has to be made partly in the dark. The awareness that something new was occurring was widespread, but there was a great temptation to refer to this newness in the old terms. The creativity I was just talking about definitely existed, but it wasn't a fully developed political creativity. What was really happening? Some people thought it was the model of the revolution itself and that we would therefore take power. The Trotskyist groups thought it was a dress rehearsal for the revolution, a little like the way the movement in 1905 had been the dress rehearsal for 1917. Still others of us, given

THINKING THE EMERGENCE OF THE EVENT"

our Maoist perspective, thought that '68 was the beginning of a long march, the inception of a new political trajectory. There were disputes and a lot of confusion, particularly because the situation was so unusual. On the one hand, there was a brand-new subjectivity, while, on the other, the State continued with business as usual. In June, the elections resulted in a solid, substantial reactionary majority. The situation of the State remained unchanged. The confusion also came from that. There was a striking contrast between activity located on some very lively fringes of society and an ongoing State situation.

In Manifesto for Philosophy *you in fact spoke about "the sequence of obscure events" with regard to the period 1965–80. Is that what it was about?*

If you consider the Cultural Revolution, May '68 and its consequences, and other political mobilizations like the ones that took place in Italy; if you add to that the radical American movements like the Weathermen or the Black Panthers; and if you push things as far as the Iranian Revolution, on one side, and the events in Poland, on the other (to take some absolutely different things), I think you have quite a long sequence, of about fifteen or twenty years, in which events of a considerable magnitude, very significant mass movements took place, although we can't ascribe any unity to them or say clearly what the sequence was. Those events were superimposed on a huge old distinction – the imperialist countries vs. the Socialist countries – without coinciding with or being explained in any way by it. This overlapping produced a period of obscure events that even today cannot be given a precise name. Personally, I'd say that, when it comes to all of this, what was really involved, whatever its colorful nature, was the question of politics itself. What is politics? What is politics if the classical Marxist idea that politics is the revolutionary form of class struggle has clearly reached its point of saturation?

Does that mean that, since 1980, we've entered into a period of silence as regards the event? That we're going through a period where things are at an ebb?

I'm not a big fan of the logic of ebb and flow because it provides too nautical a view of the historicity of politics. There's nothing new about the idea that revolutionary and counter-revolutionary periods follow one another in history. It's a phenomenon that's linked to the erratic nature of the emergence of events. So that's not really the problem for me. What has happened since 1980? The very old scheme of things has collapsed, but nothing has appeared that would revive or alter the political innovations that emerged in the preceding period. The period we're in is dominated by a sort of global stabilization and expansion of capital. There's no need to seek any particular explanation for the fact that there's been no revival of the event. Consequently, the best thing we can do is create the intellectual and practical forms of minimal fidelity to the earlier sequence and to the revival of its novelty. As I said, the *comités Vietnam de base*, the first Maoist initiatives, and so on, preceded '68. They developed elsewhere and provided a framework for the reception of the event per se. We're in a situation of that sort. I sometimes think that our situation is comparable to the 1840s. A cycle has come to an end, similar to the way that the immediate effects of the French Revolution were saturated or completed. So something else is in the works that's partly unpredictable but of which there's some hint today. The situation has not really been the same since the December 1995 strikes. Since 1995 there's been a sort of subjective shift in the situation. It began with the strike, which was based somewhat obscurely on a resistance to neo-liberalism, on the notion of public service, and on the idea that ordinary workers should be counted and heard and not treated like dirt. Then there was everything having to do with the undocumented workers, from the Saint-Bernard occupation[2] up until now. And finally there's the unemployed workers' movement, which is still trying to find a form and mode of expression for itself. We're in a period in which a potential eventual site is being developed. There are as yet no events in the philosophical sense of the word, but what we have at the very least is the development of areas of precariousness, of a partial movement that can be interpreted as heralding that something is going to happen.

To return to '68, did the '68 event constitute a paradigm for you for the implementation of your theory of the event?

Nietzsche's famous remark about a philosophy never being anything but the biography of its author should be mentioned here. It's in fact likely that the importance of the notion of the event is subjectively dependent on what I experienced. It did play an important role. It's true that, in the previous period, everyone, myself included, was geared more toward the idea of structure than to that of event.

In that regard, Pascal Bonitzer[3] recently told us that for the Cahiers du cinéma, *in the early 1970s, your Maoism was a model. Yet the* Cahiers *was influenced by structuralism, which took the form of a penetrating analysis of montage. The* Cahiers *group was influenced by Lacan, by Althusser. So what was the connection between the* Cahiers *and you?*

Intellectual history is very complicated. The exact same people were structuralists and then radical Maoists. The evental shift has to do with that, too. The Lacanians and Althusserians were Maoists. Obviously that seems paradoxical, since when you read Althusser and Lacan you have the impression that their orientation was structuralist, scientistic, and positivistic rather than evental and politically engaged. But things are a bit more complicated than that. Lacan and Althusser presented themselves as radical, renovating ruptures in the order of intellectuality. The content may have been structuralist, but the movement of thought was quasi-evental. In opposition to the dominant trends in the Communist Party, Althusser aimed to renew the reading of Marx and Marxism and ultimately the place of politics, in exactly the same way that Lacan, with his motto of "the return to Freud," waged a struggle against the American psychoanalytic establishment. Those were two gestures of rupture. That's why the people who were the most receptive to the revolutionary virtue of Marxism could identify with Althusser, just as the people who were interested in psychoanalysis could identify with Lacan. The position of the *Cahiers du cinéma*, and of many other people as well, was influenced by all of that, such that you can simultaneously see structuralist, or even formalist, tendencies in it along with a desire for rupture and radical political commitment.

In practical terms, how did you appear on the intellectual and political scene at the time for the Cahiers *group to want to seek you out?*

The connection was made by way of an article from 1967 that I'd published in the *Cahiers marxistes-léninistes*, dealing with the nature of the esthetic process. It had attracted a good deal of attention. It was entitled "The Autonomy of the Aesthetic Process." A short excerpt from it was incidentally quoted in Godard's *La Chinoise*. Since the *Cahiers* group was in search of esthetic categories, the connection was made that way. After '68 I moved in Vincennes circles, where there were lots of different people. And later on I published a number of texts, such as *Theory of Contradiction*.

Maybe we should ask what fidelity to the '68 event might be today. And first of all, is being faithful to '68 still an issue for you?

The issue still has subjective reality for me, even though the figures or modes of practice of politics are completely different. This fidelity is based on some very precise issues. In the first place, there can only really be politics, in the sense of a politics of freedom, a politics of emancipation, to the extent that you remain at a distance from the state. Philosophically, that goes so far as to say that you have to be at a distance from what I call the state of the situation. "At a distance from the state" means that the proper stakes of politics cannot be, directly, the question of power. In practical terms, this means: it's not a matter of being involved competitively in the electoral process. Politics must preserve a radical autonomy in terms of both its organization and its practice. That's what I call the need for political distance. Politics can only be constituted when it's able to create its own distance, in this case from the parliamentary state. This is something that was invented as a direct result of '68. What are the important political practices that are not crystallized or represented in what is delineated and desired by the parliamentary state? This extends to something I regard as also being part of the statist organization, namely, all the trade union apparatuses. Politics exists only if the forms of organization of local revolt establish their distance from the institutional channels of the demand. That principle, which was put forward by '68, is still valid, whatever the circumstances.

In the second place, politics exists only provided that there's a basic minimum involvement of the working-class and the common people. This may not have to do with a class framework exactly, since that framework is perhaps itself representative, in the sense of a politics referring to objective groups represented by parties. But experience shows that when there are no popular or working-class figures in the arena of politics, the hegemony of liberal bourgeois politics becomes firmly established, and that's that. These two issues are still valid. In that sense, they convey a fidelity to '68.

One of the principles of your thinking, as expressed in Can Politics Be Thought? *is "Politics is rare" or "Not everything is political." Conversely, the most famous slogan of the '68 period was "Everything is political." Does this suggest that we didn't really understand '68?*

During the '68 period, it was less a question of politics than of the ideology of politics. '68 was something really huge, which didn't completely produce the politics appropriate to it. It was above all a period of ideological militancy. I call ideological militancy the fact that there were practices, organizations, commitments (even radical and violent ones) that acted as a vehicle for systems of representation rather than stabilizing a new figure of politics. The whole problem, which is extremely complex and which would develop over time, lay in abandoning that ideologism, part of which was what you were just talking about – the equally fallacious and exciting statements such as *"Everything is political," "Sex is political," "Art is political,"* and so on – while preserving the break with the old politics.

'68 in fact raised the question of a reinvention of politics, rather than constituting a political sequence itself. That's probably why something about what name it should be given is still unsettled, even today. This doesn't prevent the fact that a certain number of the themes put forward – politics exists only if there are delocalizing trajectories, the great figures of which were the students going to work on the assembly line in factories, going into the countryside to learn from the people there and living in workers' hostels and working-class suburbs, and, conversely, the figures of the workers in the universities – are still valid.

You make a very clear distinction between politics and art. An event, you say, is either political or artistic (or scientific or amorous). But is it relevant to speak of artistic fidelity to a political event?

Artistic procedures have to be accorded their own autonomy vis-à-vis political procedures. But this autonomy may be concealed in two different ways: either under the ideological theme that was prevalent after '68, namely that *"everything is political,"* which leaves pretty vague the way things that are absolutely different from one another are politically identical, or by subjecting esthetic production to political imperatives. As far as I know, whenever a thing like that happens, the so-called political imperatives are actually *statist* imperatives. As far as I'm concerned, as you yourselves have understood, there can be no confusion between authentic political prescriptions and statist prescriptions. I can see what's meant by art's subjection to the state, but not what's meant by its subjection to politics. Art is a process of creation, and so is politics, and if they're conceived of in this way there should be no thinking of any relation of authority of one over the other. The authority of politics is only ever the authority of politics over itself.

Art endeavors to grasp the truth of something, so it also proceeds in situation and is interested in being or is required to be a *contemporary* art. After '68 the real question was: What is an art that is really contemporary with what's going on? And if what's going on involves political ideology, then: What is an art that accepts to be vitally contemporaneous with that? This is a concern you can see in Godard. Except during the extreme radical period in his career, Godard didn't subject his art to any political imperatives; rather, he tried to work in such a way that his films would be interventions whose contemporaneity could easily be seen. Let me mention the example, prior to '68, of *La Chinoise*. In no way is it a Maoist film or a film about Maoism. In this respect it's very ambiguous, and the Maoists were very unhappy about it. *La Chinoise* is simply a film that has the guts to say that it's contemporary with the establishment of Maoism. All Godard does is ask himself: What does my art make of this contemporaneity?

What was the nature of your interest in cinema and cinema criticism at that time?

First of all, we were aware – I'm taking a negative approach to begin with – of the general idea that art was also a scene in which conflicts arose. We were aware of the fact that there was a reactionary art, different from contemporaneity as we defined it. Hence my participation, around 1972–3, in the Groupe Foudre, which intervened in cinema and theater and whose primary action was polemical. This group denounced productions presenting themselves as cultural or artistic that we considered to be counter-revolutionary, reactionary, and so on. Our action sometimes took violent forms. We were very aggressive when it came to films that took a line of partial revisionism with respect to the Resistance, something that was called the "retro" current: *Lacombe Lucien*, *Night Porter*, and so on. We didn't intervene in connection with *The Sorrow and the Pity*, but we didn't like

114

it at all either. Films that called Resistance fighters' subjectivity into question on the grounds that, at the time, either everyone was a Communist or else it was purely by accident that people were on one side or the other. The ideological and historical theme of the Resistance was claimed by everyone. When we went looking for precursors for ourselves in France, that is, people who, acting on their own, had embarked on a course of confrontation, the Resistance fighters or those who had stood up staunchly against the Algerian War came to mind as models.

Aside from explicitly militant films like *La Reprise du travail aux usines Wonder* (*The Return to Work at the Wonder Factories*), a few films about the expeditions of militants to Flins, and the reference to Chinese or Soviet revolutionary films – hence films that were directly involved in militant activity – I don't remember there being any works of art that incorporated politics. I wonder whether great periods of intense political ferment are entirely conducive to artistic production. What I'm saying is a bit troublesome, but it's understandable. The intensity of things was such that the best minds were being strongly solicited by the power of politics.

Our question about the connection between politics and art was directed at something a little different. Quite apart from subordination, what might be the nature of the passages that occur between a political-type event and its artistic repercussions?

I can see no type of mediation other than what I call contemporaneity. Art, generally speaking, is a signifying formal organization of the sensible, within which it obeys its own events, its own rhythm, and produces its own historicity. On the other hand, the question of its contemporaneity is constantly being raised, with respect to the situation of art first of all but also in connection with a broader contemporaneity. The problem is never one of direct transition but rather of contemporaneity. Take a filmmaker of the year 1971: there's no way he or she could avoid the question. After '68 you have a fundamental and extremely deep split between those who thought what was happening was great and those who thought it was terrible and ought to stop.

Does this concern with contemporaneity bear the name of fidelity or is it something else?

115

Fidelity has a technical meaning for me. You can use that word if you like. In any case, the artist is forced to have minimal fidelity to his or her own subjective choice. He or she cannot do otherwise, short of finding him or herself in a schizophrenic position. At the same time, this obligation is time-bound; it lasts as long as the political solicitation is unavoidable across the board. In the years 1970–2, ultimately – and to give those years their general definition – either you were with the *gauchistes* or you were against them. There was no in-between. That's also what an event of a political nature is like: it's for everyone. There's not just a problem of contemporaneity but also an interpellation by it, something that's not the case with scientific or artistic events.

To take things in the opposite direction again, that is, from art to philosophy, what is the nature of the resonances from one domain to the other? For example, in a text on Murnau's The Last Laugh *that you wrote for* L'Art du cinéma, *you spoke of the Two, a key theme of yours, since politics (or love) can exist only in the emergence of the Two.*

Art has naturally contributed to the development of my intellectuality. It's one of philosophy's conditions for me. Art plays a major role in shaping subjectivity because it acts as a sort of impregnation. It has a powerful unconscious effect, its own distinct effect on the general structures of desire. Why did post-revolutionary states place art under such close surveillance? You can say that they were terrorist states and that they enforced censorship, but that doesn't solve the problem. Quite simply, those states gauged art's effects accurately. On the people it affects – and they can be only a small minority but it doesn't matter because it's very well known that important things always begin with a small number – art has a major impact.

For example, is New Wave cinema, apart from its subject matter, something important for you?

Yes, it's part of the political sequence. Films that, ideologically, seemed only to be about romantic nihilism with no political implications – *À bout de souffle* (*Breathless*), for example – had a real impact during the sequence, an impact that had to do with something else. It had to do with wandering and delocalization, with intense self-interrogation rather than interrogation through the intermediary of established representation, via the figure of a character who's anything but stable. In this sense, those films contributed to preparing the ground for the post-'68 delocalizations.

In your opinion, films that are genuinely contemporary with the '68 sequence are quite rare.

So it seems to me. But maybe you're going to call me out on this now.

No, that seems to be pretty much the case. You mentioned Godard. What about the Straubs' films?

Where the Straubs are concerned, their films certainly have to be included in the field of that which – since it had the force of artistic innovation – was homogeneous with the contemporary. Nevertheless, I don't see anything in their films that really resonates with the ideological militancy we were talking about. Their art is more monumental. It's pretty hard to think of Straub and Huillet as '68 directors. I see them more as timeless Marxists constructing pure forms. They were interested in the Palestinian problem, in workers, in class relations – all of that can be found in their films, but, oddly enough, not the sequence we're concerned with.

When they made Othon, *after '68, wasn't it a provocation vis-à-vis the '68ers in the guise of an appeal to memory? Such a treatment of politics always linked to the theme of memory would seem to be what pits you against each other.*

It's an appeal to memory, but it's also an appeal to structure. To the people of '68 the Straubs say more or less the following: the question of power, of class relations, is a lot older than your own sequence; it's also a lot more powerfully structured than your political activity imagines. This is what I call, with just a little exaggeration, the Straubs' lesson about timelessness. They are very forcefully didactic, in the Brechtian sense. They lecture a bit, in the good sense of the term. With respect to the sequence, they look down at it from above. Their position is homogeneous with the sequence because the Straubs were motivated by critical thinking, by a real analytical Marxism, but it's a position of looking down from above because its temporal arc is longer. I always think the Straubs' cinema is about the first sentence of *The Communist Manifesto*: "The history of mankind is the history of class struggle." It's the history of mankind, from the Greeks up until the present day; it's not the petty history of '68.

So in that case, instead of "timeless" shouldn't we say "obsolete," made obsolete by the '68 event?

I do think they failed to get something. But their cinema is a unique artistic achievement and it should be respected as such. Naturally, something of the conception I may have of politics, in fidelity to '68, doesn't feature in their films. They have a different idea: a film can capture a sort of metonymy of the power and class relations that structure History with a capital H. That's the temporal arc, which is in some respects non-eventual, within which they construct their forms. I'm thinking of the very unique role played by immobility, slowness, totality in their films. I'm thinking of the very beautiful, interminable 360-degree camera rotations in the Italian landscape of *Fortini/Cani*, which express something along the lines of: there's also the whole earth, the whole of space . . . Where I differ from the Straubs, philosophically now, would be in terms of the role of continuity and totality. In their work, everything is constructed in such a way that it appears inscribed, as it were, in a totality. But I credit them with sticking brilliantly to the idea that every question is always larger in scope and much older than we think. So they're ultimately pretty contemptuous of all circumstantial political activity.

The Straubs' latest film, Du Jour au lendemain (From Today Until Tomorrow), *was about the idea of novelty and suggested that true novelty is in fact what lasts over time.*

It's a film that I liked a lot in some respects, but it can be regarded as being downright reactionary. *Du Jour au lendemain* is an ambiguous, absolutely intentionally provocative film. It says that marriage is better than having affairs, that the institution is better than sexual opportunities, that you shouldn't give in to temptation, along with the old idea that temptation is evil. But compared with their other films – and this was already the case with Schoenberg[4] – there's a muted irony in it. That's what I liked about it: it's the first of the

Straubs' films that works a bit on ambiguity. I think it was made in such a way as to be undecidable.

To go back to the idea of false novelty: didn't '68 produce its own share of it? For example, the main effects of the use of slogans were felt in advertising. When you consider its advertising or "sociological" after-effects, isn't it possible to see what was fake about '68?

That has to do with the ambiguous or undefinable nature of '68 rather than with its essential determination. There were obviously some trivial strata of thought in '68: its somewhat festive aspect, the "sociology of youth" aspect, the belief that it was first and foremost about a sexual revolution . . . '68 was remarkably impure. What I'm talking about is only one aspect of '68, the one I regard as politically fundamental, which has to do with delocalization, the distance from the state, and so on. All of this was captured in one wildly eclectic grab-bag; you can find whatever you want in it.

Wasn't '68 the point of departure for what you very vehemently castigate in your book Ethics, *namely the bland, pointless apology of difference, the ideology of human rights, the vacuous theme of respect for the Other?*

No, I don't think so. The post-'68 years were on the contrary characterized by a very harsh critique of everything ethico-moralizing, together with a certain taste for violence, even. What's at the root of what I criticize in *Ethics* is the counter-current to '68 that began in 1976–7 with the "New Philosophers." It's a common post-evental phenomenon. Every remarkable event generates, from within itself, its own reactionary subjective figures. This is what I'm currently trying to analyze. The subjective production of an event involves, on the one hand, fidelity and, on the other, the creation of reactionary figures that are themselves truly inventions. Action has to be invented, but so does reaction.

By thinking politics as being under the condition of the emergence of events, you invite us to think it outside the notion of representation. Politics exists only when what is happening stops being a mere reflection of the overall situation. You also say that politics requires

119

delocalizations. Deleuze is the person we immediately think of here. Through the work of Carmelo Bene, for example, Deleuze thinks a non-representative art, in which representation yields to variation and the becoming-minority. Where do you stand in relation to these concepts of Deleuze's?

There are obvious points of consonance between us. What's more, as regards the fundamental choice – being with or against the *gauchistes* – Deleuze was obviously a thinker who was part of the movement. But I have misgivings about some of the categories he used to think the period in question because I believe they connect it to an overly generic vision of becoming. In "becoming-minority" I don't like either "becoming" or "minority." As far as I'm concerned, it's not exactly a matter of becoming but of a trajectory, of a topological change: what was in one place is displaced to a different place. It doesn't become something other than what it is; rather, being what it is, it becomes located somewhere else. It's not a principal of change, in the sense in which change is very important for Deleuze. As for "minority," the end result of that category, in my opinion, was the American Left. "Minority" now means "identifiable as a minority in the form of a community": women, Blacks, homosexuals, and so on. This territoriality of minorities is not exactly what it was about in '68. It was about delocalization and the construction of figures, which is something else. The conception of the '68 sequence that you can get from Deleuze's philosophy privileges the processes that were the most ideological and the least political. The basic reason for this is that, for Deleuze, there's no autonomous thinking of politics. In *What Is Philosophy?* the three systems of thought are science, art, and philosophy. Indeed, for Deleuze, politics is ubiquitous. So it doesn't constitute an autonomous register of thought. Deleuze had his own fidelity to '68, which, in my opinion, was fidelity to what was most ideological about '68.

If we take off from the question of representation now, it is striking that, at the same time, thinkers of politics (like you) and thinkers of art (like Deleuze) proposed categories other than representation. In a word, who influenced whom?

We both hail from the period of the critique of representation. But that critique began from within the artistic, rather than the political, process. It then spread to the point where it became central to philosophy.

120

Can you tell us about your history as a filmgoer? Are you a cinephile?

I am effectively a member of the cinephile generation. When I was at the École Normale Supérieure, I used to go to the Cinémathèque; I devoured everything I could of the great classic filmmakers, from the silent era right up until the present day, and eagerly followed the emergence of the New Wave. I never regarded myself as being a cinema critic, but I was a devoted cinephile.

Pascal Bonitzer reminded us that all the cinephiles went through a phase of doubt, doubt about Bazin and cinema as a whole, which was suspected of being essentially ideological and bourgeois. Did you experience a phase of doubt like that?

I never doubted cinema *qua* cinema. Of course, during the great militant period, I analyzed it above all in terms of its ability to be homogeneous with or opposed to what we were doing, which wasn't an attitude conducive to a detailed analysis of its artistic potentialities. But I never went so far as to doubt that cinema had its own artistic purpose. My doubts about it are more recent. It's the current period that's problematic for me, even though I don't impose any particular political requirement on cinema, any more than on anything else. I have trouble understanding precisely what its current artistic purpose is, in terms of trends, phases, and so on. I reject the idea of the death of cinema, since I'm always wary of the theme of the end, in philosophy as in art. In the recent past, what I was able to identify, as proof of cinema's ongoing creativity and contemporaneity, was, at a given moment, a certain Portuguese cinema, and certain Iranian filmmakers today. But these are local things, associated with retrospective assessments of historical events. Portuguese cinema was a way of dealing in thought, after the fact, with the 1974 revolution and its consequences. For a certain number of intellectuals, Iranian cinema is clearly a way of thinking the fate of their country in the post-Khomeini period. As for the rest, I'm sort of groping in the dark. What should be thought of the obvious formalism or mannerism of a certain American or Asian cinema? What is French cinema today? For all these questions I have no considered answer.

Isn't that an evental-type confusion, as was the case for politics during the '68 period?

121

During that period, there was an unshakable conviction, even if the names were unclear, that something new was happening. Today, that conviction is itself unclear. I can't determine either a continuity or a discontinuity. If I see one of old Oliveira's films, I can understand what formal history it's inscribed in. But Oliveira's a survivor. In addition, Eastwood practices a sort of identifiable saturation of something involving genres. But as for a principle of innovation that can be formally identified, I can't see any.

Even though there's this doubt you mentioned, there's a growing interest in cinema on the part of philosophers. There was Deleuze, of course, and now Rancière and yourself, but also Nancy, Lyotard, and others from time to time. How has cinema become a matter of thought for you? And then, what is implied by this interest philosophers have been showing in cinema?

You have to make a distinction between the good reasons for it and the bad. First, the "bad" reason. In the general scheme of things, cinema serves as a mediation. You have to be able to talk about common experience, after all. If you talk about mathematics (which is very important for me) you're forced to do everything: be the teacher of the math you're talking about, make sure that what you're saying is being understood and, finally, enter into its philosophical elucidation. It's the same with contemporary poetry. Cinema, on the other hand, is a term of common experience.

As for the good reasons, there's sort of an enigma of cinema today. An initial idea had first to be established, by Bazin and the *Cahiers*: namely that cinema was an art. Then there was a second sequence, dominated by the question of cinema's relationship to contemporaneity, to politics. And the third sequence is still wondering what question it's asking of cinema. The philosopher comes in where a question is lacking. He attempts to contribute to the formulation of the question. Deleuze intervened to say that the questions he was asking of cinema were wholly philosophical. For him, cinema's concepts were not internal to cinema. Ultimately, the questions have to do with time and movement, and cinema is an extremely important field in which to elucidate these critical questions. It's a normal, necessary process: a philosopher is attracted by any field in which it's clear that a question is lacking. How will the eternal question – what is cinema? – be posed anew?

122

Do you feel close to Bazin, with whom you share, for example, the notion of grace (cinematic realism or the event as grace)? Is he an important thinker for you?

The fact that Bazin was an important thinker is not even up for debate. In the period he worked in, he formulated the question and gave it its proper answer. He did so in a philosophical framework that isn't the same as mine, but that's not a problem. Something Bazin addressed, which in my opinion is still valid, is what I call the element of visitation particular to the cinema. As a viewer, I am increasingly struck by how important that point is. You have to begin with this simple problem: What goes on in cinema? What happens? You have to go back and start from there in order to deal with the enigma of cinema today. What is the passage or the visitation of the idea in cinema? Identifying cinema on the basis of the image isn't sufficient. You have to delve further into the specific way in which cinema is a thought. That thought is the coming of something: it comes, but *how* does it come? When can we determine that it has come? And how can it come today? What does cinema think that nothing but it can think? What accounts for its being something other than a phenomenon of opinion? At what point is it able to interrupt opinion and suddenly propose something else? This is my sphere of investigation. I assume that cinema is an arc of time or of passage, but what I'm interested in knowing is how there is identification in cinema based on what passes. In this sense, there's a dimension of visitation or grace in cinema that is particular to it.

What's striking about your text on Murnau are certain phrases such as "the passage of the immobile," which recall Deleuze's distinction between movement-image and time-image and suggest some aspects of Asian cinema, either contemporary, by way of Hou Hsiao-hsien, or traditional, by way of Ozu.

It has always seemed clear to me that Ozu and Murnau have something in common. In both cases, the presentation of the idea in the figure of the passage of the immobile is the key issue. But does that concern cinema as a whole or just a certain stylistics? I don't know for sure. However, at a given moment, something of the idea's eternal immobility is expressed through its passage. With some filmmakers, that passage is the main principle of the film's construction. But there are other filmmakers who construct their films in a more kaleidoscopic way so as to attain immobility by means of a fragmented mobility. That's the case with Welles. But the question remains unresolved. I'm going to ask it in a way that's rather aggressive and provocative to you: Is cinema a major art or a minor one? The relationship, which is not automatically evident, between this question and the one before is as follows: cinema is impure and this impurity is both a strength and a weakness. It's a strength because it allows cinema to have an extremely wide range of resources available to it. I'm very struck by cinema's ability to absorb things that are very remote from it, possibly even very remote from its immediate appearance. And it's a vulnerability because it allows cinema to have an inner eclecticism, meaning that we're often surprised to see that a film can be fleetingly excellent, and then be trivial. All of a sudden, the film can rely on something that comes from elsewhere but allows it to hold together. Witticisms can be injected into it, or an allusion to painting, or music that overpowers every-thing, or an always effective figure of melodrama, and so on. When I say "minor art" what that means is that cinema's essential, complex impurity is so precarious that the conditions to maintain it will have existed only gradually and under restrictive conditions. Technical development is an indefinite extension of cinema's impurity. When cinema was silent, black and white, produced in the studio, and so on, the need for it to focus on its own ends was imposed on it. Cinema is a minor art if the extension of its impurity is such that it has become very difficult for it to be anything other than a phenomenon of opinion. It's a major art if, on the contrary, what is occurring – which we can't completely make out – is the development of a new age of cinema in which, having expanded its capacity almost to the fullest, it invents absolutely new and original modes of the passage of the idea. That's the source of my hesitation. I wonder if the issue today isn't the triumph of cinema's virtuosic impurity. It's well known that virtuosity is a figure of decline. Or, on the contrary, is cinema in the position of an apparatus whose power must be harnessed in some art of the future? I often think that cinema has reached the era of the orchestra and romantic opera. You can have two hundred musicians, but you still need a Wagner or an Alban Berg to control them. At bottom, is cinema too cumbersome for its own grace? It has long been said that to receive grace you have to be living in ascesis. It's a very ancient idea: grace comes to the poor. But cinema isn't poor, and all the well-inten-tioned efforts to make it poor are artificial. It has to be accepted as it is. But is the fleeting visitation of the idea as grace and as passage still valid? That's what I'm looking into.

124

When you were talking about fragmented mobility and kaleidoscopic vision a moment ago, we were in fact expecting you to mention Hou Hsiao-hsien.

I've only seen one film of his. I don't go to the movies all that much anymore. It's not because I'm contemptuous of what's being made, but my investigation is still narrow and limited in scope. I wait, a little too long at times, I intend to go see a film and then sometimes I don't go. What I'm telling you is just an uninteresting empirical fact, but I'll take your word for it when you cite important filmmakers regarding the issues I've been speaking about.

It sounds like your taste would run more toward a cinema that was subtractive, spare, or refined in a certain way, something abstract, as opposed to an excess of virtuosity. That said, isn't there a sort of abstraction in mannerism?

Absolutely. That's what I've called formalism, but mannerism is perhaps a more appropriate term. Nevertheless, it remains to be seen for what power of thought this type of abstraction, non-representation, non-identificatory realism, which is clearly very prevalent in a large swath of contemporary cinema, serves as a vehicle. I think this mannerism is still caught up in experimenting with its own techniques rather than having found its grand design, its mighty purpose. It's still a little too much art for art's sake. But perhaps this is just an experimental or passing phase.

We think that someone like Wong Kar-wai, for example, possesses all of mannerism's tics whereas in actual fact he goes beyond it.

Yes. This question of mannerism and its destiny is key. Wasn't it in the *Cahiers* that an article was published saying that *Titanic* heralded the end of mannerism? If we identify a period in terms of the formal principle underlying it, if we therefore say that there's a mannerist period, it's because we haven't completely figured out what it's about yet. Mannerism is still too formal a category to really identify what's at stake in the period. We're still left with the question of what phase contemporary cinema is in. Isn't what's developing now in fact something like neo-classicism? I don't regard neo-classicism as a negative figure. There were important neo-classical periods in the other arts.

125

For example, between the two World Wars there was a neo-classical period that both Picasso and Stravinsky were involved in, which can be seen, as regards the earlier great transformations, to have been a necessary phase. You can find the same thing in painting, at the time of David or Ingres, between eighteenth-century mannerism and what would extend, with Delacroix, right up to the Impressionists. Once you've reached a certain degree of mastery of mannerist virtuosity you're forced to superimpose on that mastery a framework that can be identified, or represented, because, otherwise, what I call the passage of the idea becomes too erratic, too scattered over the surface of mannerism. So in this sense the neo-classical period takes in mannerism.

There is still another cinema we wanted to talk to you about, the current American cinema.

In that cinema, the formalist-mannerist power has yet to invent, from within itself, a discipline of the macro-structure.

When we watch American films – commercial, major, Hollywood films – we're struck by how relevant some of your concepts are in terms of these films' vision. In particular, this cinema is the only one that systematically struggles with the impossible, which is a key notion for you since you make it the very basis of politics. We're coming back here to a question we've already broached. In American cinema, the project always involves resolving the impossible, on the screen and during the time of the story. Is this an aspect of things that interests you?

Give me your most recent example.

Desperate Measures, *the film by Barbet Schroeder. A father, who's a police officer, has to find a bone marrow donor for his son who has leukemia. The only possible donor is a psychopathic criminal. They get him out of prison, but then he escapes. They've got to find him, but he can't be killed because he'd be of no use if he were dead. This can be regarded as a way of creating harmony, through the story, between the positive and negative poles of a country: the family and the criminal. And the action gives rise to impossible situations, to the insoluble. It's on account of this that American cinema is great, on account of the way it takes on the impossible, hence politics, on account of the way it makes a utopia possible within the time of the story. Ford's films can be regarded this way, too.*

I was thinking of Ford as I was listening to you. If you're trying to explain cinema's power other than by reasons having to do with its infrastructure and industry, look no further. American cinema is unquestionably one of the greatest artistic creations of the century. What you're saying implies that this cinema accepts being very radical in terms of the type of relationship of fiction to the real that's called the impossible. In French cinema, on the contrary, there has always been a tendency to avoid the impossible as much as possible, hence the slide into an intimist mode, in which nothing is either radical or subjected to a tension as sublime as that featured in American cinema. This is a very important problem: how does cinema frame its relationship to the real (in the Lacanian sense, not that of realism), to the point of the real, to the point of the impossible? When you claim that it's always a question of establishing a situation in which the insoluble is the main focus, you're right. The big problem, which can be tackled in America and not, perhaps, in France, is as follows: in order for there to be a fictional visibility of the impossible there have to be great, diametrically opposed categories at work. For example, the problem of good and evil has to be powerful. The visibility of the impossible can then be organized as the interweaving of two categories in a single point. A certain American manicheism may have accounted for this cinema's being so powerful, a manicheism that's often distressing but is also a source of creativity.

That's also what might make it impossible for American cinema to escape the sphere of representation.

That's perhaps the price that has to be paid: it's impossible to go any farther than making that tension visible through representation, the result of which is a powerfully representative, even allegorical, dramatic art. You mentioned utopia, but utopia goes with an allegorical stylistics, which is moreover very well suited to mannerism because it can take this general allegorism apart and disseminate it. Ultimately, the impossible can be broken into pieces. Lacan said "The real is little grains." Maybe the impossible is little grains, too. Mannerism makes it possible to have a succession of categorical collapses

127

that constantly drive the whole. But can a break with representation be located there? That's no doubt the big problem. Doesn't that sort of impossible always require a semi-epic dramatic art, which French cinema is incidentally radically incapable of?

Your Saint Paul *book is concerned with a "rare and heroic subject." American cinema has this ability to create rare and heroic subjects almost* ex nihilo, *and that's what's really lacking at this time in French cinema, which is moreover obsessed with the theme of resistance.*

I agree. To refine the question, it would be necessary to distinguish between the capacity for creating figures and the capacity for representation. How, in a system that is not necessarily representative, can figures, including heroic figures of resistance, be created? In Brecht's work, despite the criticisms that can be directed at him regarding his belonging to the age of representation, there is something of the sort: the creation of characters in a mode that's not necessarily representative or epico-narrative but sufficiently fragmented or localized to give rise to something else. I'm thinking of the character of Galileo, which is more divided into sections than created by a system of representation.

Can you give an example of that in the cinema?

I'm going to give you a really old example again: Welles. *Mr. Arkadin* unquestionably stands for an attempt to create a character other than by strictly representative means. Abstraction is achieved insofar as the character is not directly shown but is instead the object of an investigation, and this investigation is in turn subject to a sort of fragmentation and constant delocalization such that it cannot be typified in a place or closely associated with a place. There can be no cinema without the creation of a character. That's why American cinema remains predominant. And it remains so because that's what people expect from it, and rightly so. That's its deep inner calling.

Les Cahiers du cinéma, special issue Cinéma '68, May 1998

128

—19—

THE DIVINE COMEDY AND THE CONVENT

Manoel de Oliveira

Putting these two films together is not just some whim of mine. What's more, I'd like to put them together under the sign of the cosmopolitan artist in Oliveira, the artist who, understanding Portugal's uniqueness better than anyone else, extracts from it, as Pessoa does, its enigmatic universal promise. Where *The Divine Comedy* and *The Convent* are concerned, it is German art that comes to mind. Yes, there is a German streak in the great Oliveira, a way of structuring Portuguese Catholicity through the myths and parables with which Germany has been enchanting its uncertainty about itself as a nation for the past two hundred years.

This inner Germany, which is at times like a secret formalism, is explicit in *The Convent* – even if the original idea for the screenplay was Agustina Bessa-Luís' – because, circulating insistently within it, between a professor who is trying to prove that Shakespeare was really a Spanish Jew and an angelic librarian named Piedade, is a translation of *Faust*, a gift from the angel to the neurotic scholar. But this is a figure in the carpet, since the film's story (only barely adumbrated, as usual) is a freakish deviant of Goethe's play: the Faust-professor, accompanied by a Helene (Catherine Deneuve, opaque mature womanhood) whom we will see emerge from the sea like Venus at the end of the film, arrives at Mephistopheles' home, a seedy, isolated convent, where Luís-Miguel Cintra is flanked by two comical, erotically overstimulated assistants. Mephistopheles will tempt Faust twice. At the top of a mountain, he will promise him immortality. And he will offer him the Gretchen-librarian, reserving for himself the task of corrupting the blond Helene. His plot fails, because the two women get wind of it and defeat it. Helene, purified by the sea, departs with her husband, and Piedade, confessing that she is inspired only by the thirst for God, leads Mephisto off into a flaming abyss.

129

So it is true, as the last sentence of *Faust* has it, that "the Eternal Feminine leads us on high."

In *The Divine Comedy*, the matrix isn't as clear. It is nevertheless impossible for me not to think of Thomas Mann's *The Magic Mountain*. There is the same idea of gathering together a kind of sampling of the decrepit West in a hermetic medical locale (a sanatorium in Mann, a psychiatric asylum in Oliveira). The same structuring of the whole around theoretical discussions, more speculative in Mann, more theological in Oliveira. The same role played by uncanniness, underscored in Mann by isolation, snow, X-rays, unrecognizable death, and, in Oliveira, by the various character-types of madness: in the film there is a Raskolnikov escaped from *Crime and Punishment* (we even see the hatchet murder), a second-rate Nietzsche, a man who lives in his future coffin, and so forth. The same softening function of women, love and mysticism intermingled. The same transcendence of art, embodied in the film by Maria João Pires at the piano.

But what is German about these films exceeds the plot, or the material, by far. It is to the allegorical structure that attention should be paid, to an always risky manner of conferring its spiritual cohesion on the system of forms *from without*. All of German art, with the notable exception of Fontane, has been to some extent contaminated, since *Wilhelm Meister's Apprenticeship*, by this didacticism of the Idea and by an educational aim residing in the gap between the narrative or psychological elements and the emphasis on their symbolic role. Oliveira is not always any lighter. Thus, the opening scene, in which two of the inmates, naked in the garden, play the roles of Adam and Eve eating an apple, alerts us to the fact that the asylum's common folk represent Humanity suffering from the torments of sin and faith. We are not even spared the snake crawling in the grass. It can hardly be doubted that there is a touch of humor in this, but not enough to cancel out the heavy-handed insistence. Similarly, in *The Convent*, the big scene between the tempter Mephisto and the Gretchen-librarian, in a forest populated by witches, is certainly not without beauty, owing to the way the linear face of the actress is embedded in the suspicious twisting of the trees' branches. But it only reveals what the implicit matrix had long ago apprised us of: here, desire and grace face off, ambiguously, and with no certain outcome.

Ultimately, the art of these films is oblique. It stems from the eruption in the story of virtually empty shots whose function is to make us wait for the symbolic resolution. Sea, rowboat, and fisherman in *The Convent;* piano playing, armchairs, and windows in *The Divine Comedy*. As though, next to the stage on which Good and Evil set out their references and their arguments, cinema were capturing the indifferent survival of the visible.

L'Art du cinéma, Fall 1998

SURPLUS SEEING

Jean-Luc Godard, *Histoire(s) du cinéma*

What is it all about? Discussing his panorama, which he calls "programs" but which I will call "the film," Godard puts up the pretense of being an archivist, refers to Foucault, and situates his project somewhere between History and Idea. But aren't these just rehashed remarks, like one more layer, which could be added to everything bandied about the man with the cigar and the lamp (the great artist-scholar under the icon of Groucho Marx) whose return, with the clacking of his typewriter, alerts us to the fact that, in the "film," all this visual terror entitled *Histoire(s) du cinéma* is the intellectual biography of one man alone?

Or: the abstract definition of cinema is the encounter between a movement-image and a real. Is it this encounter that the "film" turns into its subject matter, by using the all-important techniques of virtuosic montage, of superimposition, of the sudden divergence between the visible and the audible, of the murmuring that we know never stops beneath the aphorisms, as though every truth were laboriously extracted from the diffuse background noise? But huge mountains of text, or big chunks of allusive knowledge, the frame frozen on a female speaker's angelic face, preclude this idea of a constant dis-encountering and re-encountering (folding and unfolding, Deleuze would have said) whose only purpose would be to dwell on the elusive rightness of the images, or on their manifest wrongness. Instead, we see a confrontation arising between an overly solitary artist and that enormous black hole of the century whose name was "World War II."

Or: Godard's subject was said to be the genealogy of cinema's power. But isn't it just as much a question of its powerlessness? The impossibility of filming certain things has always haunted Godard: the factory, sex, extermination. So the aim of this enormous palimpsest, the "film," might be to identify, by using the cumulative resources of omnipotence (we can make whatever we want of the conglomeration of images and sounds), the point of impotence, which, in the end, is cinema's entire real, and the ultimate reason for its downfall. Hence, too, the ambiguous status of the books that Godard takes down from the shelves of his bookcase in "the film," the titles or short passages of which he reads aloud. While the conglomeration of power incorporates, mixes, and inscribes books in the polyphony, subordinating their power now and then to the power cinema possesses owing to its ability to reach masses of people (numbered in the millions, while the audience for books is numbered in the thousands) and to the real dignity of filming stories (*L'Espoir*, the film, so close to *L'Espoir* the book), Godard simultaneously suggests that books remain in reserve, that their visibility is only apparent, and that this reserved availability of the written word may keep a surer watch over the real than images do.

Or: a symphonic totalization. A "complete resurrection of the past,"[1] not merely by referring to or recounting it but by combining thematic dissection (how does cinema deal with war, love, women's beauty, revolution, massacres, mythologies, countries, and so on?) and local contraction, which gathers all the available interpretations together in one point. From this there results a method of composition that can be rightly compared to Mallarmé's in *Un coup de dés* (*A Throw of the Dice*). A few key phrases, often displayed in capital letters in the frame (HISTOIRES DU CINÉMA, FATAL BEAUTY, YOU HAVEN'T SEEN ANYTHING, A NEW WAVE, etc.), elicit texts that are presented beneath them, texts that are themselves accompanied by a quasi-inaudible murmur or are metaphorized by musical themes. Meanwhile, the references to films are treated as supports for infinite variations, by means of colorization, slowing down, superimposition, reversals, cuts, miscellaneous comments, recurrences, outlining, and obvious distortions. What's more, rather than operating "beneath" the crucial phrases, secondary constructions operate right beside them, like exposed fortifications. This is particularly the case with the film titles, which, independently from all the rest, gradually compose the dispassionate, immutable roster of names of what remains.

But it is also possible to see "the film" again in terms of the exceptions to this elaborate treatment, in which the simultaneous layering of the visible and the audible multiple lifts to the surface, as the ocean does a boat, not just the semantic organization of "the film" but also all the virtually infinite associations that a constantly alert, restless mind detects in the slightest statement, associations symbolized, right at the level of the basic phrases, by attempts at combining letters or words. Take, for example, the move from NEW WAVE to A NEW WAVE[2] or the subjective injunction TOI [YOU] extracted from the word HIS(TOI)RE, not to mention the amusing little diversions like SI JE NE MABUSE[3] and many other anagrams. One exception is the quiet terror of a sequence from *The Night of the Hunter*, the sequence involving the children in the raft, which is allowed to float down the river at night without any alterations or cuts to the scene. Or the deliberate return of the machine gun sequence in *L'Espoir*. Or one moment or another in which the naked word is conveyed by a face. Or the insistence of a given passage of music, which is like the grace of serenity visited upon the hubbub of the visible. Or even the fleeting insertion of a pornographic scene, whose sudden ugliness stands out like a stain on silk. And then you can't help but think that the super-lative art of the montage, which turns the "film" into the equivalent of a multi-voice conversation crafted by God, or of a polyphonic Renaissance composition, exists only to make us want it to go on, in the same way we watch for the scattered, well-nigh imperceptible signs of a higher peace in our ravaged world.

Or: to meet the challenge of that other art of the visible, painting. There are countless moments in "the film" when the color of a Renaissance face suddenly comes alive at the edges of a scene or behind a black-and-white frame. And this ambiguity is the same as that associated with books. Does this mean – something that is often indicated by the cinematic image's opening *towards* painting's splen-dor, as though it had always been underlying it – that cinema, in fidelity to painting, continues to officiate over the stormy marriage between the savagery of history and the bodily evidence of love? Another technique, the one that creates the very rapid, almost painful alternation between a cinema image and a fragment of a painting, is more ambiguous. This might almost be regarded as meaning that, instead of being painting's successor, cinema is in fact its torture. Malraux's expression, "the coin of the absolute,"[4] is one of "the film's" crucial phrases. But one sometimes wonders whether "coin," when it comes to cinema, doesn't really triumph over "absolute" to such an extent that it would take all the atoms of all the lovers' faces in cinema's brief history to be equivalent to an *Adam and Eve* by Michelangelo.

Or: melancholy. This would seem to be the real subject of the whole "film." As we are well aware, Godard's style, pinning everyone, himself included, to a wall and forcing them to confess their morbid uncertainties, or capturing the fatal spiral of actions, or showing – through the contrast between categorical maxims (his French moralistic side, in the manner of Chamfort and La Rochefoucauld) and the graced-touched homeliness of a flat landscape or of a metal table – how little faith one should place in one's own impulses, is materially melancholy. In "the film," this melancholy is complicated. Cinema is its privileged support, since it only *seems* to be the art of its time. One of "the film's" aphorisms is: "Cinema, the art of the 19th century, created the 20th century." There is melancholy because it is always too late, especially since cinema is most likely dead, as is suggested by the inscription that comes almost at the end: THIS WAS CINEMA. "The film" also says: "We can do everything except the history of what we are doing." Thus, this "*histoire(s) du cinéma*" is either impossible or else it demonstrates that what it testifies to, the "doing" of cinema, is now foreclosed. Godard as the melancholy witness of a certain destruction of his own artistic "doing"? What would seem to be contributing to this is that the "new wave," whose benign emblem is the image of Truffaut, is designated as a sort of lost paradise, where young men, guided by Langlois[5] (that is, already, by the *histoires* of cinema), extricated an art from the deathly academic legend in which it was encased in order to expose it to the resources of the Outside.

But if considered in terms of the overwhelming real of History, this paradise was also spoiled, says Godard, since right on the edge of it were the "lost illusions," the anguish of revolutions, obscure Communism, and ultimately the unrepresentable conflation (to which Godard makes too many fashionable concessions for my taste) of the twin tyrants, Hitler and Stalin. And so melancholy backfires. Through his ability to express what has been destroyed; through his polyphonic opening of the complete file of what has been closed; through his zeal to infinitely complicate (a baroque style à la Leibniz: the monads of cinema) the foldings and unfoldings of the image and the real; through his exposing of what every fraud takes away with it in terms of truth, the artist ushers in a new age, even if he doesn't know what it is. A little like the way the retrospective saturation of Mahler's symphonies – it, too, characterized by an inimitable tone of melancholy – unwittingly ushers in Schoenberg's transformation of music. Is the expressionless face of Godard under his lamp, a face bearing a certain similarity to Mahler's death mask, that of a sad, consummate archeologist? Or that of a man possessed, with all of Switzerland's Puritanical seriousness, of the most fundamental courage, the courage to defeat melancholy with its own weapons, by turning it into the tone and the style of an encrypted promise?

Or: Godard's chaotic Platonism. It is striking that in "the film" every image is a potential index of another image and at the same time accompanies it with a number of simultaneous texts. The image never refers to any referent; all mimeticism is ruled out. Instead, the image is the gap between itself and the entire aggregate of what is taking place in the visible or in speech. "The film" is the movement of these overlapping, intertwined gaps. Cinema's true calling, it is declared, is to link together, to put things that are usually not related into relationship with one another, precisely because cinema is able to bring things together, make them consonant with one another, weave them polyphonically together, *by means of the gap itself*. Take, for instance, Jews and Arabs (ISRAEL AND ISHMAEL, as "the film" entitles it), or Jews and Germans in a single image, at a remove from itself: two young German soldiers dragging the dead body of a deportee. But then the question becomes: what is the essence of the image if it does not reproduce anything but instead distances itself synthetically from all the other images for the sake of an invisible rightness of the visible? Ultimately, the serial organization of "the film," its overwhelming subtlety of detail, and its tactical mobility comprise the means for a return to essence, for which a few suspended shots (a patch of blue in the dark, a woman's face that is slowly transposed, the lights going dark in the windows of a house, and so on) provide the symbol, and of which the constant invocations of abstract inscriptions are like guideposts, or the summaries that a Socrates converted to the essentiality of the image would provide his young listeners confused by so much obvious sophistry.

A masterpiece, yes, in the artisanal sense of the term: accomplished and complete, solitary, vaguely obsessional, weaving together several different aims, with no decidable hierarchy among them.

Do I have any objections then? Well, yes. A certain *ponderousness*, an excess of seriousness, bordering on pomposity, which is clearly indicated in "the film" by Alain Cuny's Claudelian voice. Cinema is summoned before the court of its historical responsibility and artistic destiny. Is this really fair to it? This impure art is a Saturday night art, an art of the family going out together, of teenagers, of cats on walls. It has always oscillated between the broad comedy of the cabaret and the colossal bravado of the fair, both the clown and the strongest-man-in-the-world. Shouldn't we allow that it is, for the most part, *innocent*? Like all that glitters and attracts crowds, it was propagandistic, to be sure, and promotional, and stupid. And, by virtue of a sort of inner purification of its unworthy materials, fleetingly capable of the highest purpose. As regards "the film," in which, as is always the case with Godard, the diabolical question of Salvation arises – love versus the state, the responsibility of the visible versus the dead dogs of "communication," the hard text versus the overly soft image, and so forth – what is needed is a lightened-up counter-(hi)story, in which we would see that, where cinema is concerned, we needn't make such a fuss.[6] However great it may be and however much a part of our times, this art of the general assembly is grounded in the fondness of all classes, ages, and peoples for the spectacle of an important man being doused with liquid manure by a tramp, of an enormous sinking ship, of a terrible monster suddenly emerging from the bowels of the earth, of the good guy, after many setbacks, finally killing the bad guy at high noon, of the policeman-detective tracking down the Mafioso-thief, of the strange customs of foreigners, and of horses in a field, and of brotherly warriors, and of the romantic drama, and of the naked woman torn by love. The greatest practitioners of this art, Chaplin, or Murnau, have done nothing but *accentuate* those lowly origins without ever attempting to get rid of them, quite the contrary. If the cinema is Idea, a chance visitation of the Idea, it is in the sense in which the old Parmenides, in Plato, requires the young Socrates to accept, alongside the Good, the Just, the True, and the Beautiful, some ideas that are just as abstract though less respectable: the ideas of Hair or of Mud.

Artpress, special issue, "*Le Siècle de Jean-Luc Godard*,"
November 1998

—21—

CONSIDERATIONS ON THE CURRENT STATE OF CINEMA AND ON THE WAYS OF THINKING THIS STATE WITHOUT HAVING TO CONCLUDE THAT CINEMA IS DEAD OR DYING

– I –

On the notion of "the situation of cinema"

There is no "objective" situation of cinema. That is, the situation of cinema – or, the current conjuncture of this artistic procedure – cannot be situated "in itself." "What is happening" (the films which are released) does not produce, on its own, any sort of intelligibility. There are general reasons behind this lack, but there are also reasons linked to the singularity of the cinematographic procedure.

(a) General reasons
The relation of thought to the current moment in art is one of a localized prescription and not a description. Everything depends upon the point at which one is subjectively situated, and upon the axioms which are used to support judgments. The point at which we choose to situate ourselves is called *L'Art du cinéma*, which claims a local status quite different to that of a simple review: a group of thought, possessing an orientation and particular protocols for "inquiry." It possesses two foundational axioms; drawn from Denis Lévy's work:

1. Cinema is capable of being an art, in the precise sense in which one can identify, among the undividedness of forms and subjects, cinema-ideas.
2. This art has been traversed by a major rupture, between its iden-tificatory, representative and humanist ("Hollywoodian") voca-tion and a modernity which is distanced, involving the spectator

138

in an entirely different manner. Naturally, this rupture has a complicated genealogy, which dictates the group's vision of the history of cinema

The "current situation of cinema" (or conjuncture) can then be called the legibility of an indistinct real (films which are made) on the basis of two axioms. One can then produce derived propositions, or propositions of the situation. These propositions identify the situation, not "objectively," but on the basis of engagements concerning something which has recognizable artistic autonomy. This is a little like parliamentary politics, in a given situation, only being identifiable on the basis of the statements of the Organisation Politique.[1]

In what follows what must not be forgotten is that it is the films of Oliveira, of Kiarostami, of Straub, of the early Wenders, of a certain Pollet, of some Godards, etc., which prescribe the conjuncture, or which provide the measure (whether or not it is explicitly mentioned) of derived judgments. They are what allow us to identify everything in the situation which is relatively progressive from the standpoint of art, even when this progressivism occurs within frameworks or references foreign to what *L'Art du cinéma* terms modernity. They also provide the measure of the new, precisely because they were the new. The new does not enter into a dialectic with the old, but rather with the old new, or the new of the preceding sequence.

(b) Particular reasons
The latter are attached to a thesis which has been incorporated into *L'Art du cinéma's* doctrine: that of the essential impurity of cinema. Up till the present, this thesis has signified above all that the passage of an idea in a film presupposes a complex summoning forth and displacement of the other arts (theater, the novel, music, painting . . .), and that as such "pure cinema" does not exist, except in the dead-end vision of avant-garde formalism. This thesis of impurity must be expanded and the following principle proposed: *The cinema is a place of intrinsic indiscernibility between art and non-art.* No film, strictly speaking, is controlled by artistic thinking from beginning to end: It always bears absolutely impure elements within it, drawn from ambient imagery, from the detritus of other arts, and from conventions with a limited shelf life. Artistic activity can only be discerned in a film as a *process of purification of its own immanent non-artistic character.* This process is never completed. Even better, if it was completed, thereby generating the supposed purity of experimental cinema (or even certain radical normative statements by Bresson on

"cinematographic writing"), then the artistic capacity itself, or rather, its universal address, would be suppressed. Cinema's artistic operations are incompletable purification operations, bearing on current non-artistic forms, or indistinct imagery (Rimbaud's "idiotic paintings").

The result of all this is that the dominant forms of non-art are immanent to art itself, and make up part of its intelligibility. Hence the permanent necessity of inquiry into the dominant formal tendencies within current production, and of the identification of circulating, even industrial, schemas of the visible and the audible; because it is upon the latter that artistic operations are potentially performed.

– II –

Four examples

(a) The Godardian technique of "dirty sound" (inaudible phrases, superimposition of sounds, parasitical noises, etc.) is an attempt at a formal purification of what has invaded contemporary production; that is, the constant confusion of music (in its post-rock form), brutal sounds (arms, explosions, cars, planes, etc.) and dialogues reduced to their operational ineptness. In current production, there is an imposition of sound, or a submission to the demand, characteristic of contemporary youth, for a permanent rhythmic background accompanying every activity, even speech or writing: this is what Godard transforms into an adulterated murmur. By means of this operation, what Godard does is treat the confusion of the world as artifice, as voluntary principle of the confusion of thoughts.

(b) The usage of car sequences in Kiarostami or even Oliveira's films works on an overwhelming stereotype of contemporary imagery, thanks to which the opening scene of two films out of every three is a car sequence. The operation consists of making an action scene into the place of speech, of changing what is a sign of speed into a sign of slowness, of constraining what is an exteriority of movement to become a form of reflexive or dialogic interiority.

(c) Sexual activity, filmed directly on bodies, forms a major part of what is authorized by dominant contemporary imagery. It is opposed to the metonymy of desire, which was one of the key characteristics of classic cinematographic art, and which aimed at avoiding the censor by sexualizing tiny details. The artistic problem is thus: what usage can be made of sexualized nudity in its tendentiously full exposition? The attempts at purifying such material are innumerable; whether they turn it towards speech (in contemporary French comedy), or ritualize it (certain of Antonioni's sequences), or make distanced citations of it, or render it banal by incorporating it into a genre (as Eastwood does in *The Bridges of Madison County*), or overpornographize it in an abstract manner (Godard at times).

(d)   Special effects of any kind, the formalized spectacle of destruction, of cataclysm, a sort of Late Roman Empire consummation of murder, cruelty and catastrophe: these are the obvious ingredients of current cinema. They are inscribed in a proven tradition, but there is no longer much of an attempt to embed them in a consistent fable with a moral, indeed religious, vocation. They derive from a technique of shock and one-upmanship, which is related to the end of an epoch in which images were relatively rare and it was difficult to obtain them. The endless discussions about the "virtual" and the image of synthesis refer to nothing other than the overabundance and facility of the image, including the spectacularly catastrophic or terrorizing image. Here again, attempts at purification exist, directed towards a stylized inflation, a type of slowed calligraphy of general explosion; the grand master evidently being John Woo.

– *III* –

A thesis and its consequences

One can then formulate the following principle: *A film is contemporary, and thus destined for everyone, inasmuch as the material whose purification it guarantees is identifiable as belonging to the non-art of its times.*

This is what makes cinema, intrinsically and not empirically, into a mass art: its internal referent is not the artistic past of forms, which would suppose an educated spectator, but a common imagery whose filtering and distancing treatment is guaranteed by potential artistic operations. Cinema gathers around identifiably non-artistic materials, which are ideological indicators of the epoch. It then *transmits*, potentially, their artistic purification, within the medium of an apparent indiscernibility between art and non-art.

141

Whence, to think the current situation of cinema, a number of directions for our inquiry:

(a)   Of course, we will maintain the idea that the artistic operations of modernity consist in purifying visible and audible materials of everything which binds them to the domination of representation, identification and realism. But we will add that the current challenge is that of extending this treatment to everything which binds the materials to the pure formal consumption of images and sounds, whose privileged operators today are: pornographic nudity, the cataclysmic special effect, the intimacy of the couple, social melodrama, and pathological cruelty. For it is only by purifying these operators, while recognizing their necessity, that one gives oneself the chance of encountering a real *in situation*, and thus of assuring the passage, or the visitation, of a new cinema-idea.
(b)   What is thus required is knowledge of materials in their real movement, and knowledge of the dominant tendencies which organize the latter.
(c)   Cinematic works must be dealt with and hypotheses of configuration made: this on the basis of the operations of purification and displacement of materials and their operators; operations through which cinema-ideas will occur which are effectively contemporary and which have a universal address.

At this point in time, it is quite probable that the basic unit of investigation is not so much a film in its totality as some moments of film, moments within which an operation is legible. Legibility means the following: one grasps, at the same time, the subjacent material, which assures that the film is contemporary, the protocol of purification, which is the artistic index, and the passage of the idea (or encounter with a real), which is the effect of the protocol. In the current phase of transition, within which the weight of non-art is crushing (because, and we will come back to this, in general, nothing else is opposed to it apart from a formalized distance), it is necessary to engage in the work of identification of operations, including those occurring within films which are globally deficient. In this work we will not be entirely guided by the notion of auteur, because, no doubt, nobody as yet maintains a mastered and consistent relation to the mutation of material (what is it to make films when every image is *facile*?). If such a relation emerged, then we would have a great *mass auteur* on our hands, such as Chaplin or Murnau, and without a doubt we would have such within a determined genre born from the situation. Yet nothing of the sort is on the horizon, neither in explosive neo-thrillers (despite the existence of auteurs of quality such as Woo or de Palma), nor in gore films (despite Craven's subtle displacements), nor in pornography (Bénazéraf has not kept any of his promises), nor in social melodrama (despite the efforts of a few English filmmakers).

There is thus a necessity for an inquiry into the details, guided by the sense of possible situations, by our "consumerist" visits to the cinema (to a certain degree we should share in the innocent fairground mass aspect of "seeing films"), by our instinct, and by the decoding of current criticism.

– IV –

Exceptions

One should set apart the cases in which, for a certain period of time, a vast political modification, a global event, authorized the discredit of ordinary industrial materials (let us say Hollywoodian materials, or Indian, or Egyptian), and made possible an original grasp of the evental site. During at least one temporal sequence, the cinema's mass dimension was not incompatible with a direct concern to invent forms in which the real of a country occurs as a problem. This was the case in Germany, as the escort of leftism (Fassbinder, Schroeter, Wenders . . .), in Portugal after the 1975 revolution (Oliveira, Botelho . . .), and in Iran after the Islamic revolution (Kiarostami). In all of these examples it is clear that what cinema is capable of *touches* the country, as a subjective category (what is it to be from this country?). There are cinema-ideas concerning this point, such as its previous invisibility is revealed by the event. The cinema is then both modern and broad in its action. A national cinema with a universal address emerges; a national *school*, recognizable in everything up to its insistence on certain formal aspects.

– V –

Formal operators and dominant motifs

Besides national exceptions, the inquiry must determine the situation with regard to conclusive operations practiced upon a certain number of dominant motifs, more or less coded within genres. What virtual ideas are at work in these operations?

143

(a) The visibility of the sexual, or, more generally, the motif of erogenous nudity. The question is that of knowing what this motif, purified, but without any possibility of a return to the classical metonymies imposed by censorship, can bring to bear concerning the non-relation between love and sexuality. Or how can it prove an exception (when first of all it confirms it) to the contemporary subsumption of love by the functional organization of enjoyment. What degree of visibility can be tolerated by what one could call the amorous body? A simple critical analysis of pornography is only the first stage, as can be seen in Godard's abstract pornographic scenes, for example in *Sauve qui peut (la vie)*. As yet no conclusive work has been done on this point, and the identification of some attempted operations upon this motif would be welcome.

A subsidiary question would be that of asking oneself whether pornography, X movies, could become a genre. Let us agree that what is termed "genre" has given rise to artistic enterprises. Otherwise, one can speak of specialities. Is pornography necessarily a speciality and not a genre? And if so, why? This is a particularly interesting question with regard to the very essence of cinema insofar as it is confronted with the full visibility of the sexual.

(b) Extreme violence, cruelty. This is a complex zone, which includes the theme of the torturing serial killer (*Seven*), and its horror gore variations (*Halloween, Scream . . .*), the violent neo-thriller, certain films about the mafia (even *Casino* contained shots of an unmeasured cruelty), and films about the end of the world with various tribal survivors cutting each other's throats. It is not a matter of variations of the horrifying film as a genre. The element of cruelty, the slashing, the crushing of bones, the torture, prevails over suspense and fear. It is an ensemble which actually evokes the late Roman Empire, because its essential material consists of its variations on putting-to-death.

The point is one of knowing whether all this could be exposed to a *tragic* treatment. Before judging these bloody torturing images, one must remember that tales of horrendous executions, the variety of murders, and the monstrosity of actions, were all major elements of the most refined tragedies. All one has to do is reread the tale of Hyppolite's death in Racine's *Phèdre*. After all, one can hardly better the Greek story of Atreus and Thyestes, a major narrative commonplace in tragedy in which one sees a father eat his own children. Here, our inquiry is guided by a simple question: do embyronic operations exist which announce that all this material – which acts like an urban mythology for today – will be integrated into attempts at contemporary baroque tragedy?

(c)   The figure of the worker. It is well known that there has recently been a return, via England, but also in American documentaries, of social melodrama. Even in France, all sorts of attempts, from *Reprise* to *Marius et Jeanette*, aim at giving a verdict on a certain figure of the worker, in the milieu of the PCF [French Communist Party] or May '68. The problem is then one of knowing whether cinema can contribute to the subjective generalization of the autonomy of the figure of the worker. For the moment the cinema only deals with the latter's end, and as such gives rise to nostalgic operations, like those of *Brassed Off*.

The history of this question is very complex, if one thinks simultaneously of *Modern Times* (Chaplin), of French noir romanticism (*Le Jour se lève*), of the epic Soviet films, and of the films of the sequence opened by '68 (*Tout va bien*, *Oser lutter* . . .). Today the question would be: What is the formal operator which purifies this figure's passage of all nostalgia, and contributes to its installation? That is, to its detachment from any social objectivity? What is at stake is the very possibility of a real encounter of cinema and politics; no doubt the figure of the worker would have to be the film's unfigurable real point much as it is sketched, after all, in Denis Lévy's *L'École de Mai* (1979).

(d)   The millenarian motif. This occurs in the register of planetary catastrophes from which some Yankee hero saves us. The sub-jacent real is globalization, the hegemony of one sole super-power, and also ecological ideologies concerning the global village and its survival. The fundamental imagery is that of the catastrophe, and not that of salvation. Moreover, this "genre" already comes with its own ironic version (see *Mars Attacks*). The point lies in knowing whether the motif of a general threat can provide the material for an operation which would transmit the idea that the world is prey to Capital in its unbridled form, and by this very fact rendered, globally, foreign to the very truths that it detains in its midst. This time it is clear that it is the pos-sibility of an epic film which is at stake, but of an epic whose

145

"hero" is restricted action, truth procedures' confidence in themselves.

(e) The petit-bourgeois comedy. Here we have a highly prized modern variation of the French intimist tradition. The comedy revolves around a young hystericized woman, of a certain vacuity, who is fraught by her amorous, social and even intellectual wanderings. As such, this genre is linked to Marivaux and Musset, as it is to the Marianne of *Caprices*, and given its clear delineation in the work of its founding father, Rohmer. Almost all recent French "auteurs" have been involved in this business. It is still a minor genre with regard to the American comedy of the 1930s and 1940s, which is similar in many respects, termed by Stanley Cavell the comedy of "remarriage."

Why such minor inferiority? We should be able to respond to this question. For example, it could be said that the central weakness of these films is that the central stakes of the intrigue remain undetermined. In the American films as in Marivaux there is a decision or a declaration at the end of the day. The comedy of uncertainty and the double game is articulated around this fixed point. This is what allows Marivaux's prose to be simultaneously underhand and extremely firm. If Rohmer remains superior to his descendants, it is because among his Christian allusions to grace, he occasionally finds something which is at stake. In *Conte d'Automne* it is obvious that the main motif is: "Happier are the simple of mind, the grace of love is reserved for them." Nothing of the sort is to be found in the work of a Desplechin, a Barbosa or a Jacquot. In the end, this genre only gains artistic force when it gives itself, on the basis of an unshakeable confidence in love's capacities, a fixed point, such as required by all comedies in order to tie down their internal wanderings.

Psychoanalysis, made much use of by current auteurs (including the sad Woody Allen), is a dead end, because, paradigmatically, it is the place of the interminable.

We can no longer symbolize the fixed point by marriage or even remarriage. No doubt, as Rohmer suggests, and sometimes Téchiné, it is to be found where love encounters another truth procedure. It would then be necessary to formalize a subjective ex-centring, a conversion, a visible distancing, and finally, a displacement with regard to the dominant conception, even if the latter serves as initial material, a conception which is a mix of narcissism and hystericized inertia.

– VI –

Cinema and the other arts

The generalization of the notion of impurity must not cause us to forget that it is first of all an impurity with regard to other arts. What are the contemporary forms of this question?

(a)   On cinema and music. The schema must be drawn up on the basis of rhythm. We will call "rhythm" not exactly the characteristics of the editing, but a diffused temporality which fixes, even if it is a matter of a sequence shot, the tonality of the movement (staccato, or hurried, or expanded, or slow and majestic, etc. . . .). Rhythm engages every element of the film, and not only the organization of shots and sequences. For example, the style of acting or the intensity of the colors contribute to rhythm just as much as the speed of the succession of shots. At base, rhythm is the general pulsation of filmic transitions. Music is a type of immediate commentary upon the latter, often purely redundant or emphatic. Yet it is clearly rhythm which ties cinema to music.

The twentieth century, which, after all, was the century of cinema, essentially witnessed three types of music. First, there was post-romantic music which maintained the artifices of the finishing tonality, such as found in Mahler or Tchaikovsky's symphonic melancholy, and which continues, via Strauss or Rachmaninov, right through to the current day, and singularly in cinema. Second, the great creation of American blacks, jazz, which has its major artists from Armstrong to Monk, but to which we must also attach, in its entirety, everything which falls under the term "youth music," from rock to techno. Finally, there was a continuation through rupture of veritable musical creation, which, from Schoenberg to Brian Ferneyhough, liquidated tonality and constructed a universe of musical singularities, serial and post-serial.

At the cinema, we have watched a massive movement, as yet incomplete (because every neo-classical film reclassicizes music), from post-romantic music to post-jazz music. This accompanies, at the level of rhythm, a passage from an emphatic esthetic of

147

dilation (taken to its extreme in the openings of Westerns, which are genuinely symphonic) to an esthetic of fragmentation, whose matrix, as everyone remarks, is the video clip, a sub-product of youth music.

The central problem seems to be the following: could a rhythm be invented which would tie cinema to the real of music as art, and not to the decomposed forms of symphonism or the demagogic forms of youth music? How is it possible that cinema has left aside the entirety of contemporary musical creation? Why, besides post-romanticism and post-jazz, isn't there a cinema of post-serial music? Do we not have here – it being a matter, after all, of what has been, for a century, genuine music – one of the reasons which – cinema being the essential mass art – relegates the sole restrained action of musical creation to the shadows? We must return to the few attempts at filmic and thus rhythmic incorporation of the music of our times, in Straub or Oliveira's work, in order to discern the operations which make a strength out of it, but which have also limited it.

(b) On cinema and theater. *L'Art du cinéma* has spent a lot of time working on this question. In order to progress further the best question to be asked is probably the following: What is a cinematic actor today? This is a question which traverses all the other questions. Today, an American actor is dominated by the imperative of sexual visibility, by confrontation with extreme violence and by millenarian heroism. He is an immobile receptacle for a type of disintegrating cosmos. He alone bears the latter's consistency, or what remains of it. In the end, he forms a type of invulnerable body. Moreover, this is why the actor is essentially a man, an impassive athlete. Women are almost uniformly decorative, far more so now than in the previous epoch, during which they were able to occupy the pernicious center of the narrative. Or, in the case of neo-comedy, women are mere figures from magazines, neurotic prey for "women's problems."

We should ask ourselves what exactly is going on in cinema's impurification of the theater actor. The reappearance within cinema of the subtle actor or actress – that is, one who would *divert* the evidence of the image through their acting, who would keep him or herself in reserve with regard to this evidence, and who would poeticize it – such a reappearance would be welcome news, and it is news whose traces must be tracked

148

down (they exist). Obviously what is in question in the film must allow the actor to act in such a way; this means that the gap between what is shown and the subjective fold of such showing must remain *measured*. Téchiné, for example, succeeds in doing just this in several sequences. In any case, what is certain is that one *cannot* lend support to a subtle actor if one incessantly juxtaposes him or her, as some sort of resistant *massivity*, to a visual and sonorous harassment, or if his or her body and its gestures is abandoned to the interminable plasticity of neuroses.

– VII –

A general hypothesis

At a completely global level, we can frame the particular inquiries which we have just set out by formulating, at our own risk, the following hypothesis: *The moment is one of neo-classicism.*

This hypothesis signifies three things:

– The strictly modern subtractive sequence (subtraction of the actor and of the narrative construction, prevalence of the text, indiscernibility of fiction and documentary, etc.) is saturated.
– No new configuration is perceptible *qua* event.
– What we see is an exasperated and overdrawn version of preexistent schemas, or a manipulation to the second degree of these schemas, genres included, which are cited and submitted to a hystericization of their sources. This is what can be termed contemporary formalism. Its most general signature is the mobility of the camera which steps over the notion of the shot by aiming to join together, in a single movement, visible configurations which are disparate, or classically non-unifiable.

Yet, against formalism, whose encounter with any real is improbable, or exterior (hence the ends of formalist films, which most often relapse into sugared realism, as if saying or affirming supposed a renunciation of the movement of form) one can predict an academic reaction, which has even already begun here and there.

We will term neo-classical the effort at an internal purification of the academic reaction and its regime of visibility. There is already something of this genre in the best sequences of *Titanic*, or even *Brassed Off*. It is a matter of operations which assume the

CONSIDERATIONS ON THE CURRENT STATE OF CINEMA

reactive conjuncture, but which work it on the basis of the saturated modern sequence. A little like Picasso between the cubist sequence of the 1910s, and the opening, from the 1930s-1940s onwards, of genuine non-figurative art. He accepted a certain return to representative forms, but he worked them from the standpoint of cubism itself.

Our last question will be: What are the few clues of such an effort worth today? What do they promise?

L'Art du cinéma, March 1999

—22—

THE CINEMATIC CAPTURE
OF THE SEXES

This text is of a piece with a film, Antonioni's *Identification of a Woman*. It is, so to speak, the written prelude to it, such that reading, in this case, cannot go without seeing, or hearing. It is an "*explication de film*," the way we say, or used to say, an "*explication de texte*." A genre that is not a critical but a didactic one.

I must nevertheless add: I don't think that reading a text (explicating it) amounts to enumerating the catachreses, asyndetons, metaphors, or synecdoches in it any more than I think that explicating a film requires identifying its zoom, reverse tracking, or out-of-frame shots. That sort of thing is the bogus formalism of the Diafoiruses and Trissotins[1] of cinema. But nor is it a matter, needless to say, of telling the story, hailing the actors, saying what a great time you had, and taking your leave. The discourse of journalism is not a cure for the discourse of the University.

As usual, I will attempt to use the discourse of the master, which is nothing but the discourse of the Idea, as its passage is inscribed in one form and one alone.

Let's begin with the title. *Identification of a Woman* is a true translation of the true Italian title. Let's say that it's a true title, or rather the title of a truth. Which truth? This one: what cinema is capable of with respect to sex or sexuation, or even what it alone is capable of, is giving sensible, corporeal form, not, as is too often thought, to the distribution of sexed roles or to the images of that distribution but rather – and this is infinitely trickier, and more original – to the process of identification of what being sexed means for a subject.

The fact that a woman loves a man designates that man as the identifier of that woman. Loving is a desire, hence a duty, because desire and the law are one and the same thing. Loving a woman

151

imposes on you the duty of identifying her. Will you be able to live up to that desire, to that duty? This is not at all a question of a role, or of a type, since it is a question that constitutes a subject.

In Antonioni's film one of the two women subject to identification, Ida, the second one, played by Christine Boisson, says to her male identifier, the believable Niccolò: "I'm a human being like you. It's only a matter of chance that I'm not the same sex." I like to think that what is really at issue in the cinema, where sexuation is concerned, is that chance, the capture of that chance, and of all its consequences: being of one sex or the other.

What Ida claims is that, prior to the chance determination of sex, there is a humanity that is everywhere the same, a generic humanity, a humanity based on identity or resemblance, not on difference or mystery. A particular image of this idea is moreover featured in the film. The male character is a filmmaker, as in Fellini's $8\frac{1}{2}$, with which Antonioni's film, perhaps unconsciously, carries on a dialogue of sorts. The filmmaker has a very vague idea for a film that would be about a woman, or would be based on a woman. Consequently, he is looking for a woman's face. On the wall of his apartment he puts up photos of women – Louise Brooks, obviously, a sort of hopeless nostalgia, and other photos that he cuts out of magazines. The one he likes best is the photo of a terrorist, a member of the Red Brigades most likely. It is the only photo in which the woman is paired with a man, her man, her lover, who is also a terrorist. Both of them are in prison. Niccolò the filmmaker tells Ida: "These lives are coherent," and he comments that those two have the same world view, they face the same risks, they share everything they are and do. So we can imagine them, or identify them, as representatives of a humanity of identicality and sharedness. We can imagine that the chance difference between the sexes does not undermine that paired identity of a humanity of identicality.

There is one fundamental art that defends the idea of a generic humanity protected by identity, an art in which the universality of human types triumphs, albeit with great violence. That art is the epic, the epic narrative of self-affirmation, the heroic negation of the negative. Cinema joins forces with affirmative humanity when it accepts to take on the epic, its space, its taciturn heroes, its duels in which the Same confronts the Same for the glory of Sameness. This sort of thing happens more than once with Griffith, Eisenstein, or Ford. It doesn't happen with Antonioni. What is at stake in the film under consideration is only allusively and fleetingly that generic orientation, that humanity whose burden, if there is one, is that of commonalities, not differences. In Antonioni's cinema, and ultimately in cinema as a whole, the chance addition of sexuation gives rise to radical, painful alienation, to passionate ignorance, to a sort of disordered estrangement. Above all, the contingency of sex foregrounds the need for an identification of the other sex, for an analysis of the *heteros*, or heterosexuality, whose actual scene, or real process, is nothing but love, or the attempt at love, but of which cinema endeavors to be the privileged artistic witness.

In this sense, cinema, or at least one kind of cinema, albeit an essential one, is an art of love, a witness in thought of love as the identification of difference. The novel, too, is an art of love, but the novel treats love as fate. It inscribes that fate in the gap between the sublimity of renunciation and the lost illusions of symbolic fusion. Cinema of course pays tribute to the novel and therefore to renunciation and to lost illusions as well. But I would at least like to suggest that that is not its own particular genius; that the aim of cinematic capture, which both depends on and elucidates the visible and speech, luminous bodies and dark signs, is identification, the story of identification; and that it concerns the chance determination of sex as such and legitimates it as chance and as a consequence of chance.

Through the exhibition and the evasiveness of bodies, and with its constant repetition of signs, cinema asks: If sex is the contingent supplement that weakens and divides generic humanity, is there any hope of connecting that supplement to that genericity? Is there a human element in sexuation or is it essentially non-human? This question can only be answered by showing how the identification of the other sex, in situations both unique and typical, occurs from within love, or what is assumed to be love. For if that identification were possible, nothing would prevent it from being connected to generic humanity's capacity for identity and similarity. If it were impossible, however, the split would be irreparable, and the very idea of humanity would be hurt, injured as regards the minimum of identity it requires.

The question can also be phrased as: Is love the scene in which the fundamental Two of the sexes laboriously produces an identifying thought of its own duality? Or is it always the tortured witness of an impossible identification, of a Two that exists only in mystery and alienation when it comes to love?

Or: Is love human or non-human?

The fact that this is one of cinema's key questions, and the reason why this is so, is attested by one major example: sex scenes, which are both the obsession and the real test of this art of the visible.

Cinema is the only one of the arts that can claim to capture, pin down, and convey the sex act. There are pornographic novels, of course, but imagination is more than enough for them. The power of words to name the non-existent can turn all the paragraphs you like into pornography. There is no need for real sex organs. But cinema testifies, and increasingly so, to the real of organs, positions, cries, and sweat. It arranges their repeating visibility. And for a very long time, under the strictest censorship, cinema announced that it could capture and convey the sex act, that it alone could really do so, and that all it had to do was show, but really show, an ankle, some cleavage, a black stocking, or a symbol for everyone to thrill with pleasure at the idea that everything was visible and that there was nothing intimate that couldn't be violated and exposed by cinema. In this regard, as has often been remarked, cinema in its essence, or rather in its essential possibility, is pornographic.

Nevertheless, as art, cinema sets up a question, not a business. It does not sell sexual spices. And the question it asks is very clear: Is pornography – understood as the exhibition of sexuality, but taken in terms of its connection to love – human or non-human? Can there exist an exhibition of sexuality – or even just of nudity – that bears witness to a process of identification of difference? Or does any exhibition of sexuality refer to the objective non-humanity of that which involves no thought?

Antonioni courageously confronts the problem in the film's three sex scenes, which he takes right to the edge of pornography, especially if we consider the date the film was made, 1982. The chief difficulty, as we know, is that the subjectivation of the sex act offers it its only chance to be humanized. Yet how can the signs of such a subjectivation be found in the visible when cinematic capture narrowly circumscribes within the frame the excitement of the bodies or the too prettified, too painterly display of their relaxing after the race? This difficulty is exacerbated by the fact that – as opposed to what some libertarians, for whom sex is multi-faceted liberation as such, would have us believe – there is nothing more monotonous, closed, and finite than the repertoire of sexual positions. It would seem almost impossible to conclude from this that there can be a process of identification of differences in cinema, when the slightest nude scene immediately produces an overwhelming feeling of déjà-vu and what we want more than anything is for the actors to hurry up and get out of that bed in which they are unrecognizable, in which, as opposed to any identification, their identities hardly matter or other ones can be substituted for them. Or when, as has long been the case thanks to the use

154

of body doubles, they are not purely and simply replaced by a surrogate.

The problem can be expressed as follows: How can a sex scene be filmed in immanence? How can it be subordinated to the identifying process of love?

Antonioni attempts to give three different answers to this question. But, when all is said and done, he answers in the negative, in my opinion. Sex, the film tells us in its very attempt to say the opposite, cannot be the locus in which the sexes are identified. The sex act is blind to sexual difference; when it comes to the identification of a woman, it is the locus of the greatest obscurity. But let's describe Antonioni's three attempts. All three of them concern the woman who is difficult to identify *par excellence*: Mavi, the woman who runs away and disappears, the aristocrat who is possibly also a lesbian and a prostitute, unless those categories are only the man's projections.

The first sex scene involves classic sexual positions. The man performs cunnilingus for a long time on the woman, who is fondling her breasts. Then he penetrates her from on top, with her knees raised and her clutching him between her legs. Prior to this, there was the woman's initiative, the woman making the decision, standing in only her panties on the bed and extending her hand to the man. The filmic supports of subjectivation do not have to do with the succession of sexual positions here, nor with what can be inferred from the faces or the words. They lie above all in the establishing of a distance that is not really one, since the bodies are filmed from too close up for there to be any true objectivity to the scene, any real long shot, any real description, and from too far away for it to be regarded as a pornographic close-up. Rather, everything suggests that the scene's very passionate and tense physical violence is also a sort of blind linking-up of the amorous subjects and does not lead to any genuine identification.

In the second scene, Mavi's body is filmed with her lying on her stomach now, and it essentially involves her being masturbated: the woman guides the man's hands to her buttocks, and we will later see, without any real close-up again, that the man thrusts his fingers, almost roughly, deep inside the woman. Here, too, the distance is both too short and too long. In addition, there are several interpolated shots of the woman's hands, of the way they grab the sheets when she is on the point of coming. This scene is in any case more about orgasm than about desire. It needs to be linked to the remarks made by a young woman in another of the film's scenes, a scene that takes place at a strange swimming pool.

155

This young woman claims to have slept with Mavi and thus gives rise to the lesbian order of identification. When she is questioned by the male protagonist as he is searching for Mavi, who has disappeared, the young woman says three things. First, that chastity might be a solution since she, the young woman, is incapable of love; next, that there is nothing better than masturbation; and finally that masturbation is nicer when performed by a woman than by a man. The scene I was discussing a moment ago is a counter-position to these three notions, because it connects the sex act to the possibility of love; it includes masturbation in a broader spectrum of acts; and it is heterosexual. It is nevertheless true that orgasm in the scene is connected with a violence in which the man, the service provider, is so to speak erased and in which it may well be that he could be replaced by a woman. Thus the lessons of the pool are anticipated via their sexual reverse, as a sort of retroactive curse.

The third scene abandons any attempt at a convincing reproduction of sexual activity. The two bodies are lying beside each other, filmed in a long shot this time, with the woman in front and the man lying against her back, and they move fluidly as in a horizontal dance, immersed in the fluttering of white sheets before them, in the wind coming from nowhere. For the first time we will see, albeit innocently, the woman's pubic hair, and even fleetingly, for only a second, the man's penis, completely flaccid. This time what is involved is an explicit estheticization, in which nudity is at the service of the image and of movement, and all of it is really offered to a presumed gaze, at the cost, though, of it all being asexual. In other words, this scene abandons immanence at the same time as it abandons the sex act per se. It tells us, in the sphere of sublimation, that there is no sexual relationship and therefore that there is never any identification whatsoever at the moment of the act.

So Antonioni's thesis, demonstrated filmically, is indeed that sex, at any rate, never dispels the mystery of sexuality.

The question is whether this thesis has to do with cinema or with the real. Remember that the hero is a filmmaker looking for a woman's face for his film. Does this then mean that in cinema the identification of a woman cannot come about by way of the exhibition, however refined, of the sex act? Or that what cinema is capable of testifying to is that the sex act never contributes to the identification of a woman? Antonioni's film takes great care to leave something undecidable about this issue. If we accept that displaying the intra-amorous process of identification of a woman in the visible is what defines a whole swath of cinema; and if it is clear that in cinema the sex act, however under- or over-represented it may be, does not involve that process of identification, then we will tend to think that the thesis of Antonioni's film is a cinema thesis about the real, a linking of cinema to the real of love. And that, all in all, the truth is that sex is what needs to be identified, not what identifies.

Let us even say, more generally, and to the extent that cinema is the art of stripping bare, that stripping a woman bare is unrelated to identifying her.

In addition to the sex scenes, there is a high frequency, in Antonioni's film as in countless others, of female nudity, and especially of scenes of stripping or getting dressed again. In connection with the second woman, Ida, now, there is even an exceptionally indecent scene. At the end of a corridor, filmed from a distance, a totally naked Ida gets up from the toilet, wipes herself, and walks out of the shot. What is the point of this? In the discreet economy of the film, these are all inflections of one essential point, which is that a woman's *intimacy* is not at all part of her identification. This restrained critique of intimacy and intimism, as the supposed loci of the identification of sexed positions, is highly relevant. Basically, the mystery is a public one and should be treated as such.

How, then, does identification operate, once it has been purged of any intimist hypothesis and therefore of all psychologism, including sexual? What are its terms? I would like to show that what Antonioni's film, as a film – in its places and its cuts, in its colors and its slow pacing – encourages us to think is that, in love, the process of identification of a woman involves a capacity for *decision* on the part of the man, which he more often than not lacks. Or that we think a woman is a mystery to the extent that we think it is a matter of knowing her. But it is really a matter of deciding her.

Consequently, the aim of the cinematic capture of the sexes is to deal with the interrelationship among three terms in the visible: decision, disappearance, and mystery. Rather than saying, it is a matter of showing, and therefore of demonstrating, that it is wrong to think that it is a woman's mystery, as evidenced by her disappearing, that makes it impossible to decide for love. On the contrary, it is the lack of decision that turns everything into a mystery and leads to the woman's disappearing.

Antonioni's genius lies in plunging us into the ideological order of male representation, which puts mystery in charge, and in discreetly showing us that a real decision would have cleared everything up. It is for the purposes of this demonstration that the main formal techniques that define Antonioni's style are brought to bear. It is a style that could be called an understated mannerism or, inversely, an ornate narrative. In the film under consideration, three formal devices in particular can be noted that are clearly connected with the theme I just highlighted, the triangulation among mystery, disappearance, and decision – a triangle in which the process of identification of a woman operates and ultimately fails.

(1)   The most well known of these involves making the mystery visible by means of the distanced gaze, or distancing, which can change the meaning of a fragment of the world, depending on how it is framed. That was the theme of an entire film, *Blow-Up*. Here, too, there is the man who, from a green, or blue, car, is possibly, probably, watching Niccolò's apartment from the street. In a high angle shot from the window, we see him, a tiny figure, partly hidden by the trees. In the long party scene at the home of the upper-crust friends of Mavi, the woman to be identified, there are also the whispers, the ambiguous glances, the enigmatic group scenes, dissolving slowly into one another with a kind of drawing-room formality à la Visconti, while the confusion and uncertainty of the character thus observed by what he is observing grows. Above all, as a symbol of this opacity introduced by distance into the real, there is a strange object in the branches of a pine tree outside the window, an object that is neither a bird's nest, nor a pine cone, nor quite a wasps' nest either, and whose real identity we will never learn. With this object we have the true symbol of non-identification.

But what is important, on balance, is that this undecidability introduced by distance into the gaze hinges entirely on the hero's inability to decide to do what has to be done to put an end to it. Even when he leaves his apartment to walk over to the supposed spy, it is only because Mavi has suggested the idea to him. He will never go look for the object in the tree. He will not put a stop to his growing anxiety by asking serious questions of the people at the aristocrats' party. At bottom, mystery suits him. It suits him as a substitute for decision. Why? Because mystery presents the real as a problem of knowledge, whereas the real is always of the order of the act. But the male character isn't interested in this real act. As a result, identification is presented as a detective-novel problem and, at the same time, eluding the act that alone has the power to found it, it necessarily ends up in a reassuring acknowledgment of failure.

(2) The second formal technique is the dispersal of the identification process in either an empty or obscure space, or both, a space in which everything is reversible and the very traces of the process disappear. First, there is the interminable scene in the fog. For once Niccolò has decided something: he is taking Mavi to an isolated house in the country. But fog blankets the road; the car is stopped by strange, luminous roadblocks. We see flashing high beams; we hear the rumors being spread by the drivers lost in the fog: "they" fired shots, "they" found a body in the river, and so on. Niccolò alternates between brief inquiries in the fog and pointless bursts of anger. A kind of blue-gray shroud of fog makes everything disappear. Fed up with all these trappings of obscurity, Mavi takes off on foot and instantly disappears. A strange apathy then takes hold of Niccolò, who has gone back to his primal indecisiveness. Mavi will return to the car and the lovers will eventually find the house (a big, freezing-cold building ridden with emptiness), but, with joy and enthusiasm gone, everything is ruined, and the final sex scene (the most estheticizing one) will turn out to be the prelude to the ultimate loss of Mavi.

The other scene, with Ida now, likewise bogs an ostensible decision (to spend a few days together in Venice) down in an unsuitable space. This is the scene in the "open lagoon," the place where the waters of Venice open out onto the sea, a white and gray place with no landmarks, where the lovers go boating and Ida feels nothing but fear and desolation. The lapping of the waves, the only sound in this place (as the man notes), is like a funereal rhythm, or a meaningless monotonous chant. Niccolò apologizes and attributes his fondness for such a deserted place (the gray desert, after the red one) to his quest for cinematic inspiration. But here, too, space is like a time just before the end. The break-up will occur that very day.

(3) The third and final technique, the crucial one, places the pure moment of non-acting in a closed, or very cramped, space. It is the moment when a gesture will not be made or a word will not be spoken, and identification will fail definitively, along with the love that included the possibility for it. This can be called the mode of counter-flight. Let me explain what I mean by that term. In Antonioni's films, and in many other works of art, it at first seems as if a woman's essence is to flee, to disappear.

Take Mavi, for instance, the aristocrat, a woman being closely watched perhaps, a kept woman perhaps, a lesbian perhaps, who will disappear one fine day. And the same goes for her counterpart, Ida, who we will learn at the very end of the film is pregnant by a friend and who had thus concealed, or removed, an essential part of herself from the view of the male protagonist. Yes, the pattern – a woman fleeing, disappearing, and a man wandering around looking for her – does seem to be the plot of many films, and especially Antonioni's.

But if we take a closer look at it, and if we watch everything again in terms of what I call the filmic moment of non-acting, our opinion will have to be different. In reality, the woman flees in order to create a space of decision for the man she loves but who, precisely because he fails to make any decision, she can't be sure loves her in return. If she disappears, he will at least have to decide to look for her. And, as Pascal says, if he looks for her it means he has really found her, that is, loved her. Similarly, in Ida's case, if she reveals what was hidden – the friend by whom she is pregnant – the hero will have to decide whether he loves her enough to disregard that and to take on, with her and for her, fatherhood and friendship, not just companionship and sex.

Yet what does the character, the man, do? He doesn't even really look for Mavi. The one who understands that that must be his desire is Ida, and it is she who will find the trace of the woman who has disappeared. But now there is the key scene, the filmic moment of non-acting. We are in a narrow staircase, whose spiral form, filmed abstractly, is reminiscent of a labyrinth. Besides, wasn't it Ariadne-Ida who was able to lead our weak Niccolò-Theseus to the Minotaur, the woman he has to identify? He is all the way at the top of the stairs, on the landing, just above Mavi's door. She arrives, can't get the door open right away, suspects his presence, smokes a cigarette . . . In short, she once again gives him time to make a decision. But he doesn't move, he lets her go in and shut the door, and he leaves, with his shoulders looking as narrow as the spiral staircase. From the window above, without our being able to tell if she is visible to him or not, Mavi, a dejected look on her face, watches him as he walks away down the street.

And when Ida, between two glass doors, tells Niccolò about the state of affairs (the friend, the baby she is expecting), he says nothing; he acts as though his silence were eloquent; he uses the fake, very male art of eloquent silence, and leaves without our being able to

160

THE CINEMATIC CAPTURE OF THE SEXES

know what he would or could have made of the real that is activated in this way.

Thus we are informed – by the well-organized force of the forms, the blue fog, the distance of the images, the slowness of the rituals, the melancholy sound of the sea, the flight of the women, the indecisiveness of the men, the immobility of the *objets d'art*, the impotence of the words – about what foregrounds, and leads to the failure of, the central theme of cinema since its invention, the identification of a woman.

What foregrounds the theme is the chance amorous encounter, whereby two fragments of indivisible humanity suddenly become players in the game of difference and its thinking. The sudden sexuation of everything owing to a chance encounter: this is what leads one, above and beyond the aporias of the sex act, into the labyrinth of identification.

But what leads to its failure, at least as far as Antonioni (but many other directors as well) is concerned is, in a word, a philosophical contradiction. For the male polarity – and this is perhaps what is most essential to it – to identify is to know. And since there is in reality nothing to know, since even pornographic nudity provides nothing to know about a woman, there is necessarily mystery, which gradually permeates the whole world. For the female polarity, the whole point is for love to be explicitly decided, if only by a declaration of love. It is the act that matters this time, not knowledge. If too much indecision introduces too much mystery, the latter will be compounded by withdrawal or disappearance, thus affording, through a deliberate increase in mystery, a last chance for a decision to be made.

Antonioni's exceptional mastery has to do with this process of mystery and with the issue of the missing act, which would dispel its bitter charms. That is why he is really a filmmaker of the identification of a woman, inasmuch as, such an identification being impossible for the man, it remains one of the rare forms of the real still available to him today.

"La différence des sexes est-elle visible?" ed. Jacques Aumont
Conférences du Collège d'histoire de l'art cinématographique
(Paris: Cinémathèque française, 2000), pp. 127–37

—23—

AN UNQUALIFIED AFFIRMATION OF CINEMA'S ENDURING POWER

Hugo Santiago, *Le Loup de la côte ouest* (*The Wolf of the West Coast*)

What is a film? An impurity that can only be purified by the admixture of the Beautiful.

In *Le Loup de la côte ouest*, the film Hugo Santiago offers us (because, for the viewer, a true film is always an offering, and a visitation as well), he piles on the instances of impurity at will. But his mastery of the labyrinth of scenes could not be more satisfying when it comes to a higher kind of purification.

The genres, first of all. It is a crime thriller: the hero is a detective and there are guns, intrigues, mysteries, shady deals, meetings, people being tailed, and so on. It is a historical, or war, film: a meditation on what the life of the American occupiers and mercenaries in Saigon was like during the Vietnam War in terms of the lasting effects of soul destruction. It is a romantic film: over the multi-faceted, glittering image of a woman from thirty years ago, with whom everyone was in love, is superimposed the woman of today, an attorney who is both direct and evasive. It is a porn film: the orgy in Saigon, filmed in black and white, extracts the latent poetry from the sexual dance captured in its rawness. It is a melodrama of masculinity: the men who thirty years ago were bound together by a bond stronger than the circumstances meet up again, amid the present-day entanglements, with the sort of taciturn stolidity, the powerful distance between bodies that is so typical of Hugo Santiago's art and his vision of men. It is a literary film, a novelistic meditation on time: one is reminded, often enough, of Proust, although the filmic material is poles apart from his work. It is a critical film, a sort of report, clear and mysterious at the same time, about what that strange imperative – to make a film, to tell a story, and to go far beyond that narrative, using the techniques of cinema – might be today. It is a theatrical film: the acting wrests itself away from all effects of realism through the abrupt oscillation (in which something of Antoine Vitez's teaching can be sensed) between a subtraction from all effect, a simple, over-whelming presence, and a sudden, momentary vehemence. A wonder-ful combination of the meditation on bodies and the decision made by souls. It is a prophetic film: the tracing of influences of the past, the prose of an old woman that gradually becomes clear, the switch-ing between different locales (Paris, the Atlantic coast, America, Saigon, and so on), the complicated maze of investigations, the mys-terious deaths: everything proclaims that you have to try to live, try to make sense of what is happening. That you have to endure.

There is also the impurity of the style, ultimately condensed in the nocturnal power of baroque paintings but imparted at first by a sort of survey of resources, a meticulous inventory of possibilities. The lighting of a building, a patch of yellow throwing the inky darkness of the night into relief; the uncanniness of a garden gate; the ocean, like a dark-blue gel; the quays of the Seine, a distribution of lights, hidden staircases, solitudes: the never-seen-before in the very same place as the always-seen-before; living rooms cluttered with cryptic objects; dealings observed from too close up for the bodies to reveal the meaning of what is going on; cars, guns, staircases, doors, glasses of liquor, beds, windows: all those hackneyed symbols used in ordi-nary films are here revisited, reconstituted, projected into the slow construction of time. Here, too, Santiago's cinema carefully achieves an infinite expansion of the visible. It deliberately involves retaining things – platitudes and evasions, stale visuals, a slew of TV images – that shouldn't be retained.

This is one of the miracles of the film: to proffer the grace of eleva-tion – I would almost say of redemption – to what everywhere else would only be corrupt images.

May I be permitted to say, simply, lamely, that cinema combines stories, performances, places, sounds, and colors? And that the assemblage of all of this should take us right to the verge of the Idea, to what must be called its passage? On that condition, I can become the guide to this monument that I urge you all to visit without delay: Hugo Santiago's film *Le Loup de la côte ouest*. So here's my pitch:

"Ladies and gentleman, it is my pleasure to present to you a work that is exceptional in every way, in these times when cinema is taking a pounding due to something that can only be called kitsch. Devoting ourselves to the pleasure of seeing, taking in, visiting the film for which I am serving as guide amounts to giving an answer to the very tough question: 'How can we filmgoers avoid being completely kitschified?'

As far as the plot is concerned, this film tells the story of an investigation, seemingly of people and crimes but in reality of the substance of time, and of the long-range consequences of powerful, corrupt pasts on uncertain presents. This is why everything that is told you in the film should be understood in the future perfect tense: what will be (a love? a return somewhere? a liberation? a disappearance?) is immersion in what will already have been (corruption, war, death, secrets), whereas what will have been is finally only clarified by what happens.

As far as the performances are concerned, this film obliges the actors, after strenuous exercises, in the direct line of descent from Bresson and a few others, to show how they might act if they were being natural, and yet never to act that way. Because they, too, must endure. Endure in the gestures and voices, in the filmic materiality of the image and the sound, without their ever being immobilized by the psychological rigidity of a role. They are all marvelous, given over like this to the film's power, which constricts them but at the same time shows them off like human gems in the hard jewelry case of the world.

As far as the locations are concerned – streets at night, silent façades, cliffs overlooking the sea, secret gardens, Parisian settings, crammed apartments, secular confessionals, quays of separation – this film incorporates them all in a chiaroscuro of its own invention. Naturally, we recognize Caravaggio in it, but a Caravaggio altered, re-lit, with dabs of mobile gaiety as well as motionless depths in which, as Wagner says in *Parsifal*, "time and space are one." This is because the Idea is passing through the place, the Idea that, although we have been scattered and are astray in the exiles imposed on us by history, although everything in our lives is uncertainty and chiaroscuro, we must not give way on light. The film must be made.

As far as the sounds and colors are concerned, the whole point is to secretly match them to the film's overall construction. They are not mere ornaments added to it after the fact but its very truth. For the sounds highlight the liberation from time, while the colors express the plasticity of the visible, which we mold to both our illusions and our beliefs. We will relish the subtle interplay of classic, nostalgic, and daring references through which the music and voices reveal that the soul is but the unfolding of a mystery, the mystery of the influence of the past and of the difficulty of becoming free of it. And we will learn the art of colors at night, namely that yellow stands for waiting, blue for steadfastness, white for uncertainty, black for the past . . . Or red, the red of velvet or wine, for friendship.

164

As far as the montage is concerned, this film is in the richest tradition, the tradition of Orson Welles, but without the hysteria. Because what I particularly like about this film, as I did about *Invasion*, the film Santiago made thirty-three years ago, is the amazing calmness with which the most radical decisions, improbable quests, and terrible risks are all woven together. The film is in the tradition of Eisenstein, but without the epic. Because what I particularly like about this film is its narrative proximity, which makes us share, as the film unfolds, the secrets it creates and dispels, as though they were our own. And finally there is Hugo Santiago's ability to hold on with an iron grip to the contrast between scenes and to give us the essence of the story only in fragments that dovetail so well, while being at the same time so unexpected, that it makes you think of the inventions of cubism.

Ladies and gentlemen, I hope I have convinced you. Follow the guide, follow me right this way for cinema, which endures in this film as the desire for art and thought; for your pleasure, because this film is delectable and fascinating; for your salvation, to which this film will contribute; for the struggle against kitsch. Let's all go through the doors of the movie theater now to see *Le Loup de la côte ouest*!"

Unpublished text, 2002

—24—

PASSION, JEAN-LUC GODARD

This film, *Passion*, expresses or attempts to express, through music, an intermediate world, an in-between world. What's more, in-between situations recur repeatedly as one of the film's leitmotifs. How can an intermediate world be expressed through music? And first of all, what does "through music" mean? "Through music" implies the mystery of the work's construction, because *Passion* is clearly a film based entirely on themes and variations. It is not based on the typical order of a story but neither is it based on an instantly intelligible symbolic order. It is really based on themes and variations, as well as on expositions, developments, and conclusions, which are also borrowed from music. If you pay close attention, you can discern these three movements, the three classical movements of a concerto, in almost every scene.

The film can therefore be said to present a twofold articulation, which no doubt requires being seen or experienced several times. First, there is an articulation based on recurrence or return, something that could be called the canonical image, the image that comes back, the image that is like a matrix of the film's development. Then, there is a second articulation based on progression, on linkage, at which point we get what could be called a resolving image. I think that this twofold pattern – on the one hand, the use of repetition, and on the other, by means of this repetition, something like the search for a resolving image – is really the key to the film's meaning.

"Through music" also means, of course, that music properly speaking plays an essential role, namely the series of successive musical themes, contrasting and coupling with the image, those great musical passages – Ravel, Mozart, Beethoven, Dvorak, Fauré – along with a theme that clearly revolves around the idea of the requiem. It is moreover on Fauré's *Requiem* that the film concludes as everyone returns home.

The question posed by the film becomes: a requiem for what? What is being commemorated here, albeit commemorated in the manner of the commemoration of the dead, of the Last Judgment? This is my second subject. The film really attempts to express an intermediate world, a world between two worlds, a world in which something is finished, or most likely finished, and in which something is trying to begin but hasn't really done so.

Some further clarification is necessary here. *Passion* dates from 1982. Even in terms of Godard's career it is a film between two periods. It obviously comes after his period of absolute politicization of cinema in the 1970s, which extended, roughly speaking, from 1967 (from *La Chinoise*, which, in my view, completes the period just before) to 1979, the year of *Sauve qui peut (la vie)* (*Every Man For Himself*). Between 1967 and 1979, Godard went so far as to disappear *qua* Godard and melt into a cinema collective, the Dziga Vertov group. The film you have just seen is situated after that period and before another great phase, when the filmmaker would be increasingly committed to a kind of reflective cinema, a sort of retrospective and prospective meditation on what cinema is and what the image is, with *Histoire(s) du cinéma* really representing the peak of that trajectory.

Passion is typical of what could be called the period of the 1980s in Godard's work, which began with *Sauve qui peut (la vie)* and ended, to my mind, in 1987 with *Soigne ta droite* (*Keep Your Right Up*). This period included four main films, *Passion*, *Je vous salue Marie* (*Hail Mary*), *Prénom: Carmen* (*First Name: Carmen*), and *Détective*, all of which have something in common, but of which *Passion* is really the focal point, the sensitive plate, with all that that term can connote in terms of mystery or complexity.

Essentially, the film attempts to depict the early 1980s and to depict them as an intermediate, enigmatic, elusive period. The general question it poses is: Where do we stand, in the early 1980s, in terms of the possibilities for thought and life? It is a film about possibilities, which is also why it is not easy to understand, because it is less about reality or the fragments of the real than about possibility. Where do we stand in terms of the possibilities for thought and for life, or for life as the thinking of life? That is really the film's theme.

Cinema would provide Godard with the means for creating a sort of allusive poetics of this question. This is also why *Passion* is both a fragmentary film and a musical one. Actually, Godard's method,

167

particularly in these films of the 1980s, could be said to consist in changing questions into situations, that is to say, in finding a cine-matic situation that is the equivalent of the question (although without asking it explicitly): "Where do we stand in terms of the thinking of life and the relationship between thought and life?"

The film is a series of situations. I need to explain what is meant by "situation." In reality – and this is one of the film's themes – Godard refuses for the film to be constructed on the basis of a story. In the film, an Italian producer shows up demanding a story, "*una storia*." There may not be a story, but nor is it a matter of the story as such being eliminated, or, for example, of something that would replace the story with haphazard successions of moments. In reality, what Godard intends to do is extract schematic or typical situations from the notion of story. These situations, which are completely familiar and bound up with the history of cinema, are no longer presented as stories but as the skeletal structure, kernel, or matrix of a story.

Let me give two examples of this method.

(1) *Passion* is concerned throughout with one of Godard's major questions, namely where do we stand in terms of love? More to the point, where exactly do we stand in terms of sexual differ-ence and its effects in life and, ultimately, where do we stand, if we are men, in terms of the cinematic representation or figure of women? To express this, instead of taking a story that would relate such a thing Godard takes a completely ordinary concept: a man between two women. Jerzy, the director of the film-within-the-film, is between Isabelle Huppert and Hanna Schygulla. The man between two women has given rise to count-less film plots. Cinema has nearly always explored the issue we are talking about by using the situation of a man between two women. So Godard will go about it in the ordinary way in this respect, except that he will retain only what is ordinary about this ordinariness. He will keep only the concept of "a man between two women" without developing it in any plot or story. This could be called the reduction of the story to the situation, of the story to its concept. And, as a result, this concept can be polymorphous since it is no longer attached to a story but is reduced to its kernel. Something can spread through the film or take it in several different directions. For instance, this man between two women will also be the man between a bourgeois woman and a factory worker (Hanna Schygulla, the hotel owner,

168

and Isabelle Huppert, the worker character). We thus go from the initial question about love, about sexual difference, to the question of class relations, of the relation between bosses and workers, which had preoccupied Godard so intensely in the 1970s. Here, then, is the possibility for a simplified concept, borrowed from a traditional story in film, to reorient a theme or enable another theme or question to be developed.

The film thus allows for different questions to be interwoven on the basis of little matrices that are, at bottom, tired old stories, reduced to their pure cinematic situation.

(2) How has cinema usually approached the social issue (let's call it that), namely the question of work, class relations, relations between workers and bosses? It has usually done so by depicting its dramatic moments: revolts, uprisings, strikes, demands, and so forth. And it is usually an epic or semi-epic treatment that the issue has been given in film. Here, Godard goes about it in a completely different way. He'll take up the question of struggles, protests, strikes, and so forth again, but instead of giving it an evental dimension, an epic dimension, he will reduce *it* as well and turn it into a sort of little microcosm. The factory is reduced to two or three machines and a few women workers; the boss is the only boss there is; the police are represented by a single police officer whom the boss will go seek out; and politics is concentrated in a sequence devoted to a quasi-virtual meeting of the workers, at which what they would like to say, write, and declare is discussed. As for political action per se, it boils down to an almost slapstick chase scene in the pseudo-factory, where the rebellious worker is chased around by a caricatural policeman and the factory owner (Piccoli is an old hand at playing this type of character). This set-up bordering on slapstick functions as a reference, reduced to a microcosm, to the ordinary treatment of the workers' struggle issue. I will conclude on this point, but this is the method of legibility of the film, meaning that it must always be seen in such a way that you can discern in it something that functions not as a story, but as the matrix of a potential story within a reference to cinema's ordinary ways of treating the situation in question, regardless of whether that situation involves sexual difference and love, or social struggle and the worker-boss relationship.

Now that the method has been established, I think we can turn to the various types of questions the film runs through, the types of questions that it frames. I will deal with just a few of these in order to show how extraordinarily complex the film is and what I mean when I stress that it expresses an intermediate world though music.

First, as we have just seen, the film deals with the question "Where do we stand in terms of love and the historicity of the situation?" It does so in a variety of ways and concludes (if you can call it a conclusion), as so often with Godard, that the issue is caught between the opacity of women, which is usually shown by the interrogation of a face, and an abstract erotics represented by the pictorial style of the various instances of nudity in the film. It is in this interplay between the two that the interrogation emerges. The film is split between an attempt to signify femaleness as thought, as interrogation, as representation, in Hanna Schygulla's or Isabelle Huppert's face (there are some very beautiful shots, shots of pure opacity, mystery, questioning), and, on the other hand, Godard's contemplation of the erotic act, which is a little icy, a little detached, a little mechanical. Between these two aspects the new situation of the question of sex and love appears.

Second, the film weaves this together with the question "What meaning does the word 'worker' have in politics in the early 1980s, what meaning does 'class struggle' have, what meaning does 'social struggle' have, and what meaning does the generic function of work have?"

The question of work is a key issue in the film, whose subject, in essence, is the passion for work as a figure linked to love. You could say that the key subject comes down to the maxim that is heard in *Passion*: "One should love to work or work to love." This is ultimately the destiny of humanity, which lies between these two terms.

Naturally, the issue of worker/boss/class struggle will be represented by Isabelle Huppert's character, by the situation in the factory, by the other women workers, by Piccoli as the factory owner, by the workers' meeting, and will be dealt with abundantly. It is important to understand that the year is 1982, in other words, when the 1970s and everything that came after '68 were coming to a close. This was the time of what could be considered the last political experience with significant working-class content, the Solidarity movement in Poland – Poland, a signifier that will become a crucial element in the film for this very reason.

One might wonder whether the other question running through the film – and it is one that may still be of interest to us today – isn't

170

the following: Is an orderly exit from actually existing socialism possible, a way out that doesn't simply amount to a collapse? Is there a possibility for a way out of socialism? At a given moment Poland inspired hope of that sort, namely that in actually existing socialism, the countries under the control of Communist parties, there might be workers' political movements so significant that they could change the situation in a way that wouldn't merely amount to its collapsing and the state of things being replaced by some anarchic form of capitalism or other. *Passion* is a film that attempts to capture this "Polish way," whereby an alternative to actually existing socialism that was not a ruthlessly capitalistic one might ultimately emerge in the workers' movement. This is of course the reason why everyone leaves for Poland at the end of the film, to see whether there might not be something else there besides the terrible choice between an actually existing socialism that has collapsed or is on the verge of collapsing and the unbridled capitalism that was in the process of being established there.

Third, the film naturally deals with the question "Where do we stand in terms of the arts?" Love, politics, and the arts. Or rather, where do we stand in terms of the impure place of cinema as compared with the situations of the other arts? *Passion* puts forward some complex propositions concerning this issue. To begin with, it clearly shows that cinema is linked to a temptation exerted by America. This is another way of seeing the film, as suspended between America and Poland. At the end, will they go to America or to Poland? Some of the people go to Poland, the others to America. That has to do with cinema's impurity. It also has to do with the fact that money issues are a constant obsession. There is never enough money. But the all-important meditation in the film is the meditation on the relationship between cinema and painting. And it is a masterstroke of cinematic invention, I believe, to have placed at the very heart of the film, and as an elusive project at that, the recreation of great masterpieces of painting.

One after the other, we see Rembrandt's *Night Watch*, a painting by Goya, and Delacroix's *Entry of the Crusaders into Constantinople*, by means of images that are rather baffling because, at bottom, their real intention is absolutely enigmatic. It is a matter neither of a simple display of the paintings nor of something that is their exact equivalent. Rather, it is the filming of live bodies recreating something that already existed as an image within the painting. This is an interrogation that amounts to saying that painting and cinema have a number of elements in common, first and foremost the question of light, which is an essential leitmotif in the film. How is light distributed in such a way that it does justice to the visible, and is cinema's destiny in this respect superior, or equal, to painting's? Godard experiments with this (the movement of light in the visible world) by constructing cinematic equivalents of well-known paintings, in an attempt to understand whether or not light distribution in film can elucidate light distribution in the masterpieces of painting.

Fourth, there is an interrogation of language: in this enigmatic world, in this in-between world, what can language still say? This is the reason behind the "Say your line" sentence. You also find this theme of the forcing of the line in both the issue of sexual relations (a scene involving sexual relations during which the man is extremely brutal and the woman says, "Say your line," a line we won't hear at all or will hear only imperfectly) and social relations, inasmuch as Isabelle Huppert will question her old grandfather by saying to him, too, "Say your line, say your line." Here, the line will be "As a rule, the poor are right," which the film in a way constantly seeks to question or challenge.

This is the question of the sentence as a sexual or political one. In the world being interrogated here, is there a sentence that could express *jouissance* or desire? Is there a sentence that could express the relationship of justice and injustice between the rich and the poor? Likewise, we hear: "We need to make a declaration," to which Isabelle Huppert replies, "We need to see what we say." The problem of the relationship between seeing and saying is also one of the major issues in Godard's cinema, which, along with its whole battery of words, quotations, and clippings, was suited to the situation of the 1980s.

But the film is shot through with anxiety about the power of speech, about the possibility of expressing those essential experiences of love, on the one hand, and class struggle, on the other. The most important symbol of this is Isabelle Huppert's stuttering, which must be taken at face value. The working class stutters, the working class is no longer able to speak, no longer has a candid, straightforward, confident way of speaking. The stuttering it suffers from is ultimately the stuttering of the political situation itself. Let me remind you that 1982 was the year after the Left's return to power, and the stuttering is probably also related to that return, the stuttering of the Socialist government.

Of course, there are still other basic themes in the film, which I will just mention briefly. One of them in particular seems very important to me: where do we stand in terms of human turmoil? In this case, too, Godard treats the issue through a unique capture of cine-matic material, such as in the scenes where people run around in different directions. This is one of the film's leitmotifs, one of the ways it resonates: shouting people run over to cars and Jerzy's assis-tant calls him to say "Jerzy, you've got to come right away." This is truly an interrogation of the pointlessness of turmoil with no real purpose, an aspect of modern life captured on film by all this abso-lutely desperate activity around the cars to no apparent end. It all concludes with the purely farcical episode involving a sort of free-for-all in which people start hitting each other without anyone having the slightest idea why. It's perfectly obvious: if you want to treat human turmoil in film, broad comedy is surely the most appropriate and effective means of doing so.

I also need to mention the lateral themes, the themes circulating between the themes, such as the connection between love and work, which is constantly elucidated in the film, including with the hypoth-esis that, at bottom, neither love nor work can really be filmed because they are the same in terms of their gestures. Isabelle Huppert says, "I notice that films never show people at work." Her interlocu-tor replies with a down-to-earth answer: "Filming in factories is not allowed." Isabelle Huppert then comments, "I'm right, it's because the gestures of work have something in common with the gestures of love." That is why work can't be filmed. Here, the idea is essentially that the ultimate real of human experience, which lies between love and work, in the common space of love and work, is something that in a certain way is inaccessible, still in 1982, to the operations of cinema.

There is clearly one final theme, which takes in all the others: the theme of the sacred. It is on this theme that the film opens, with the sky and the moving line of the jet's exhaust trail, which, little by little, cuts enigmatically across the image of the blue. And it is also on this theme that *Passion* ends, with the great upward movement toward the final image of the painting, an ascent toward an implicit transcen-dence, a transcendence that is unnamed, unnamable, but clearly an essential resource of the film.

All of the foregoing shows the extent to which *Passion* is the film of a passage, of an in-between space, because to none of these ques-tions does Godard give a tenable, considered answer. The film essen-tially depicts a time when the old politics, the old hope cherished by politics, lives on only in its last possible forms. Whether it is the Polish workers' movement or the Left's coming to power in France, the fact remains that this is the unsettled closing of a certain period of politics,

173

and, by the same token, an enigmatic period in the relationship between men and women and in the history of desire.

So there is another way of defining the film: it is a compilation of uncertainties. That is why it is about gaps and difficulties in understanding. But this compilation of uncertainties nevertheless lets something come through, it seems to me, something like two different kinds of power. There is a compilation of uncertainties, but the diagnosis is not entirely a foregone conclusion: two kinds of power are at work in this compilation. First, there is a definite power, a power that I would say is basically Godard's last refuge, in every period of his work, namely the power of the light of the visible, as the enduring possibility of a contemplative distance independent of life's incidents or ups-and-downs. This power is very evident in the film. I already mentioned the white line at the beginning of the film, that first image of the sky; one could also mention what I consider to be the extremely powerful scene in which Hanna Schygulla watches her own image in the video. This effect of delayed or distanced self-contemplation is filmed with extraordinary subtlety, with that way of turning partly away from your own image, letting it linger on sort of tenderly and at the same time leaving you a little out of sync, as it were, with it. There are also, to be sure, the images of Isabelle Huppert walking beside the stream, which also possess that quasi-sacred quality coming from the light of the visible, or of the snow at the end of the film, in which they are leaving for a Poland at once emblematic and totally uncertain. So that is the first of the two powers, a purely cinematic power, the passage of the illuminated power of the visible.

But there is another power, which, back then, at that time, was still only hypothetical: the power of work. Work remains the common feature, the common reference point, the name that is common to love, art, and politics, through the successive figures – the woman factory worker and the other female characters – of the film's uncertainty. So there is a definite power, the light of the visible, which is partly metaphysical, and a hypothetical power, still kept alive in 1980, which is the question of the agency of work. Everything is played out in this in-between space, and the montage is indeed a compilation of uncertainties.

Passion – and I will conclude with this – never fails to make me think of a tremendous play by the young Ibsen, *Emperor and Galilean*. It is a play devoted to Julian the Apostate, the Roman emperor who, after Constantine and after the Roman Empire's adoption of Christianity, wanted to restore the old gods. At a certain moment, Julian, in despair, realizing that his enterprise is futile, says, "We live in a world in which the old beauty is no longer beautiful but the new truth is not yet true." *Passion* is a film about just such a thing. Something of what there was before no longer exists, but something of what is supposed to come hasn't come. That is the space the film inhabits, and its genius lies in changing it into a form of themes and variations, all the while borrowing its power from the light of the visible.

Lecture delivered at *Le Lieu unique*, Nantes, November 2001
(The text was transcribed from a video recording)

—25—

"SAY YES TO LOVE, OR ELSE BE LONELY"

An interview about Paul Thomas Anderson's
film *Magnolia*[1]

Unity and multiplicity

Élisabeth Boyer: What I was struck by in *Magnolia* was the multiplicity of spaces, the multiplicity of characters, all of them main characters, and the multiplicity of performances, all very strong ones. There's something really new about this aspect, but what seems very different and yet a lot like one of John Sayles' first great films, *City of Hope* from 1991, is precisely this multiplicity of spaces, characters, even stories, all intertwined and interwoven. In Paul Thomas Anderson's film, the montage is still very technical in terms of juxtaposition; it's a classical montage that's highly complexified yet still with relatively analogous sequences. What's very different in Sayles' work is that there's this same multiplicity but with montages within shots, within space. That's why it's a thinking of the world today, of separate spaces, of their lack of connection. What's your opinion of the coherence of such a montage in terms of the need today to think the coherence of the world despite all the different spaces and worlds?

Alain Badiou: I think there's a tension between the desire for multiplicity and a counter-tendency toward unity in *Magnolia*. The multiplicity is very striking, of course, in terms of the stories, the characters, the characters' acting style, and the way the stories are interwoven, but at the same time it seems to me that this multiplicity doesn't really negatively affect the issue of shot composition. It's a technical issue in effect, albeit an important one. Furthermore, in the final analysis, the multiplicity is subordinated to a principle of unity, only this principle of unity is always presented as a result rather than as a given, and as a partial result at that: every time you think you've got unity, it's nevertheless a little undone or thwarted by something else. The

most glaring example of this is that, just when the stories all inter-
twine and connect with one other, if only on a narrative level, the
rain of frogs occurs like an element over-determining the narrative
unity and making it ultimately a bit pointless, since it's an element
that could be called symbolic.

The film is contemporary in terms of its capture of multiplicity and
disconnection, of the impossibility of holding on to an ideological or
subjective narrative point that would encompass everything. But I
think that the desire for unity is strong enough for an argument possibly to be made that it's a neo-classical film. And that's the case, it
seems to me, for two reasons. First of all, because however many
things there may be, we never lose sight of the fact that in the final
analysis they do in fact constitute a story in the multiple sense of the
term: a narrative but also a symbolic story. Second of all, and maybe
more important, each of the stories ultimately constructs a familiar
theme. It's still, at bottom, a film about father and son, which is an
absolutely basic organic feature of American cinema. If American
cinema has a classic theme, it's surely that one, even if there are others
of a similar sort. The great intersubjective characters of American
melodrama are all depicted in this film. None of them is the subject
of the film in the usual sense, but that's still what it's all about.

Daniel Fischer: The tendency toward unity can effectively be seen in
the father–son issue, but also in the community that the film creates.
There's an explicit operatic dimension: for example, when the characters sing the same song in unison – that's very American, too. How
does that differ from John Ford's plot of a community created by the
film?

Alain Badiou: You could say the same thing as a moment ago. The
theme of the community's creation by the film, or even the theme of
the time of the film being the time of the community's creation, is
actually a bit fractured, a bit fragmented, but it can nevertheless be
found in the film. Quite simply, it's more abstract, because the community is not an epic, or narrative, one, in a very broad sense; it's a
community that shows that it's been produced by the film: this is an
element of modernity injected into the classicism. There's never any
attempt to make us think this community is a *real* construction. We're
shown very clearly that the film creates it. Nevertheless, the theme is
also a classic theme. I simply believe that here, particularly because
the film uses abstract means, the director's idea is that this community
is humanity itself. It's not a specific narrative community involved in

a story; rather, it's allegorical of humanity as a whole. That's why it can be stricken by something like a plague of Egypt.

The film is located on a really interesting plane, since just below it (that is, within it, as a potential plane) can be found certain traditional themes of American cinema. It could be an elaborate film, after all, but dealing with father–son relations or with the community. And just above it there could be something that would turn it into an abstract, symbolic film. In my opinion, the special genius of this film lies in its not being exactly one or the other. It floats around, with a varyingly emphasized possibility of, or potential for, shifting onto a plane of very substantial symbolic – or even completely unreal, fictional, in the strongest sense of the term – abstraction, when it comes to the business about the frogs or the chorus, or some of the connections between stories that are too implausible or artificial to really function narratively. It can be abstract like that, but it can also be really virtuosic in some scenes, or almost reminiscent of ordinary melodrama in one scene or another.

Still, the film won't reveal much of what it is if you isolate just one of its scenes. In this regard, it's a montage film, in an essential way, precisely because the shot isn't really negatively affected by multiplicity: except in a few rare cases, certain scenes or parts of scenes can be regarded as being absolutely like classic cinema. One of them comes to mind at random: the scene where the son is crying at his father's bedside. If you isolate it, it'll seem like conventional melodrama. There are a lot of scenes like that.

Father and son

Slim Ben Cheikh: Would you say that that's the key scene, this story of the son and his father?

Alain Badiou: It's a very important one. It exerts a certain influence, which is why I stressed the father–son theme, because it's not just present in that scene alone. There's the story of the little boy, and so forth. As regards father and son, the counterpoint is very important. But the story of the wife of the father, the old man who's dying, is not merely peripheral, or tangential, relative to an issue that's central, nor is the incest story. These stories are in effect not exactly of equal weight. The father–son theme is still the central organizing theme. It predominates, but a certain balance is maintained; the rest is not just tangential. There are several different threads,[2] even if that one is the main one. It's all done with perfect awareness that the father–son theme is a basic theme in American cinema. (*Magnolia* is an exceptionally self-reflexive film, with a very powerful intellectuality.) Anderson is aware of this and provides an important, centrally organizing version of it, but one that you have to realize is also extremely condensed, bordering on abstraction. Not necessarily in individual scenes but overall. Take the big scene of the son's macho lecture: if you isolate it, you get something that's impossible to understand at the moment, even in terms of the father–son story.

Slim Ben Cheikh: But then there's the interview with the reporter, which is very striking and works on several different levels. It lets us shift over to the son's relationship with his father while it simultaneously expresses something else about contemporary America, the America of journalism and the media. Each sequence is linked to the others, and stands on its own.

Alain Badiou: That's one of the great strengths of the film, whereby it remains involved in real multiplicity. What's really interesting is that the scenes have an intensity of performance that's particular to them; they can stand on their own, even with several different meanings at the very moment of the scene. Yet, at the same time, what I said before is still true: if you isolate them, in some cases they can seem like moments from masterfully directed great narrative cinema. I'm thinking of a very striking scene when the old man's wife is in the pharmacy. The scene is very skillful in terms of its composition, the distancing play of the gazes, the way the camera remains half-way above and shows the face from a distance. You can admire this scene; it has an intrinsic intensity about it. But if it isn't considered as part of the montage, connected with the whole constellation of the film, it will function as a neo-classical scene, that is, extremely brilliant, innovative, and so forth, but treating something that's closed up on itself, that has its own narrative intensity.

Slim Ben Cheikh: In connection with the question of linking to the whole, do you think that the prologue acts as a sort of key, or that it stands on its own? It's unclear: even if you consider it as a key, it's not one that's easy to grasp.

Denis Lévy: It's a little like the abstraction of the whole.

Alain Badiou: The prologue warns us, it alerts us to the fact that the film is actually something other than its sequential literalness. I agree with Denis: it indicates abstraction. I have to stress this point: I think the film lies exactly between, on the one hand, a melodramatic mosaic that's completely recognizable piece by piece, in terms of various themes, and, on the other, an abstraction resulting not only from the combining of the pieces (because they have to be put together, literally) but also from the fact that the community created is in actual fact humanity in general. Even the father–son theme tends toward allegory; it's not just a family story.

Between neo-classical and baroque

Daniel Fischer: We might wonder about the title, *Magnolia*. Is there a connection between the abstract structure of the film and the shape of the flower?

Denis Lévy: There's a magnolia flower in the credits, a flower that opens up and suggests the radiating form of the film.

Alain Badiou: It suggests the construction of a totality made out of complexity, something along those lines. As a tree, the magnolia is characterized by each of its leaves being very glossy and very independent of the others. There's the organic unity of the tree, and the closing up of each leaf on itself, even in terms of its brilliant, glossy appearance. The director sees himself like that: each scene is very polished, very glossy, but the living thing is the tree.

Annick Fiolet: That's the "flashy" aspect of the film that some of us had problems with . . .

Alain Badiou: But I think there's a very deliberate, overdone glossiness, which I would attribute particularly to the fact that there's a fairly systematic exaggerated quality about the intensity of the acting. That peculiarity, in terms of the actors' performances, is a striking feature of the film. There are entire bits that are bits of actor intensity. In my opinion, Anderson is very well aware that he could be accused of piling on the affectation, and it *is* in fact possible to accuse him of that. There are moments when the actor is so naked that you could say he's really getting off on it. For example, Julianne Moore's half-hysterical scene in the pharmacy or Tom Cruise's big sex lecture scene. Each of the actors has his own aria, as in an opera, a moment when he gets to show off what he can do. I think this is a sort of veneer applied to the scene, an almost excessive intensity that will ultimately have to be reincorporated into the life of the whole. That's what the film is made up of, but it can't be reduced to that. It's true that, in this regard, we're in a bind. We say that the film is neo-classical for a number of obvious reasons, but on another level we're tempted to speak of baroque, really, in the "classical" sense of baroque. Baroque and classical are opposites, but the baroque also has a certain classical dimension. I get a sense of a baroque esthetic, that is, the whole is constructed on the basis of an intensification of the parts and not just on the basis of a subordination of the parts to the whole. Each part has to be intensified and it's only on the basis of that intensification that it will find its principle of connection to the other parts. The more unique each story is, the greater the chance it has of being connected to the others, and not at all in terms of its having to be watered down in order to link up with the others. Anderson managed to carry that off, which is hard to do, because usually, in films with a lot of different interlocking stories (something he didn't invent), in order for all the components to be connected to each other, each individual one has to be watered down. Here, on the contrary, they're all connected by virtue of being intensified. Take the example of Tom Cruise's interview, which will make it possible to transition to another node of the story: it's accomplished violently, not at all by smoothing its edges.

Confession

Alain Badiou: There's one feature that's unusual. There's something about the form that's been preserved from melodrama, something that comes from the theater. A good many of melodrama's plots come from Eugene O'Neill and Tennessee Williams; they're the original sources. There's a trope that's borrowed from O'Neill's theater, the trope of confession. It's a basic *topos* of American melodrama in terms of its theatrical reference: the moment when something is finally going to be able to be *said*, when, in a sort of nighttime group therapy session, something will be able to be revealed. This sort of confession figures prominently in the film: "I cheated on you," and so forth, along with both the pain and the liberating function of confession. But what I'm struck by here is that

181

confession is separate from the theme of reconciliation, whereas it's usually always connected to it. I think *that's* contemporary. Reconciliations are only apparent: the father and son make up with each other, the old man's wife finally confesses, but it's too late. The former whiz kid admits he's gay, but it doesn't change a thing. There's a network of confessions that's absolutely typical of this kind of cinema, but usually the confession is constitutive of the community's reconciliation. The community was broken apart, divided by secrets that couldn't be expressed, and the thing has to be expressed in order for the community to have a chance of coming back together. It can be the conjugal community, incidentally, the story of a couple.

In *Magnolia*, there are big scenes involving confession, but they take place within a community that never really comes together. That's also why there are the frogs raining down: it's all presented as a potential path for humanity but for a humanity that can't be totalized, that won't come together. The role of confession is severed from its ordinary purpose. A lot of features of traditional American melodrama, including ones that derive from its theatrical origins, function that way in the film. They're there, but in the service of something a lot more abstract than usual. Ultimately, all these stories are stories of confession, but the confession has a sort of abstract value, a value of compassion, not of reconnection or reconciliation.

Élisabeth Boyer: There's another trope, too: the sensitive cop's and the young drug addict's declaration of love, which is quite hystericized in terms of speech. They say "Let's tell each other everything" so that they won't have any confessions to make to each other, so that they can avoid having to make dangerous confessions. The pledge they make to each other is a pretty amazing declaration of love, in which one of them admits she's an addict and the other that he's lost his gun.

Annick Fiolet: The declaration could be seen as leading to a love process, but at the same time it remains abstract. The confession exceeds the object of the confession; it's connected to the declaration itself. The declaration is moreover a little separate; it functions on another level, it opens something up.

Élisabeth Boyer: The film ends with them, it ends on the girl's smile.

Humanity is love

Alain Badiou: We might ask, in keeping with our good old method, what the subject of this film is. We identified a whole series of tropes that function not as the film's subject but as its materials. It's not a film about the father–son relationship, or about the inadequacy of confessions, or about the conditions of the declaration and of love, even though all those things can be found in it and all of them are the basis on which we'll say something about the film.

I think the question the film is asking is whether humanity exists or not. It has an abstract Christian thesis (which is why the registers are those of melodrama), namely that humanity is love. That's how I understand it, even in terms of the film's ending, in terms of its future. I call it "abstractly Christian," which is what justifies there being allegorical moments in it, or quotations from the Bible, even if the film isn't strictly speaking a Christian film. Insofar as humanity exists (which is an unresolved question, incidentally, because the film also says that there's a big risk that it doesn't), insofar as humanity exists, its only real figure is love. Ultimately, for the little boy, the main issue is that his father won't have loved him; the woman's despair derives from the fact that in her own eyes she won't have really loved the old man as she should have. By contrast, an incredible difference between them notwithstanding, the police officer and the girl will have the chance to declare their love. But the father and son won't have loved each other, and the TV show host will have wrecked his daughter's love for him by incest. The cinematic thesis of the film, which dictates its montage, its hesitations, its complexity, is not just *"Does something like humanity exist today (via the question of the multiple, of separation, and, at the same time, of unity)?"* but is also a hypothesis: *humanity is love.* When there's no love, then there's no humanity, there's only disconnection, in the strict sense of the term. There are stories that are in danger of having no relationship among themselves, that are in danger of coming apart amid a potentially riotous chaos, in which, in a way, the only thing that counts anymore is performance.

I think that one of the meanings of the use of the actors' intensity is that it's a metaphor for the question of performance. When you're alone, all you can do is perform your own number. Numbers like that have a certain legitimacy in the film: they're linked to the question of humanity. Anyone who's alone – without love, in other words – can only affirm him or herself through performance, whether it's a given character's hysteria or the incestuous father's TV performance. The father is revealed through the drama of that exhibition; his sickness is tantamount to his being totally trapped in performance, owing to the unspoken story. These are all people trapped in solitary exhibition. The kid is shown as someone who's been trained from childhood for such a thing. It's a harsh critique of the idea that humanity might be able to fulfill itself as a collection of performances. And performance is shown as the non-human form of man because the price of performance is non-love. It's in that sense that the kid's story is exemplary. Each of the stories is key because each contributes little by little to the key theme of the film. That's what constitutes true equality among these stories: each story is really a typical example of the film's subject, namely that if there is no love, we have a different conception of humanity, a defeated humanity given over to performance. This is shown even in the characters: to the extent that he doesn't have love, the sensitive cop is trapped in performance. He's absolutely not like the others, but he has no way of being represented other than by doing his job as a cop really well and thoroughly, by being a perfect cop, through and through. That's why losing his gun will be a tragedy. With the male nurse, it's compassion as performance; it's the absolute of Tolstoyan goodness. And ultimately, insofar as it's no more than that, it doesn't lead to a way out of solitude. Some characters can be good guys, others bad guys, but the film says that that's not the issue. There's the incestuous character, the compassionate character, the kid, the hysterical woman, the excellent cop, the drug addict, and so on, and at any moment, from the standpoint of the image, you can say they're good or bad, decent or not, putting up a horrible cynical front, and so forth, but that's not the issue.

Élisabeth Boyer: The little black boy who asks the policeman a riddle at the beginning of the film has his own performance, too, his rap number, but the good cop can't relate to it: he's kind, but the two of them don't relate.

Alain Badiou: Absolutely. But the film says that regardless of whether you have great inner goodness or you put up a big cynical front, regardless of whether you're a character who's very much in view or a socially very minor character, none of that constitutes a principle of judgment. It's a humanistic film from that point of view. There's no morality in terms of rules, the law, and so forth. "Say yes to love, or else be lonely": that's basically what the film is saying.

184

Emmanuel Dreux: The question of ineffectual confession, the fact that confession doesn't lead to melodrama's usual reconciliation, could be connected with the question of performance you were just talking about. Confession in classical melodrama, where everything is resolved in a somewhat artificial or forced way, might only function as performance today.

Alain Badiou: I quite agree with you because it could be argued that one tendency of classical melodrama is to turn the confession itself into a performance with therapeutic value. I have in mind those great confession scenes in Hitchcock, in *Rebecca* or *Under Capricorn*, those magnificent scenes where everything will be cleared up because the original secret will be revealed. And also the great confession scene in Mankiewicz's *Suddenly Last Summer* or Huston's *Night of the Iguana*. There's a whole bunch of films you can think of, which are implicitly based on O'Neill and Tennessee Williams, in which there's a great moment of solo performance by the actor, which is identified as such. In *Rebecca*, I'm thinking of the great camera movement revolving around Laurence Olivier. Those are virtuoso scenes in which the actor has to carry the story all by himself, sometimes for quite a few minutes. And that's what has therapeutic value, whereas Anderson's thesis, in my opinion, is exactly the opposite. Performance, in the fictional sense, will be shown as the moment of greatest *alienation*, not at all as that of the resolution of truth. The moment of that resolution is, on the contrary, the moment when someone stutters, or is shy, when speech is halting, or difficult. The great performance scenes are on the contrary scenes of solitude. There's a down-playing, and it's interesting because it's not split between form and content. It's really the actor's performance as an index of emptiness.

Élisabeth Boyer: There's a remarkable scene, the scene of the rain of frogs, which reconstructs the unity. The child, surrounded by his books, is the only one who's not frightened. We get the feeling that someone who's a thinker, someone who's immersed in his books, possesses a certain superiority, and that's not an ordinary perspective today. The cop isn't very scared either. He's surprised, but he just goes on doing his job, arresting the thief in a very realistic scene. When it comes to the child, the rain of frogs doesn't have the same realistic aspect; there's an aspect of someone who knows, who eludes the pure awareness of the game he's involved in, which portrays the world in a sort of nihilistic way. Those games are a somewhat depressing view

185

of humanity. He underscores that: there's a fairy-tale dimension to the moment.

Annick Fiolet: There's an element of the fantastic about the atmosphere: the light of the scene in the library contrasts with everything else.

Élisabeth Boyer: The film ends like a fairly classic film, with the hope that inheres in the love between the cop and the drug addict, with the difference between the two characters. It's an open-ended ending: the smile of a woman who's recovering from what the world is increasingly haunted by: drugs, a kind of self-destructiveness, loneliness, suffering. The child tells his father "You need to be nicer to me," but the father can't hear him. Yet his loneliness is made more bearable by books, by the fact that something else exists: that figure brightens the film up a little.

Alain Badiou: I agree. You have to take that into account along with the possibility of the opening afforded by love, something like the opening afforded by thought. It's implicit in the film, but it's there. The scene with the kid being coached for the game shows attempts to show that there's a true kind of knowledge and a false kind, true thought and its simulacrum. The kid is presented as someone who's not allowed the field of true thought and true knowledge because he's being coached, in the name of that knowledge and thought, for something else. The kid is shown as having an ability to be really interested in the things he talks about; the coaching is on top of something that's shown at the end of the film as the possibility of books, of reverie, of true thought.

Slim Ben Cheikh: But opening exists in most of the characters. The ones who've been hurt the most are not yet trapped in loneliness; they haven't given up. For instance, the cop and the drug addict are both so eager to escape their loneliness that they practically throw themselves at each other, whereas they have nothing in common.

Alain Badiou: In that regard, the film's hypothesis is nevertheless that humanity is possible, in every one of us.

Slim Ben Cheikh: But with a real sense of urgency. The film says we're on the brink. Later, it will be too late.

Alain Badiou: It's a film that serves as a warning of urgency and that says: "Make no mistake about it, what's at stake is the question of humanity itself; it's really under threat." That's also one of the meanings of the frogs: humanity is on the verge of the plagues of Egypt . . . It's not saying that it's a divine punishment. You can take it however you like. But as frogs are one of the plagues of Egypt, you can regard it as meaning quite simply that humanity is in danger. I regard it as a Paulinian film in a certain way, a film saying: "Careful, the question of love – love one other, and so forth – is a matter of humanity's survival and fate. It's not a matter of morality that's just tacked on. I'm going to show you that the humanity of performative disconnection is a monstrous, endangered humanity, and that everyone is capable of something else." That's stated clearly. The film shows that capacity to different degrees and in different realms of possibility. This isn't a film that discriminates. It takes a range of very different characters precisely in order to show that each one of them, whatever his or her own situation, possesses an opening, a capacity that he or she can take advantage of or not. But things are effectively urgent; it all risks ending badly and, to some extent, it all does end badly. You could say that the sensitive cop, at least, leaps at the chance: he encounters his chance for love and he grabs it. Anderson claims that that's what humanity is, that humanity only exists under such conditions. Everything else is only a matter of ferocity, loneliness, absurd competitive performance, devastation.

Maybe the film is biased with respect to that issue, but it's still something we'll agree with overall. Its critique of the world of loneliness and performance is a very profound one because it's not sociological or ideological. It's not a general critique; it has its level of abstraction, but it does give subjects their chance. There are only subjects, of whom there are a pretty extensive network, but there's only individuality. We see how the world of solitary performance destroys that individuality and, conversely, how something can happen, how there can be an encounter, some grace that allows it to be restored, together with a complicated dialectic concerning the role of confession; confession's not everything. And ultimately – this is very Paulinian again, although not classically Christian – repentance is useless. That's a very forceful, rather harsh idea. In the case of the incestuous father, or of the old man's wife, repentance is not a virtue, as Spinoza would say.

Élisabeth Boyer: The incestuous father is loathsome when he confesses, not because he makes a confession of something loathsome but just because he makes it.

Daniel Fischer: He's pathetic because he plays his last card and it's no good.

Alain Badiou: That's actually a very striking point. It's very Paulinian yet again: what matters is not repentance, what matters is accepting grace and turning it into love. Confession and repentance, which are closely related things, are shown as not being a recourse for humanity. That's a critique of traditional melodrama, internal to *this* melodrama, because traditionally, after confession or repentance, you can make a fresh start.

Élisabeth Boyer: Let's talk about Cruise's way of performing, about the seminars he's giving at the beginning of the film to educate men about their relationship with women. The scene is tremendously unsettling. You can't tell what it's all about. You can take it as a macho scene, but there's something else to it. When he takes out his brochures, you get the impression that there's something other than sex involved, that you can think your relationship with someone, that you can be nice, that you need to have a plan of action and not rush things. It's more than simple machismo.

Alain Badiou: It begins with the fact that the scene is way too macho. It's such a blatant dramatization of machismo; he's performing it and he shows that he's performing it. What's more, Cruise is absolutely terrific. Actors have moments of pure genius and there's an element of true genius here. It's overacted and to the extent that it's overacted it can't literally mean what it means. So what *does* it mean? We find out only gradually, but the figure of masculinity is confused, where this character is concerned, because the stamp the father put on it was twisted, screwed up. Cruise invented a fictitious biography for himself and later it will be reversed and we'll see him crying at his father's bedside. Each of these pieces, and this one in exemplary fashion, is conveyed with such intensity that its meaning is never its explicit nature. Here, you can understand it not as a macho speech but rather as a desperate one on the question of the possibility for love, the possibility for a relationship with women. It's expressed as cynical self-confidence that's actually just the opposite.

Slim Ben Cheikh: At the same time it's about the war between the sexes. It's certainly not a macho speech but a speech that intends to be liberating for men after the misdeeds of feminism. It goes no farther than war, its subject isn't love. Basically, it's despair, to come

188

back to what you said. With Cruise's character, the theme of the father–son relationship is key. There's a certain Hollywood-type Freudianism about it . . .

Alain Badiou: Since his masculinity wasn't developed in the classical Freudian way, shall we say, the result was a total breakdown in his relationship with women, which manifests as a kind of cynical, warlike, combative self-assurance, whereas in reality it's desperate and screwed up. What's so brilliant is how Cruise plays *both* of those things. The excess of affirmative performance reveals the flip side, so that, later on, when the interviewer throws him a curve, we get the impression that he's doing an about-face and that we're going to see that flip side we sensed, in his silence, in his reticence.

Anaïs Le Gaufey: In that scene you can immediately sense that there's a power struggle going on between the two characters. Cruise calls the shots at first, then he seems a bit unnerved by the reporter's accusations, right up to the very beautiful tracking shot over his face. The immobility of that face, its muteness, the insistence of the camera's gaze all creates a "Kuleshov effect." But the shot, which enables us to read Cruise's inscrutable face, is composed of both the reporter's voice-over and the viewer's imagination, which has been activated by the very rapid pace of the introductory scenes. During the tracking shot, you have the impression that you're taking a break from the story while at the same time you're looking at, you're getting the feeling of a distillation of the ambient violence of the scene and of the film in general, and that you're being looked at. Cruise's silence gradually strips the reporter of all credibility, and the interview turns into a revelation of the pettiness and arrogance of a certain voyeuristic brand of journalism.

Annick Fiolet: In connection with that scene again, in terms of the urgency we were talking about, the war theme seems to me to be related to that. You exit the macho speech through that aspect of urgency. Men are now in such desperate straits that something very affirmative is needed: fight back, get a grip on yourself, take your white brochure and your blue brochure and you'll succeed. The idea of love passes through the scene completely unconnected to the question of sex, subtracted from it. The combativeness has more to do with love than sex, ultimately. You mentioned the montage as a whole, but in this scene there's something of the multiple at work, in the montage, between Cruise and his audience, who all seem to be at a loss and offer a vision of that flip side you were talking about. The men are in Cruise and at the same time Cruise is in the men.

Alain Badiou: In the scene with the reporter, there's also a subtle balance owing to the fact that Cruise is shown with all the appearance of an unlikeable guy, even if it's overacted, and *she's* the one who becomes unlikeable. Why? Because the filmmaker's thesis, linked to the idea of confession, is that a confession shouldn't be forced out of someone. It's larger than the question of journalism; it's the question of confession that's important. Confession may have its role, but it's not confession that constitutes love; it's love that constitutes confession. Forcing a confession out of someone is about performance; it has no value. The critique is based on the idea of confession being forced. It has a general value; it's not just a critique of sensationalist journalism, which the film is moreover shot through with. There are an unbelievable number of themes in this film. There's also a whole take on the media in it.

Slim Ben Cheikh: The idea of performance is often associated with the idea of the media. The fact that he chose a black reporter is a little additional complication.

Annick Fiolet: She's the symbol of the "positive" character that can't be attacked.

Alain Badiou: That's the whole aspect of the film that criticizes political correctness: just because you're a woman or you're black doesn't make you right.

Annick Fiolet: There's a certain mixture of tones in the film. *Magnolia* doesn't completely repeat melodrama. There's an alternation with comedy so that in the most melodramatic scenes there are some explosively funny moments. When Cruise goes to his father's bedside there's a comic interlude with the dogs that cuts into the melodrama. The dramatic tone is contradicted by comic moments, even in the scene of the rain of frogs.

Alain Badiou: Yes, it's comic, symbolic, allegorical, and a bit of a gore film all at once. There's a deliberate tonal indecision that's bound up with the multiple.

Slim Ben Cheikh: There are even moments of downright anxiety. When the cop loses his gun and the delinquents are looming there like menacing shadows, it's like a thriller. I wanted to discuss the film's contemporaneity, but you already mentioned it: it's what's said about love in connection with the idea of performance.

Alain Badiou: I do think that's what it is, and it's in effect completely contemporary. It's a thesis about today's world, a partial thesis no doubt but one that has its force. A thesis that says that "true life is absent to the extent that love is withdrawn." Its contemporaneity lies in showing that humanity cannot really exist in the figure of performance, and in showing such a thing cinematically, even within the actors' performances, which is quite remarkable.

It's an anti-individualistic film that says: "The individual today has been abandoned to his figure as an individual given over to performance. His life is a sham and the only means of gauging the extent of that sham is love." That's the film's thesis, but without any moralism. Love is the encounter, a different way of seeing the world. It's not political correctness, the respect for differences, and so on and so forth. The black reporter is no more than a cop. She's all about performance, too, and that relationship doesn't amount to anything that can involve humanity, so it only deserves the rain of frogs.

There's some uncertainty in what Anderson is saying about the question of the father. There, too, in a certain way, the question of the father in classic melodrama is a long-established, fundamental question. The son has to acknowledge the father one way or another, and vice versa, whatever the potentially extremely dramatic vicissitudes of that acknowledgment may be. In keeping with one of contemporary psychoanalysts' current theses, we might ask whether the film isn't saying that this story of fathers and sons is over, that that's not where we need to be looking. If you look at the three fathers, they're all disasters. That's quite a harsh accusation against fathers, and in this respect, too, I'd regard the film as Paulinian: the law of fathers is over, the world's not based on that anymore. We've got to find something else. We'll turn to random encounters, exactly the way Christianity said "It's the world of the son now, not the world of the father any longer." The father–son issue is a fundamental one, but it's nevertheless very specific. If we wanted to complete the film's subject we'd say: "What is it that makes humanity hold together as a world, given that it no longer seems to be respect for the law of the father?" It's not that anymore but rather the chance nature of love. That's what we're reduced to, there's nothing else, with all that entails in terms of riskiness and the absence of law.

Denis Lévy: *Magnolia* would seem to answer to the imperatives of "affirmationism" as you articulated them.[3]

Alain Badiou: Yes, the determining factor of *Magnolia* from that point of view is the relationship between idea and construction. It's the conviction that if you want to bring about, in the world as it is today, something that takes a stand on a possible meaning of generic humanity, even if you're using traditional materials, the path has to be that of *construction*, not deconstruction. I think *Magnolia* is faithful to this idea of mine. The key point is: to reveal the meanings of the world, is the path that of deconstructing established figures, critiquing and exposing them? That's not what *Magnolia*'s all about. This doesn't mean that it doesn't go about it locally by using, misusing, or deviating from traditional materials. We might see a melodramatic scene destabilized by some element or other, but the whole doesn't consist in ironically deconstructing established forms. The whole is really a construction. Whatever the complexity, the performances, the overly intense character of the actors, and so on, might be, it's a construction, a partly baroque one but still a construction. So, regardless, I would classify it as affirmationism.

Cinema is a harsher critic than is generally believed. The deconstructionist figure has had a lot of trouble becoming established in it and in the final analysis has hardly become established in it at all. Deconstructionism has remained avant-gardist to some extent. That doesn't mean that everything that's been positively affirmed has been good: kitsch has had quite a field day! But it's true that cinema hasn't been the privileged witness of what I'm describing as the flip side of kitsch, that is, post-modern deconstructionism. Avant-gardism was able to establish itself securely and even be hegemonic to a great extent in the visual arts, but that hasn't been the case in cinema. Cinema's special genius is more kitschy than avant-gardist.

L'Art du cinéma, Winter 2002–2003

DIALECTICS OF THE FABLE

The Matrix, A Philosophical Machine[1]

Morpheus: "Remember, all I am offering is the truth,
nothing more . . ."

– *I* –

Against empiricism, and with Platonism, one must always verify that
the visible – the apparent figure of what is certain (we must see to
believe, like St. Thomas) – is really nothing but an especially aleatory
index of the real.

It follows that at the cinema we must verify that this artifice –
cinema – can only put philosophy to the test with some degree of
rigor if it demands *a variation in the regime of the sensible*. Basically,
we must verify that the cinema enjoys a certain aptitude for the
concept, once it has the power to render the certainty of the visible
visibly uncertain. Or, to project into images the idea that the image
is nothing but semblance, even the semblance of an image.

– *II* –

By "verification" in this text I refer to certain convergent
annotations.

These annotations concern three films, all of which were released
in France in 1999: *Cube*, a Canadian film by Vincenzo Natali,
eXistenZ by David Cronenberg, and *The Matrix*, by Andy and Larry
Wachowski.

The (philosophical) method is that of the ordinary viewer, not that
of the cinephile. By this I mean:

– that I am basing myself on films that I've seen, like everyone else,
  because they were out in the cinema, without taking any distance
  – and not because I thought they exemplified the *art* of cinema;
– that I am not seeking a singular grasp of their quality;

193

- that I work starting from my recollection of the films, and not on the basis of their analytical re-vision (with a VCR, for instance);
- that I give a certain primacy to the fable, to narration, that is, to an exercise which after all is fundamental to social life: to retell a film.

– III –

In these three films, the fable is explicitly connected to time-honored philosophical questions. In France, we would even say, to essay subjects. For example: reality and semblance. How can one break with the seductive regime of appearance? Is knowledge of the mathematical parameters of the real the precondition for effective action? Calculating rationality and mystical intuition. Freedom and values. And so on.

The difficulty is that such a connection is not the prerogative of cinema. In actual fact, it is characteristic of a genre which does indeed span a whole section of cinematic activity, especially today, but whose origin is purely literary: science fiction and its by-products. Science fiction is obliged to construct a world, and by this very token, to elicit a comparison with the one that we already know. This comparative construction is always related – as was already the case in Plato with the Myth of Er at the end of the *Republic*, or even with the cosmology of the *Timaeus* – to a kind of conceptual epic woven out of images. It is demiurgic (creating the Whole) and normative (judging what is, on the basis of what could be or could have been). Science fiction resembles a metaphorical disquisition, because it elaborates a judgment about what is on the basis of a global fiction in which we experience the momentous question of the relation between the structure of the world and the reality of the choices that one believes oneself to be making within it, or the freedoms that one imagines to be exercising within it.

– IV–

For a fine study of the speculative significance of science fiction, see Guy Lardreau's book *Fictions philosophiques et science-fiction.*[2] Lardreau studies two great novelistic cycles: Asimov's *Foundation* and Herbert's *Dune*. He compellingly demonstrates how the latent thesis that undergirds these cycles – the thesis of the existence of other possible worlds – finds its concept in the most experimental aspect of the philosophy of Gottfried Wilhelm Leibniz, that of distinct universes presented simultaneously in the divine intellect. Above all, he examines how these philosophical and/or novelistic experiments concerning the Whole and its presumed variations help us to discover that our immediate belief in the world that we know (the "natural" world), in the Whole with which we are familiar, must be questioned with regard to its presuppositions.

Lastly, for Lardreau, every imaginary variation of the conditions of the given world puts to the test what amount to frequently dissimulated philosophical *postulates*. Furthermore, it also subjects the supposed *coherence* of the consequences of these postulates to different verifications and falsifications.

In novels, narration is that which makes postulates explicit, but it is also, through the vicissitudes it recounts, that which puts their consequences into play. That is why, when it comes to the philosophemes that are fictionalized in these novels, the key inquiries concern the hypotheses that you are asked to accept (thereby letting you know that, in order to believe in the real world, you *also* accept hypotheses) and the degree of "robustness," the logical solidity, of the outcomes (to make you examine what type of logic sustains your relationship to the spatial and temporal continuity of the ordinary world).

– V –

We can apply this method to the three films we've selected. We can easily distinguish within them the narrative postulates and the logic of their vicissitudes. Narrative postulates are the expression of the *conditions for a fundamental experience of what is and what appears.* In sum, they are axioms relating to the crucial ontological distinction between being, on the one hand, and that which in being gives itself through the fundamental experience in question, on the other. The progression of vicissitudes concerns what a *regulated conduct* could be (one that is effective, just, good, and so on) in a world governed by a determinate narrative postulate governing the relationship between being and appearing.

– VI –

The narrative postulates of our three films are different and institute different worlds.

In *Cube*, the postulate presents itself from the outset as a postulate. In effect, the film begins with a group of characters who awake in an artificial world, made up of a gigantic superimposition – in the guise

195

of a rotating tower – of booby-trapped (or not) cubes, with possible, albeit precarious, passages from one cube to the adjoining one. There is absolutely nothing to connect this world to the "natural" world from whence the characters come, and no explanation is ever given for their "abduction" from the natural world and their transferral into the cubes. It is clear that the characters thus transported are subjected to a kind of experiment, but the experimenter is totally absent from it. Thus, there is something Kafkian about the apologue: the possible rationality of the postulate remains *upstream* from the narration, and the meaning, if there is one, is strictly coextensive with the character's vicissitudes. We can therefore say that the natural world is purely and simply *abolished*, concept-less, in favor of a fictional totality whose rationale and laws are, at the outset, entirely unknown to all.

In *The Matrix*, the postulate is progressively uncovered. Its character is eventual, and it comprises three givens. First of all, in a world that seems to have reached the end of the road, the machines have seized power, in the sense that they utilize the biological energy of humans reduced to a larval state (asleep, drugged, plugged to cables like so many little power stations). What's more, there aren't many images of this real, and scanty anecdotal validation for this part of the postulate. That is because what interests the film's authors above all are the other two components. First, the fact that machines entertain in the brain of the larvae-humans the numerical ("virtual") fiction of a world that is essentially similar in detail to the one that we (the spectators) know, which is also the one that, in the film, has disappeared. Second, that there exists a handful of "living," resisting humans who circulate between the "real" world (that is, the reign of machines pumping energy from enslaved human bodies) and the "virtual" world (the "Matrix"), these bodies' artificial consolation. This time, the natural world has been entirely *destroyed* (to the benefit of a despotic mechanical world stripped of meaning), but it has also, as such, been *turned into semblance*. The postulate principally and painstakingly bears on the structure of appearing, its numerical engineering. We see screens where what is otherwise visible and apparently inhabited – a banal world – testifies that its being is reduced to nothing but green integers. Obviously, it is difficult not to be struck by the resemblance between this postulation and the Platonic fable of the cave. Plato too shows us humans enslaved by fiction. He too envisages that some resistants may circulate between the solar real and the cave of semblance. He too takes every care (at the price, like in the film, of more than a few hitches) when it comes to the artisanal production of appearing.

196

In *eXistenZ*, we could say that the postulate is *realist*. In effect, the projection into another world has a very simple cause: you are asleep, and a game projects you into this fictional world by means of different connections to your nervous system. In sum, we are dealing with a ludic realism that mobilizes the neuronal structure of dreaming. Moreover, the fictionalized universe is not globally other (than the natural universe), as in *Cube*, or globally the same, as in *The Matrix*. It is simply marked by some differences. We could say that the experimentation is local, that the "other world" is a bastard one, as behooves Cronenberg's genius, which always seeks to graft ordinarily heterogeneous elements onto one another (in general, the mechanical and the biological), rather than creating a global universe from scratch. We must nevertheless add – this time following the classical schema of the *mise-en-abyme* – that in the fictional universe wherein the game projects its protagonists there is, precisely, a game. Or rather, the universe of the game is itself perhaps the consequence of the hypothesis of a meta-game. The end of the film is ambiguous in this regard. In fact, we see some assassins, partisans of the pure actual, enemies of every virtual world (fanatical anti-Deleuzeans . . .) massacring the presumed authors (and participants) of the new game (the one in which the vicissitudes of the film take place, including the game within the game), without thereby being able to exclude the possibility that this massacre is a sequence of the meta-game itself. So that in the end we are obliged to say that the natural universe is neither obviously *abolished*, as in *Cube*, nor historically *destroyed*, as in *The Matrix*, but rather *suspended*, since nothing can prove its global difference with regard to the virtual world of the games. Existence (as in the title of the film) is not an obvious fact, but only a predicate hovering between reality, the game, the game within the game and the meta-game.

– VII –

We thus have three variations with distinct postulates: the abolition of the natural world for the sake of an artificial totality; the presumed destruction of this world for the sake of a virtual copy; and finally the suspension of its existence for the sake of a possible hierarchy of fictions.

These three postulates give rise to three philosophical inquiries.

Cube deals with the question: what is a subject, if the totality of the natural world is taken away from it? We could call this a Kantian or transcendental inquiry: what happens if we modify from top to bottom the minimal conditions of experience? What constituent structure remains? We should note that the film's answer is also entirely Kantian. What remains is on the one hand pure mathematics – in this case, as we'll see, the theory of prime numbers – and on the other pure intuition, whose precondition is sainthood (or idiocy).

The Matrix deals with the question: what is a subject who struggles to escape the slavery of semblance, which is in turn the subjectivated form of biological slavery? This program is obviously Platonic: how do we exit the Cave? The response is not yet provided in the first episode, but it seems like it will have to go in the direction of the neo-Platonist commentaries. "The One" is programmed to wage the Manichaean battle of the real against semblance, a semblance which, consistent with neo-Platonist theology, is nothing but the being (which is to say the non-being) of Evil.

eXistenZ deals with the question: what is a subject who, with regard to the environing world, cannot lay hold of a stable clause of objective existence? In sum, what is the subject of transcendental *épochè*, of the suspension of the judgment of existence, for the sake of the pure flux of representational consciousness? This is obviously a Husserlian or phenomenological question. Cronenberg does not provide an assured response, and this hesitation is one of the film's weaknesses. Nonetheless, it seems that the film points towards a subject of the unconscious, a monstrous, violent, sexual projection of an "Ego" revealed by the ludic erasure of objectivity.

– *VIII* –

The form of the films and the genre to which they chiefly belong are determined by the logic of vicissitudes and therefore by the philosophical inquiry, which is itself the consequence of postulates concerning the world (abolition, destruction, suspension).

Cube draws its schema from the catastrophe film. A motley group of ordinary humans, entirely unprepared for anything exceptional, is faced with an ordeal "at the limits" – buildings ablaze, falling planes, subways burning underground, cable cars blocked at great heights by potent winds, and so on. Besides the effects of suspense and terror, the aim is to reveal what each is capable of, on the basis of axioms that change the world. In Natali's film, the catastrophe, internal to the artificial world, is the booby-trapping of the cubes. Under the horrified gaze of the survivors, in order to escape, one or other incautious member of their group passes into the adjoining cube, only to be sliced to bits by a harrow, or burnt alive by a ray. The whole ordeal to which the group is subjected is to move through regardless, if possible by discovering the law according to which one cube is booby-trapped and another not.

The Matrix is more closely related to the "patrol" film, which in the main derives from the western and the war film: a group of rebels (or of accidental heroes) – in every case featuring an ideological leader, a mysterious convert, a seductive woman, a traitor and someone endowed with exceptional fighting abilities – tries to crush an enemy a thousand times more powerful than itself. In the film, in order to organize its combat, the patrol uses a spaceship that circulates in the "real" (the world dominated by machines) but from which one can also enter the "virtual" (our world as transformed into semblance). None of the ingredients are missing: neither the charismatic leader nor the mysterious convert ("The One"), neither the seductive woman nor the traitor, nor of course the exceptional fights, whose style is borrowed from Asian choreography (an amalgam of Kung-Fu and John Woo).

Finally, *eXistenZ*, whose form is looser, nevertheless resembles a chase film: a couple (the mandatory subject for this genre of film) traverses the oddities and perils of the world of semblance, of its *mise-en-abyme*, and of the semi-monsters inhabiting it.

– IX –

We could say that the Kantian fable involves the exploration of the capacities and limits of ordinary consciousness; the Platonic fable involves the heroism of conversion, which violently turns you away from semblance; and the Husserlian fable involves the idealist uncertainty of the object, its submission to interpretations (or, at best, to the assent of this essential Other which is the partner).

– X –

Nevertheless we must recognize that the three films have a problem in common, which is simply the fundamental problem of cognition: what is it that, from within our own capacity to know, testifies that it is indeed the real that is at stake in our cognition?

In *eXistenZ* and *The Matrix*, it is a matter of finding a discriminating procedure, from within a regime of appearing (the game, or the Matrix), between what is real and what is only a semblance of the real.

In my view, this question is watered down in Cronenberg's film by the paradigm of the game. To pose the ludic virtual as an undecidable rival of the real amounts in effect to an inexact banality. As "realist" as it may be in its representations, every game is played from within an irreducible consciousness-of-gaming.

By way of contrast, in *The Matrix* the question is posed in a radical fashion. In effect, what is at stake is not how to move in the midst of indecision, but *how to endure the ordeal of the real faced with semblance*. The One is in effect he who knows how to identify semblance from within semblance – the one who, *in the Cave*, succeeds in knowing that the shadows are nothing but shadows.

In *Cube*, in conformity with a Kantian type of postulation, the problem is that of the limits of cognition, of the impossibility, for human understanding, of determining the being of what appears. To escape the cubes' traps, one must discover the law of the (artificial) world, to find at the surface of things that which distinguishes them (that which makes one cube lethal and another harmless). Mere prudent and pragmatic know-how is not enough. A wily man first throws his shoes into the adjoining cube to see what happens. He manages to avoid the bad cubes for quite some time. But in the end, it turns out that the trap is only triggered if it detects a gaze. The shoes will be spared but the man's eyes and face will be ravaged by a ray. Nor does pure discipline suffice: authoritarian and organized leaders will reveal themselves to be either inept or treacherous (agents of the Tower of cubes). The key to the problem, as with the post-Galilean physical universe, is mathematics. In every cube there is a brass plaque marked by a number, and, in order to tell the cubes apart, it is a question of knowing the decomposition of this number into prime factors. The knowledge of a young mathematician will protect the group for a while. But in the end rational knowledge too is not enough, because calculating the decomposition of very large numbers takes too long. The film maintains that the highest form of mathematics is a kind of mysticism: a Dostoyevskyan idiot of sorts immediately knows, without calculating, the being of each number, and leads the survivors of the group into a pure light (which does not stop them from noticing that their journey was in vain: they are back at the starting point, which all alone has turned towards the opening. Are we to understand by this, now following Bergson, that mysticism is nothing but a coincidence with real movement?).

– *XI* –

As far as I'm concerned, the greatest filmic force is to be found in *The Matrix*. Doubtless this is because it avoids – for the time

being . . . – both the somewhat limp undecidabilities (the phenomenology of *eXistenZ*) and the mystical *coup de force* of *Cube* (which
is nonetheless endowed with an astonishing terrorizing power,
obtained by sober, abstract means). I obviously like the fact that the
most robust of these cinematic inquiries is the Platonist one.

– XII –

But why is it so robust? Because the question of challenging the image
on the basis of the image itself, in the direction of its foundational
beyond, is the very question of cinema. *The Matrix* contains an
admirable sequence: a child, taught by a kind of inspired prophetess
(the Diotima of the *Symposium*?), stares long and hard at a spoon
until it bends, thereby showing that it is not a solid object belonging
to the real world but an artificial composition, an inconsistent virtual
effect. Thus, from within the world, by means of a critical dialectic
that prepares an ascending dialectic, you can say, in a Platonic style:
this spoon is not the real spoon. The real spoon is not visible, it is
only thinkable. The principle of the art of cinema lies precisely in
subtly showing that it is only cinema, that its images only testify to
the real to the extent that they are *manifestly* images. It is not by
turning away from appearance, or by lauding the virtual, that you
will have the chance of attaining the idea. Rather, it is by thinking
appearance as appearance, and thus as that aspect of being which,
by coming to appear, gives itself to thought as a disappointment of
seeing. *The Matrix* at its best sets out this giving and this disappointment. It therefore sets out the principle of every idea.

– XIII –

"The cinema, as a preparation of Plato," as Pascal would have said.
If only he'd known.

Text published in *Matrix, Machine philosophique*
(Paris: Éditions Ellipses, 2003)

—27—

CINEMA AS PHILOSOPHICAL EXPERIMENTATION

Cinema has a unique relationship with philosophy: we could say that it is a philosophical experiment. This raises two questions. First, "How does philosophy regard cinema?" Second, "How does cinema transform philosophy?" The relationship between them is not a relationship of knowledge. Philosophy does not enable us to know cinema. It is a living, concrete relationship, a relationship of transformation. Cinema transforms philosophy. In other words, cinema transforms the very notion of idea. Cinema basically consists in creating new ideas about what an idea is. To put it another way, cinema is a philosophical situation. Expressed abstractly, a philosophical situation is the relationship between terms that usually have no relationship with each other. A philosophical situation is an encounter between terms that are foreign to each other.

Cinema is a philosophical situation

I'd like to give three examples. The first is from one of Plato's dialogues, the *Gorgias*. Callicles suddenly intervenes forcefully in this dialogue. The relationship between Socrates and Callicles is a philosophical situation, like a philosophical theater of sorts. Why? Because Socrates' thought and Callicles' thought have no common measure. They are foreign to each other. And the discussion between Callicles and Socrates consists solely in showing that we have two kinds of thought here with no common measure, a relationship between two terms that are foreign to each other. Callicles argues that might is right, that the happy man is a tyrant, the man who prevails over everyone else. Socrates argues that the true man is the just man. Between justice as violence and justice as thought, there is no real

202

relationship. The discussion isn't a discussion; it is a confrontation. Everyone who reads the dialogue understands that there will be a winner and a loser, not that one of them will have convinced the other. In the end, Callicles is defeated, but he is only defeated in the dialogue staged by Plato. Incidentally, this is probably the only time that Callicles and what he stands for is defeated. Such are the joys of theater.

So that is a philosophical situation. What is philosophy in a situation like this? Philosophy shows us that we have to choose, to choose between two types of thought. All of us have a decision to make. We have to decide whether to be on Socrates' side or on Callicles' side. Here, philosophy is thinking as choice, thinking as decision. Philosophy is a matter of making this choice clear, of clarifying it. So we can say that a philosophical situation is the moment when a choice is clarified: a choice of existence or a choice of thinking. That is the first definition of a philosophical situation.

Now for my second example: the death of the great mathematician Archimedes. This Greek from Sicily had taken part in the resistance against the Roman invaders and occupiers. But Rome was ultimately victorious. Archimedes is one of the greatest minds ever known to humanity. To this day his mathematical texts are amazing. He had already reflected on infinity; he practically invented infinitesimal calculus, many centuries before Newton. He was an extraordinary genius. When the Roman occupation began, he resumed his activities. He was in the habit of drawing geometrical figures in the sand. One day, as he was drawing these complicated figures, a Roman soldier came and told him that the Roman general wanted to see him. The Romans were very curious about the Greek thinkers, a little like the way people are curious about an intelligent animal. So General Marcellus wanted to see Archimedes. I don't think Marcellus was very good at mathematics, but he wanted to meet this thinker of international repute. Archimedes didn't budge, so the soldier repeated: "General Marcellus wants to see you." Archimedes still didn't answer. The Roman soldier, who was probably not very interested in mathematics either, told him for a third time: "Archimedes! The general wants to see you." The Greek looked up slightly and replied: "Let me finish my demonstration." So the soldier repeated again: "But Marcellus wants to see you! What's all this nonsense about your demonstration?" Archimedes resumed his calculations without replying. After a certain time, the soldier, who was by then absolutely furious, killed him. Archimedes fell down dead, right on his geometrical figure.

Why is this a philosophical situation? Because it shows that between the right of the state and creative thought there is no common measure, no real discussion. In the end, power is violence. And creative thought knows nothing but its own rules. Archimedes is caught up in his own thought. And he is outside of the action of power. That is why violence will ultimately be used. There is no common measure between power, on the one hand, and truths, on the other, truths as creation. So we will say that between power and truths there is a distance – the distance between Marcellus and Archimedes. Philosophy must clarify this distance. It must reflect on and think this distance.

My third example is a film, an extraordinary film, *The Crucified Lovers*, by the Japanese director Kenji Mizoguchi. It is possibly one of the most beautiful films about love ever made. The story is simple. A young woman has been married off for financial reasons to the owner of a small workshop, a decent man but one whom she neither loves nor desires. Enter a young man with whom she falls in love. You can see how banal the story is. The story takes place in the Japan of the Middle Ages. Adultery is punishable by death. The adulterous lovers must be crucified. They end up fleeing to the countryside. They take refuge in a sort of poetic nature. Meanwhile, the good husband tries to protect them because he doesn't want there to be any violence and because he himself is guilty in the eyes of the law if he doesn't report them to the police. He tries to buy time, explaining that his wife has gone off to the provinces. He's really such a good husband. But the lovers are nevertheless captured and taken to be tortured. Then there are the final images of the film. The lovers are riding on a mule, tied back to back. The shot frames this image of the two lovers heading to an atrocious death, with the hint of a smile on their faces. It is truly an extraordinary smile. This isn't the romantic idea of the fusion of love and death. They never wanted to die. Quite simply, love is also what resists death, as Deleuze and Malraux said about the work of art. No doubt this is what true love and the work of art have in common.

The lovers' smile is a philosophical situation, for it shows us that between the event of love and the ordinary rules of life – the laws of the city, the laws of marriage – there is no common measure. What will philosophy say to us now? It will say: "We must think the event." We must think the exception. We must know what we have to say about what is out of the ordinary. We must think change in life.

We can sum up the tasks of philosophy as regards situations. First, to clarify the fundamental choices of thought. And it is always a choice between what is interested and what is disinterested. Second, to clarify the distance between thought and power, the distance between the state and truths. To measure that distance. To know whether or not it can be crossed. Third, to clarify the value of the exception, the value of the event, the value of the rupture. And to do so in opposition to the invariability of life, in opposition to social conservatism. These are the three great tasks of philosophy, as soon as philosophy is something that matters in life, something that is more than just an academic discipline. Philosophy is the link between the three – between the choice, the distance, and the exception. This is a philosophical concept, in Deleuze's sense of the term: something philosophy creates. On closer inspection, we can see that it is always a link, something knotting and unknotting a problem of decision, a problem of distance, or gap, or a problem of exception. The most profound philosophical concepts always tell us something like this: "If you want your life to have meaning, you must accept the event, you must remain at a distance from power, and you must stick resolutely to your decision." In this sense, philosophy is that which helps you change your life. Rimbaud said: "The true life is absent." At heart, philosophy makes the true life become present, because the true life is present in the choice, in the distance, and in the event.

In these three examples there is a relationship between heterogeneous terms: Callicles and Socrates, the Roman soldier and Archimedes, the lovers and society. We are told about a relationship, but in fact that relationship is not a relationship; it is the negation of relationship. And so, ultimately, what we are told about is a rupture. To relate a rupture, a relationship has to be related. You'll have to choose between Callicles and Socrates. So you'll have to produce a rupture: if you're on Socrates' side you won't be on Callicles' side. If you're on Archimedes' side you won't be on Marcellus' side. And if you're with the lovers right to the end you won't be on the side of societal rules. So we can say that philosophy is concerned with relationships that aren't relationships. Deleuze called this sort of thing "disjunctive syntheses." There is philosophy every time you want to think a relationship of this type. When all is said and done, philosophy is the theory of ruptures.

This is what Plato already said when he explained that philosophy is an awakening. But the awakening is a rupture with sleep. In this sense, philosophy is the moment of the rupture reflected in thought. Every time there is a paradoxical relationship there can be philosophy. I must stress this point: it is not because there is something to think that there is philosophy. I agree with Deleuze: philosophy is not a reflection on anything whatsoever. There is philosophy, there can only be philosophy, when there are paradoxical relationships, ruptures, decisions, distances, and events.

Philosophy is the thinking of ruptures or of relationships that are not relationships. But this can be put another way: philosophy is what creates a synthesis, what invents a synthesis where the latter is not given. Philosophy creates a new synthesis in the very place where there is a rupture. It does not just involve observing differences but inventing new syntheses, which are constructed where there is difference. If I take the example of Mizoguchi's *Crucified Lovers* again, a synthesis also occurs with that image of the lovers being taken to be tortured. Naturally, the lovers are in conflict with social law, but in the unity of their smile another possible society is being heralded. It is not just a matter of the disjunction with social law; it is the idea that social law can change. There is the possibility of a social law that would integrate, rather than exclude, love. These lovers are universal because that synthesis, the synthesis between their status as exceptions and the ordinary law, exists. We understand that every exception, every event, is also a promise for everyone. And if it weren't a promise for everyone, that artistic effect of the exception wouldn't exist.

So we can say that whenever philosophy thinks the rupture, whenever it thinks the choice, whenever it thinks the distance, whenever it thinks the exception or the event, it invents a new synthesis that of course forces you to choose. Nevertheless, there is something in your choice that preserves the other possibility. Of course, you are for distance. Truth is completely different from power. But there is a power of truth. And of course you are for the exceptional event, but there also exists a universal promise. This is what I call the new syntheses of philosophy. "What is universal about a rupture?" is essentially the great question of philosophy. The question of rupture is fundamental, but what philosophy tries to discover is the universal value of rupture. That universal value always requires a new synthesis, which explains why the moment of synthesis was so important for Plato. Why is it necessary to prove that the just man is happy? Why isn't it enough to say that there is the just man, on the one hand, and the sophist, or the criminal, on the other? Because, in reality, when Plato says "The just man is the happy man," he means "Justice is possible for everyone." You can be for justice. That point seems very important to me as regards the relationship between cinema and philosophy. If philosophy is really the invention of new syntheses, of syntheses within rupture, then cinema is very important because it alters the possibilities of synthesis.

So the definition of cinema is paradoxical, and that is why cinema is a situation for philosophy. Cinema is a unique relationship between total artifice and total reality. Cinema is really both the possibility of a copy of reality and the completely artificial dimension of that copy. This amounts to saying that cinema is a paradox that revolves around the question of the relationship between "being" and "appearing." It is an ontological art. Many critics have long said as much. André Bazin, in particular, demonstrated early on that the question of cinema, the problem of cinema, was really the problem of "being": the problem of what is being shown when you show something. That is the first reason why there is a question, or a problem, of cinema.

What is a mass art?

I'd like to enter into this question in a very simple way and begin with a fact, namely that cinema is a "mass art." An art is a "mass art" if its masterpieces – great, indisputable works of art – are seen and loved by millions of people, at the very time they were created. Adding "at the very time they were created" is important because we know that there can be an effect of pastness. Millions of people can go to museums because people love treasures and because tourism is also the tourism of treasures. But that is not what I'm talking about. I'm talking about the love for a work of art at the very time it was created, about when millions of people love a masterpiece at the time it first appears. We have indisputable examples of this in the cinema: Charlie Chaplin's great films, for instance. This is a well-known but interesting example. Chaplin's films were seen all over the world, even by the Eskimos. And everyone instantly understood that these films were speaking about humanity, were speaking in a profound and crucial way about humanity, about what I would call "generic humanity" – in other words, about humanity beyond its differences. Charlie's character, although perfectly situated in a particular context, is representative of generic humanity for an African, a Japanese or an Eskimo. This is a striking example, but there are others as well, which are not limited to comic, slapstick, or romantic films. For example, Murnau's *Sunrise*, an extraordinarily condensed, innovative film, which remains to this day one of the greatest poems ever created in the cinema, was in its own time a hit comparable to *Titanic*. We know that all sorts of very great films, films by Lang, Hitchcock, Ford,

Hawks, Walsh, and many others, were loved this way by millions of people.

It is quite simply beyond dispute that cinema is capable of being a mass art, unmatched by any other art. In the nineteenth century there were writers of the masses, poets of the masses – in France, for example, there was Victor Hugo, who is even today a writer of the masses, incidentally – but never on the scale of cinema. Cinema is unsurpassable as a mass art. But "mass art" implies a paradoxical relationship. It is not at all an obvious relationship, because "mass" is a political category, a category of political activism, whereas "art" is an aristocratic category. This isn't a judgment, merely a statement of the fact that "art" encompasses the idea of creation and requires our having the means for understanding that creation, requires some proximity to the history of the art in question and therefore a particular kind of education. All this accounts for why "art" remains an aristocratic category, while "mass art" is typically a democratic category. In "mass art" you have the paradoxical relationship between a purely democratic element and a historically aristocratic element.

All the arts were once avant-garde arts. Painting was an avant-garde art up until the time when it entered museums. You can also regard works by Picasso as a treasure. Music was an avant-garde art and still is. Poetry was an avant-garde art. The twentieth century can be said to be the century of avant-gardes. But it can also be said to be the century of a mass art. In that era of avant-gardes the first great mass art appeared and developed. So there is a paradoxical relationship in cinema, a relationship between heterogeneous terms. Art and the masses. Aristocracy and democracy. Invention and familiarity. Novelty and general taste. That is why philosophy is concerned with cinema. And so, here too, we need to search. To search for the choice, to search for the distance, and to search for the event.

The five ways of thinking cinema

How might it be possible for philosophy to think cinema? How can the question of cinema be entered into? How can the question of this paradoxical relationship be entered into? In other words, how can cinema be thought in terms of its capacity for being a mass art? Because cinema is not always a mass art: there are avant-garde films, there is an aristocratic cinema, there is a difficult cinema which presupposes knowledge of the history of cinema. But there is always the possibility of a mass art in cinema. And philosophy must enter into that question. That is, it must enter into the question of a relationship that is not a relationship. In the history of humanity, what has cinema represented in terms of rupture? What did humanity break with by inventing cinema? Is humanity with cinema different from humanity without cinema? And what is the intimate relationship between the emergence of cinema and potentially new forms of thought?

I believe there have been five major attempts to think cinema. Or rather, five different ways of entering into the problem. Cinema can be studied, this paradoxical relationship can be thought, in terms of the question of the image. That was the traditional starting point: cinema as an ontological art. It can be thought in terms of the question of time. It can be thought in terms of the question of the historical succession of the arts, the series of the arts, by comparing cinema with the other arts. It can be thought by studying the relationship between art and what is not art. And, lastly, it can be thought from the perspective of the question of ethics or morality, of cinema's relationship with the great figures of human existence. I'd like to say a word about each of these attempts.

First, the question of the image. To explain why cinema is a mass art – let's not forget our question – we will say it is an art of the image: it has the ability to captivate everyone. In this case, we are regarding cinema as the fabrication of a semblance of the real, a sort of double of the real. We are trying to understand cinema's ability to captivate people in terms of the ability of images to captivate. To put it another way, cinema is the high point of an art of identification. No other art allows for such a force of identification. That is the first possible explanation.

The question of time was fundamental for Deleuze, but it was so for many other critics of cinema as well. We could basically say that cinema is a mass art because it changes time into perception. It makes time visible. Cinema is basically like time that can be seen: it creates a feeling of time that is something other than the lived experience of time. Naturally, we all have an immediate lived experience of time, but cinema changes that lived experience into representation. It shows time. You will notice that, in this interpretation, cinema approaches music, because music is also an experience of time, a way of showing time. We could simply say that music makes time audible while cinema makes it visible. Cinema makes it audible, too, because music is incorporated into cinema. But the essence of cinema is to make time visible. Image and time would be two philosophical ways of entering into the question of cinema as a mass art. But they're not the only ones.

The third possibility involves comparing cinema with the other arts. We could say that cinema retains from the other arts precisely everything that is popular in them, and that cinema, the seventh art, takes from the other six what is most universal, what seems addressed to generic humanity. What does cinema retain from painting? The possibility of the beauty of the world of the senses. It does not retain the intellectual technique of painting or the complicated modes of representation but rather a sensory, well-regulated relationship with the outside world. In that sense, cinema is a painting without painting, a world painted without paint. What does cinema retain from music? Not the difficulties of musical composition exactly, nor ultimately the great principles of musical development or of the theme, but the possibility of accompanying the world through sound: a certain dialectics of the visible and the audible, hence the charm of sound when it is placed in existence. We all know that there is a musical emotion in cinema that is connected with subjective situations, a sort of accompaniment of the drama, like a music without music, a music without musical technique, a music borrowed from, then given back, to existence. What does cinema retain from the novel? Not the complexities of psychology but the form of the narrative: telling great stories, telling stories to humanity as a whole. What does cinema retain from the theater? The figure of the actor and the actress, the charm, the aura that has transformed them into stars. We can say that cinema is that which changes the actor into a star. So, when all is said and done, cinema does indeed take something from all the arts, but it is usually what is most accessible in them. I would even say that cinema *opens up* all the arts, strips them of their aristocratic value and delivers them over to the image of life. As painting without painting, music without music, the novel without psychology, the theater with the charm of the actors, cinema is like the popularization of all the arts. That is why it has a universal calling. This, then, is a third hypothesis, which would make the seventh art the democratization of the other six.

The fourth hypothesis involves examining the relationship between art and non-art in cinema. Cinema is always located on the edge of non-art; it is an art affected by non-art, an art that is always full of trite forms, an art that is always *below* or *beside* art with respect to certain of its features. In every era cinema explores the border between art and what is not art. *That is where it is located.* It incorporates the new forms of existence, whether they are art or not, and it makes a certain selection, albeit one that is never complete. And so, in any

210

film at all, even a pure masterpiece, you will find banal images, trite materials, stereotypes, images that have already been seen elsewhere, clichés. That may not necessarily prevent the film from being an artistic masterpiece, but it does facilitate its being understood by everyone. Every film viewer can enter into the art of cinema from what is not art, whereas for the other arts, the opposite is the case: you always have to start from the greatness of art in order to understand them. In cinema, on the contrary, it all begins with the most ordinary feelings, in order to arrive at refined and powerful things, whereas in the aristocratic arts, you are always afraid of falling. Cinema is the great repose of art: you can go to the movies on Saturday night to relax. Bad painting is bad painting: there is very little hope of its turning into good painting. It is a fallen aristocracy, whereas at the cinema, you are always a democrat hoping to attain an absolute. That is cinema's paradoxical relationship with aristocracy and democracy, which is ultimately a relationship between art and non-art that is internal to cinema. This also accounts for the political significance of cinema: a cross between ordinary opinions and the work of thought, a relationship that you won't find in the same guise anywhere else. Cinema is always on the verge of being on the other side.

There is one last hypothesis for thinking cinema: its ethical significance. Cinema is an art of figures. Not just figures of space, not just figures of the outside world, but great figures of humanity in action. It is like a sort of universal stage of action. Powerful, embodied forms, great values are debated at any given moment. Cinema conveys a unique sort of heroism. And, as is well known, it is the last bastion of heroes today. Our world is so unheroic, and yet cinema continues to feature heroic figures. It is impossible to imagine cinema without its great moral figures, without the battle between Good and Evil. There is obviously an American aspect to this, the political perspective of the ideology of the Western, which is sometimes disastrous. But there is also an amazing side to this capacity for heroism, amazing in the way that Greek tragedy could be: presenting typical characters of the great conflicts of human life to an enormous audience. Cinema deals with courage, with justice, with passion, with betrayal. The major genres of cinema, the most coded ones, such as the melodrama and the western, are in fact ethical genres, genres that are addressed to humanity so as to offer it a moral mythology. In this respect, cinema is heir to certain functions of the theater, of the theater at the time when it was a theater for citizens.

From the question of time to the question of metaphysics: a round trip via love

I'd like to give a few examples to illustrate these five different ways of thinking cinema philosophically. Let's consider the question of time, which has always been a great question about synthesis. There are some very well-known arguments of Kant's concerning this issue. But let's keep things very simple: time is the synthesis of experience. Our experience is synthesized in time. Now, in cinema there are operations on time, in particular some very different ways of showing time. For example, there is time as construction, time as an active synthesis of different blocks, a time that can be said to be "made of imbrications." This is obviously linked to the fact that cinema is an art of montage. So it can make the montage of time visible. There are countless examples of this, one of the most classic being Eisenstein's *The Battleship Potemkin*, in which the temporal construction of the event (the uprising, the repression, and so on) is entirely organized by montage. It is a construction of time because it rearranges things that are happening simultaneously. What we have in this case is a unique kind of time, constructed and imbricated time. But there are also temporal constructions in the cinema that are totally different from that one, the opposite of it, even: for example, a time that is obtained by being stretched out, as if, space being immobile, it were space itself that were stretched out in time. This is the case in long sequences where the camera is either still or rotating in space as if it were unwinding the spool of time.

One example that has always struck me occurs in Alfred Hitchcock's *Rebecca*. *Rebecca* is built on a mystery, which will eventually be resolved by a confession. The hero, played by Laurence Olivier, confesses to a crime, owing to Hitchcock's extraordinary fondness for confession. Hitchcock loves it when someone relates a crime, because he only likes guilty characters and he especially likes telling us that we're all guilty. The most cunning element in Hitchcock's films is that the innocent character is guiltier than the guilty character, which is the case in *Rebecca* since the crime turns out to have been justified. So the guilty character is innocent. But the scene that concerns us is the confession itself. It is a long sequence, a long story, and the camera revolves around the story. The time of the story is a sort of long virtuoso scene stretching out, without any montage, without any divisions, very similar to the pure flow of duration. Here we encounter a different conception, a different thinking of time. It would seem that cinema basically proposes two conceptions of time:

time as construction and montage, and time as an immobile stretching out. There is something of Bergson's distinctions here, since Bergson essentially contrasted an external, constructed time, which is ultimately the time of action and science, with a pure, qualitative, indivisible duration, which is the true time of consciousness: *The Battleship Potemkin*, on the one hand, and the confession in *Rebecca*, on the other.

Just as an aside with regard to the confession in *Rebecca*: what is utterly fascinating is that there is a parallel scene in another Hitchcock film, *Under Capricorn*, where there is a long confession scene with a very similar temporality. The only difference is that it is a woman speaking, not a man. If you watch both scenes very carefully, you could even go so far as to say that Hitchcock filmed the difference between male and female duration.

But cinema's greatness doesn't lie in reproducing Bergson's division between constructed time and pure duration; it lies in showing us that a synthesis between the two is possible. What cinema offers is precisely the ability to combine these two types of time. In the greatest films – I'm thinking of Murnau's *Sunrise*, for example – you can absolutely show how moments of pure duration are inscribed within the "assembled" construction of time. There is an absolutely extraordinary scene in *Sunrise*, a trolley car coming down a hill. This pure movement filmed from inside the trolley car is an utterly intense feeling of duration, at once fluid and poetic. But the film is otherwise very much constructed, very much assembled in terms of montage. In the final analysis, what cinema offers, and I think it is the only art that does so, is the possibility of the presence of pure duration within temporal construction, which can really be termed a new synthesis.

Metaphysics has often been defined in terms of the use of opposite categories, basically in terms of a dualism, of major oppositions: finite and infinite, substance and accident, soul and body, sensible and intelligible, and so on. Bergson's opposing of the pure duration of consciousness and the external time of action and science is one of these great oppositions, which makes Bergson a metaphysician. So we could perhaps say that there is something anti-metaphysical about cinema, or, more precisely, that cinema is the art of the end of metaphysics. It is basically an art that might have suited Heidegger. I think he regarded cinema as an art of technique, hence as a metaphysical art, ultimately. But, at heart, cinema's new syntheses are not metaphysical syntheses. On the contrary, they run counter to metaphysical dualism. Let me give a very quick example. What is the difference, in cinema, between the sensible and the intelligible? There isn't any,

213

in actual fact. The intelligible, in cinema, is only a heightening of the sensible, a color or a light of the sensible. This is also why cinema can be an art of the sacred, as it is an art of the miracle. I'm thinking of Rossellini's or Bresson's films. Do Rossellini and Bresson separate the sacred or the intelligible from the sensible? No, they don't, because cinema makes it possible for the sacred or the intelligible to appear as the purely sensible.

Look at Rossellini's film *Journey to Italy*. It is another film about love. (I wonder what cinema would do without love, and what we ourselves would do without love.) It is the story of a couple that is falling apart; we're all familiar with that situation. They take a trip to Italy in the vague hope that things will improve, but of course they don't. The man is tempted by other women. As for the woman, she seeks isolation, solitude, in the city of Naples or in nearby nature, around Mount Vesuvius. But the film ends with their love really being revived, which is actually a sort of miracle. What Rossellini is trying to tell us is that love is stronger than will, that when you make an effort to save your relationship you are merely involved in something abstract, and that in reality something about the couple must save itself on its own, as if love were a new subject, not the object of a negotiation. Basically, what Rossellini is trying to tell us comes down to a radical proposition: love is not a contract; it is an event. If it can be saved, it will be saved by an event. In the last scene, Rossellini films the miracle. You can film a miracle in cinema, and it may even be the case that cinema is the only art that has the potential to be miraculous. Painting a miracle is difficult, telling the story of a miracle isn't easy, but filming a miracle is possible. Why? Because you can film the miracle from within the sensible, simply by making some minor adjustments in the value of the sensible and in particular by using light. Cinema can make the inner light of the visible appear. And at that moment, the visible itself becomes an event. This is one of the great syntheses that are possible in cinema, which is basically a synthesis of the sensible and the intelligible.

I think there is an intimate relationship between cinema and love, first of all because love, like cinema, is the eruption of the miraculous in life. The whole problem is whether or not that miracle can last. As soon as you say "It can't last," you fall into a cynical and relativistic conception of love. But if you want to have a positive conception of love you have to maintain that the miracle can last forever. The amorous encounter is the symbol of discontinuity in life; marriage, on the contrary, is the symbol of continuity. This raises the philosophical and cinematic question: "Can a synthesis be created within rupture?" Love, along with revolution and cinema no doubt, has always been a typical example of this problem. Furthermore, cinema is similar to love because it is not an art of speech. Please don't misunderstand me: people speak in the cinema, speech is important. But let's never forget that cinema could be silent, it can be quiet. So speech is very important, but it is not essential. Cinema is also an art of silence, an art of the sensible and an art of silence. Love, too, is silent. Let me suggest a definition of love to you: "Love is the silence that follows a declaration." You say "I love you," and then all you have to do is keep quiet, because, in any case, the declaration has created the situation. This relationship to silence, this presentation of bodies is tailor-made for cinema. Cinema is also an art of the sexual body. It is an art of nudity. That creates an intimate relationship between cinema and love.

And so I think that cinema is a movement from love to politics, whereas theater is a movement from politics to love. The two trajectories are opposite ones, even if the problem is ultimately the same: What is a subjective intensity within a collective situation? To illustrate this, let's take some examples involving World War II and the question of the relationship between the situation of love and that of war. There are two very different, paradigmatic films on this topic: a classic film, a melodrama, *A Time to Love and A Time to Die*, by Douglas Sirk and a modern film, *Hiroshima, mon amour*, by Alain Resnais and Marguerite Duras. In *A Time to Love and A Time to Die* there are some extremely powerful scenes dealing with the war on the Russian front and the ruins of Berlin. In *Hiroshima, mon amour*, the atomic bomb that was dropped on that Japanese city is the issue and so is the German occupation of France. The historical and political situation is very important. But you enter into these figures through the words of love, through the encounter of bodies, through the intensity of intimacy. And that, I think, is cinema's real movement. Theater's movement is different, because the theater must ground the general situation in language and construct individuals on that basis.

You can also see that when you go from love to politics, when you go from love to History, the technique of the image is twofold. On the one hand, you have the image of intimacy, which is necessarily a compact image, a tightly framed image, and, on the other hand, the image of History with a capital H, which is an epic image, an open image. Cinema's movement involves opening up the image, showing how, within this intimate image, there is the possibility of the larger image. This trajectory of opening up is typical of cinema: its genius

215

lies in such opening up. It could be shown that the problem of theater is associated with condensation while the problem of cinema has to do with opening language up.

Cinema and the invention of new syntheses

Finally, let's take the question of the multiplicity of the arts: cinema proposes new syntheses. Even before people began to talk about multimedia, the cinema was itself a kind of multimedia. For example, there has always been a problem with regard to the relationship between visual and musical values. It is a problem that runs through the whole history of art. How can there be a synthesis of visual and musical values? That is the whole problem of opera as a genre. Cinema does in fact propose such a synthesis, however: it is the great resource of slapstick films, for example. Go see or see again the Marx Brothers in *A Night at the Opera* . . . Or Visconti's *Death in Venice*, especially the beginning of the film when the character arrives in Venice. We don't know a whole lot about him. We see him arrive with his luggage, get in the boat, and move through the canals of Venice. Naturally, we experience intense visual values, associated with the esthetic relations existing between Visconti and Venice. But these are not just beautiful images of Venice; it is already a sort of mortal poem, a magnificent, melancholy journey. And Visconti incorporates into the sequence what will become the musical leitmotif of the film, the *Adagio* from Mahler's *Fifth Symphony*. Now, what is extraordinary is that at no time is it ever just decorative. Between the character sitting motionless in the boat, whose face we see, and the impression we feel (Venice, the canals, the buildings, and Mahler's *Fifth Symphony*) there is a synthetic fusion that produces a unique effect belonging to no other art. It is not an isolated musical impression, it is not just a pictorial impression, it is not a psychological or literary impression; it is really a cinema idea, and that idea is a synthesis. This is why I say that "cinema invents new syntheses." It invents them, as usual, where there is a rupture, where there is in fact a disjunction between pictorial and musical art. This sequence in *Death in Venice* in no way involves eliminating the difference between music and painting – that would be meaningless. On the contrary, we see the difference, but we also see a synthesis within this difference, and this is really something created purely by cinema.

When we consider the question of the relationship between art and non-art, we also encounter new cinematic syntheses, in particular via

216

cinema's use of the great popular genres and its transformation of these unique forms into artistic materials. Let's talk about the circus, for example, which gives rise to a real cinematic transfiguration that deserves to be examined closely. Whether in Chaplin's *The Circus* or in Browning's *The Unknown*, Fellini's *The Clowns* or Tati's *Parade*, or actually in many other films as well, the circus is treated as a popular genre, but it is simultaneously integrated into a new artistic synthesis. These films aren't mere documentaries about the circus; they aren't just a copy. They feature a synthetic integration of circus techniques into a different, more cinematic context. The same goes for cabaret or variety shows, which were legion at the dawn of the seventh art. Thus, the Marx Brothers were at first associated with a variety or cabaret-type show. But if the Marx Brothers had only put on a cabaret show, we would probably not remember them now at all. There is a unique operation in cinema that consists in providing cabaret with a universal stage, integrating it into a new synthesis. It is the same for the detective novel, the crime thriller, or even the sentimental novel, which were all materials that enabled the cinema to produce masterpieces. Cinema can show the open nature of the question of the popular. The clearest example of this is Orson Welles' *The Lady from Shanghai*. This film shows the woman's darkness, her negative image, but it also shows her reflection. Basically, cinema is capable of showing metaphysics and of showing (by taking it apart) its deconstruction as well. All of Orson Welles' films are open to that twofold, open-ended, poetic interpretation of showing both a metaphysical mythology and the destruction of that mythology by the same cinematic process. That is incidentally why Welles used all the resources of montage as well as all the resources of still frames. He is both the great montage director and the great sequence-shot director, not for formal reasons but because he is at once someone who proposed mythologies and someone who proposed the inner destruction of mythologies. And with that, I believe, we have something absolutely novel for contemporary philosophy.

I'll complete this overview with the moral role of cinema. There are basically two apparent possibilities in cinema for staging great ethical conflicts. On the one hand, there is what could be called the "wide horizon form," in which the moral conflict is set in an adventure, in a sort of epic, the Western, the war movie, or a great story. In this case, the conflict is enlarged: the role played by the setting – nature, or space, as in Kubrick's *2001: A Space Odyssey*, which is a metaphysical Western – allows the values to be visible against the backdrop of the immensity of nature in exactly the same way as the heroes in Westerns stand out against the horizon. This cinematic possibility amplifies the conflict. It is a very old question that can already be found in Greek tragedy. Why, when the Greeks lived in a democracy, were there always kings and queens in tragedy? Clearly, for poetic reasons: because kings and queens were amplifying symbols; they stood for something with great symbolic import. This is amplification through the role. In cinema, there is amplification through the horizon. The characters are ordinary people, but in order for the conflict not to be an ordinary one, it is set in a unique space.

The other possibility, on the contrary, is the "confined setting," the closed circle, the little group. In this microcosmic case, everyone stands for one value or position. Cinema can also work in a stifling space, and certain cinematic techniques make it possible to flatten space. Orson Welles often used this kind of technique: filming very near the ground so that there was no horizon, with all the characters flattened in space. And yet, he, too, filmed conflict. He achieved the intensity of the conflict by means of confinement. In this respect as well, cinema is capable of synthesis: it can move from enlargement to confinement, from an infinite horizon to the flattening of a confined setting. In some great classic Westerns a combination of this sort can be found. Take Anthony Mann's *The Naked Spur*, for example. It is a classic Western, an iconic story. A small group of characters, with two sworn enemies in its midst, has to move from one place to another. The film makes the trip, the space opening onto the magnificence of nature in the American West (the waterfalls, the streams, the mountains) coexist with the confinement in a little group, along with the heightening of tension and violence, the duel within the microcosm. It is a brilliant synthesis in that it shows how it is possible, and even desirable, to use the method of enlargement in conjunction with that of shrinking in order to examine moral conflicts. At one and the same time you can be in Greek tragedy and in Sartre's no-exit situation; at one and the same time you have kings and queens and two characters in a cellar. And in both cases, great conflicts are explored. The genius of cinema lies in being able to move between the two.

We can therefore conclude as to this point: cinema is a wonderful invention for creating synthesis. But does that transform philosophy? While philosophy involves inventing new syntheses, I think that it hasn't completely understood cinema yet. It is a process that is beginning, that is underway. The relationship between philosophy and cinema was an esthetic relationship at first: is cinema an art? And if cinema *is* an art, why and how is it one? That constituted the first

218

big debate, an esthetic debate. It was a first skirmish. However, that question isn't the most important one, which is rather: What does cinema bring with it that is new? Now, I think that cinema brings an upheaval with it. At the heart of this upheaval new syntheses are created, syntheses of time, syntheses among the arts, syntheses with what is not art, syntheses in the operations by which morality is represented. I venture the hypothesis that the passage between cinema's ideas and philosophy's concepts always poses the question of syntheses. If we are able to create philosophical concepts from cinema, it is by changing the old philosophical syntheses by bringing them into contact with the new cinematic syntheses.

Let me give an example of that process. Cinema shows that there is no real opposition between constructed time and pure duration since it can install one within the other, something that is always done by the great filmmakers, really only the greatest ones – Murnau, Ozu, or Welles, for example – because it is very difficult to do. Only the greatest poets of the cinema are capable of doing it. It is an extremely important question because it poses the idea of a rupture in time. And since the question of philosophy is the question of ruptures, the relationship between ruptures and time is a fundamental one. It is also a political question. For instance, it is the question of revolution. Revolution was the very name of the rupture in time, like a new synthesis within temporal ruptures. It is also a philosophical idea, in particular the idea of a new existence, of a new life. Now, cinema in its turn tells us: there are new temporal syntheses. For example, there is no complete opposition between constructed time and pure duration. And also: there is no complete opposition between continuity and discontinuity. Or: discontinuity can be thought within continuity. And also: the event can be thought immanently; it is not necessarily transcendent. Naturally, cinema doesn't *think* this; it *shows* it, or even better, it *does* it. It is an artistic practice, an artistic thinking; it is not a philosophy. There is no theory of continuity and discontinuity in cinema but rather the creation of new relationships between continuity and discontinuity.

I think this may be the most important point: cinema is an art in which what happens is both continuous and discontinuous. In mediocre works, it is neither continuous nor discontinuous; it is merely a matter of images. But in great works, there is something undecidable between continuity and discontinuity. Continuity is created with discontinuity. Or, if you prefer, cinema is a promise, a promise that may have no equivalent: we can live within discontinuity. And that gives rise to a new image, an absolutely new one, which is the continuation

219

of the poem by images. Cinema exists for that very reason, on account of that reason. You could take numerous examples, such as those great films whose continuity is indisputable but which still make room for sudden appearances, for complete surprises, for bolts out of the blue. I'm thinking of Ozu's *Tokyo Story*, the story of an old man. (This is a big theme in cinema, as is the case with *Death in Venice* or *Wild Strawberries*, and old men should be grateful to cinema, which has given them so much.) In *Tokyo Story* the basic pace is particularly slow, and this makes the old people's temporality, which is stretched out but ultimately secretly fast, visible. Ozu shot it wonderfully: a few still frames, a patch of sky, train tracks, telephone poles, and electric wires. This next-to-nothing quality constitutes the sudden appearance of the new. It is an extraordinarily simple, exactly right symbol of the synthesis between continuity and discontinuity. The sudden appearance of something is always possible, and cinema tells us that the possibility of that miracle really does exist: such is the promise it makes to the film viewer. Cinema is the miracle of the visible as an enduring miracle and as an enduring rupture. This is without a doubt the greatest thing we owe to cinema, and philosophy should try to understand it with its own devices.

So cinema is a philosophical situation, and this is so for two reasons. First, for an ontological reason: cinema creates a new relationship between appearance and reality, between a thing and its double, between the virtual and the actual, so that a film like *The Matrix* is a Pythagorean film. Pythagoras would have been glad to see it. He would have said: "You see, the sensible world is nothing but numbers." It is a film that shows how appearance is digital. Once again, cinema is the revenge of old ideas: cinema is a totally recent invention but it corresponds to very ancient dreams. The second reason for the relationship between cinema and philosophy is a political one: cinema is a "mass art," and this affords a new relationship between democracy and aristocracy.

I'd like to illustrate the ethical thinking of cinema by way of its relationship with the figure of the lawman, which is a basic theme in cinema. The lone lawman can be the hero of a Western, or an old police officer, or the citizen who stands up on his own against injustice. It is an infinite resource in cinema. If you put all these heroes together you get a crowd, a crowd of solitudes. But the lawman is an essential character. Why? Because cinema has a special connection with the question of the law, and America, more specifically, has a strong relationship with the theme of the law. Cinema plus America equals an altogether essential relationship with the law. It derives from a relationship between the law and retribution. The American idea is basically that the law is important, but it is almost always powerless. In particular, it doesn't allow for just retribution. The lone lawman is the one who can repair the inadequacies of the law. He is the hero of the law but only where there is no law anymore, where the law is missing, where the law is deficient. Cinema follows this lonely hero in his relationship with a lawless world. And the reason why these images are such powerful ones is that they are simultaneously the images of one particular hero – who ends up coinciding with one particular actor – and those of a somehow deserted or violent world, which the cinema uses all its great resources to depict. We re-encounter that typical cinematic relationship between something solitary, something subjective, and the vastness of the world, the general figure of the world. And so this theme of the lone lawman is tailor-made for cinema. This figure is so iconic that the lone lawman may often kill more people than the criminal does. That is because redressing the crime is difficult: to kill the real bad guy you first have to kill dozens of other people. This is a special culture, with a delicate balance between law and retribution. Now, what strikes me is that this problem of the relationship between law and retribution also happens to be the oldest problem in theater, since it is precisely the subject of Aeschylus' great trilogy, the *Oresteia*. In the latter, Aeschylus tells how the law must replace retribution, through the creation of a public tribunal. Theater begins pretty much with the idea that retribution has to be replaced by the law. The cinema, at least a certain American cinema, tells how retribution can replace the law, via the figure of the lone lawman. At bottom, this cinema of the lawman can be said to be situated *before* theater, before the creation of the relationship of justice in the theater. The relationship to the law is not of the same nature in theater and in cinema.

One final way of thinking the cinema philosophically involves asking the following question: "Is cinema a thinking of the Other?" This is a very important question, and I think that cinema is in fact a new thinking of the Other, a new way of making the Other exist. The simplest argument consists in recognizing how cinema allows us to know the Other. There are entire situations today that we only know about through cinema. Take Iran: what would we know about that country without Kiarostami? And the same goes for Asian cinema. Japan, Hong Kong, Taiwan – what are they for us, if not Ozu, Kurosawa, Mizoguchi, Wong Kar-wai, Hou Hsiao-hsien, and others? This is very important: the Other in the world is presented to us by cinema. He is presented to us in his private life; he is presented to us in terms of his relationship with space; he is presented to us in terms of his relationship with the world. Cinema thus expands the possibility of thinking the Other enormously. If philosophy is the thinking of the Other, as Plato says, then there is an essential relationship between philosophy and cinema.

A Tribute to Gilles Deleuze[1]

I'll begin with one of Deleuze's statements, from the beginning of *Cinema 1: The Movement-Image*, where he writes: "With certain ideas in cinema, concepts can perhaps be produced." This is a difficult statement, because Deleuze terms "ideas in cinema" the content of cinematic creation, which has nothing to do with philosophy. And he terms "concepts" the content of philosophical creation, which has nothing to do with cinema. How can concepts be produced with ideas in cinema? This is a very complicated issue. In Deleuze's important books on cinema, *Cinema 1: The Movement-Image* and *Cinema 2: The Time-Image*, a partial solution to this problem can be found, because the new concepts Deleuze proposes have to do with time and movement and are illustrated by the analysis of films. However, they don't come from this analysis; in actual fact, they originate in a discussion of certain of Bergson's writings. This is why classifying Deleuze's book is complicated. There are cinema-ideas, analyzed with true genius; there are philosophical concepts, chiefly about time and movement but also about the ritual; and finally there is the idea of a passage between cinema-ideas and concepts.

What is the relationship between cinema and the image, Deleuze wonders? To begin with, the term "image" has to be defined correctly. A first meaning of "image" is a word from the psychology of perception: to have an image of something is to have a mental copy of it. The image is a relationship between knowledge and reality. It basically indicates the separation between consciousness and the outside world. If you accept this definition of "image," you pose the question of cinema in psychological terms: What relationship does consciousness have with the image? Or: What image do we have of images? Because the cinema spectator is someone who has images of images. This is similar to the experience of talking about a film. You get together one evening and talk about a film. "Yes, it's good . . . It's not bad," and you describe the film. What we then notice is that everyone has images of the film and yet they're not the *same* images. Sometimes it is even hard to be sure you're talking about the same film. All of this happens because we only have "images of images." And these images of images are not the same thing as the film; they express the relationship to the film. They are ultimately relationships between images. I think that, in order to really talk about cinema, you have to change the use of the word "image" and try to forget about the psychology of the image. This is one of Deleuze's basic contributions: he tries to define the image, and ultimately cinema, independently of psychology. He turns "image" into a word about reality, not consciousness.

To that end, Deleuze begins with Bergson. What was Bergson's great discovery? Let me quote Deleuze: "Movement as physical reality in the external world, and the image, as a psychic reality in consciousness, could no longer be opposed." This is really a key issue. To think cinema, says Deleuze, the opposition between external movement and the internal reality of the image must be abandoned. Consequently, what Bergson discovered is that movement and the image are one and the same thing. Deleuze synthesizes that discovery in his key concepts of "movement-image" and "time-image." This is once again a synthesis, and we remain within the general definition of philosophy. Where there is a rupture between image and movement, Deleuze establishes a new synthesis, based on Bergson. This is essential since it makes cinema a reality and no longer a representation, because if the image and movement are one and the same thing, the image is not the representation of movement. It is "movement-image," so cinema is no longer a representation; it will be able to be a creation.

In this sense, cinema is indeed produced with images, but the image is not a representation. The image is what cinema thinks with, since thought is always a creation. Let me quote Deleuze again: "The great directors of cinema think with movement-images and time-images instead of concepts." This is a very clear conception that I'll sum up with a series of short propositions: Cinema consists of images; these images are not copies or representations; they are the same thing as movement and time; and when we create "movement-images" or "time-images" we are creating a thought, which is a cinema-thought; and which is not philosophy because philosophy thinks with concepts. Therefore, cinema as thought is the production of movement-images and time-images.

What is a philosophical thinking of cinema? Cinema thinks with images, while philosophy thinks with concepts. So there is a rupture. What is the possible synthesis between these two different modes of thought? Deleuze proposes the following path. I quote: "This study"

– he is talking about *The Time-Image*[2] – "is a taxonomy, an attempt at the classification of images and signs." What philosophy can do, then, is provide a classification of images, something requiring concepts. And that is something cinema can't do: cinema produces images, not classifications of images. The objective of Deleuze's work is clear: it supplements cinema by producing, thanks to it, a classification of images and signs. And that is why the second key thinker, after Bergson, is the American philosopher Pierce. Bergson proposed a theory of the image and Pierce, a theory of signs. In philosophy, if you produce a classification of images and signs based on cinema, you must necessarily come after Bergson and after Pierce. Deleuze's books on cinema ultimately offer a synthesis of the theory of signs and the theory of images, and this synthesis is a classification. You have three kinds of movement-images, for example. The first is "the perception-image" (the cinema directors cited by Deleuze will then be Grémillon, Vigo, Vertov, et al.). Next, you come to the "affection-image" (Griffith, Sternberg, Dreyer, Bresson, et al.), and you end up with the "action-image" (epic films, on the one hand, which are the large form of the action-image, and, on the other hand, comedies, which are the small form of it). Each category can be illustrated by certain directors, so that the films and directors become examples of the classification. The classification itself, of course, involves philosophical concepts.

With Deleuze we thus have primary philosophical concepts: the concepts of time, movement, image, and signs. Corresponding to them are films that produce time-images and movement-images. And finally we come to the synthesis between the two, a classification with a twofold use. First of all, a certain order is provided for the history of cinema – schools of cinema that produce affection-images or perception-images, or even action-images – which will enable Deleuze to speak liberally about German cinema, French cinema, or Russian cinema, not as national categories but as categories of the image per se. For example, Deleuze mentions the great Soviet epic cinema, which is a particular form of the action-image. So this is the first use of the classification, and it enables Deleuze to perform the extraordinary feat of talking about virtually all international film directors, by means of very close analyses, thanks to a conceptual order that he himself invented: that of the classification of cinema.

But there is a second use of the classification, a purely philosophical use, because this classification naturally changes our thinking of the image. Thanks to cinema, we can make much finer distinctions. Not only will we have the movement-image but we will have different *kinds* of movement-images, and we would probably never have been able to think these kinds if we hadn't had cinema. The classification is a classification specific to cinema, but it makes it possible to transform the concepts of philosophy. The overall result of the enterprise is itself twofold. In one respect it is an ordering of cinema, a conceptual classification of the time-image and the movement-image. In this regard, Deleuze's analyses of the details are extraordinary. In another respect, you get a philosophical creation that is ultimately a new theory of the image. It is really and truly a synthesis. In one of his lectures Deleuze said: "Filmmakers do not need philosophy in order to think." This is obvious, since they don't think with concepts. But Deleuze shows that philosophy can make use of cinema in order to think, that there can be a synthesis based on that rupture, and this produces a transformation of philosophy itself. Let's take a very essential issue, the conception of time. For Deleuze, time is being as such. Therefore, cinema has ontological consequences. It makes possible a transformation of the thinking of being and a fundamental transformation of philosophy.

One major hypothesis of Deleuze's is: cinema thinks with images, "image" meaning the presence of time. But does cinema *really* have to be thought on the basis of the category of images? That is the problem I'd like to raise, although not to criticize Deleuze, because his work on cinema is essential, introducing as it does creativity and freedom into philosophy. Not to criticize Deleuze, then, but simply to wonder if there isn't something else in cinema, another philosophical resource, a broader possibility than that of the image as transformation of the thinking of time. I'd like to examine the exact role of the notion of "image" in cinematic creation, to investigate the conditions of production of the cinema image.

Cinema, an absolutely impure art

To write a poem you need pen and paper. You may also need to be familiar with the whole history of world poetry. But the existence of that history is virtual. It is not something physically present. To paint a picture, you also begin with an absence, a surface – and the whole history of the visual arts, as a basic potentiality. But beginning a film is not at all the same. The conditions of production of the movement-image or the time-image involve a unique assemblage of materials. You need technical resources, but you also need to marshal extremely complex and, above all, heterogeneous materials. For example, you need locations, either natural or constructed ones; you need spaces; you need a text, a screenplay, dialogues, abstract ideas; you need bodies, actors; plus you'll need chemistry, and editing equipment. And so you need to make use of a whole collective apparatus, a whole collection of different materials, which you'll have to master, at least to some extent, through the resources of their inscription within the image. This is a completely banal point, but a very important one, in my opinion. Cinema is an absolutely impure art and is so right from its conception, because the system of its conditions of possibility is an impure material system.

This impurity is reflected in a well-known fact: cinema requires money, a lot of money. Money is what unites things that are totally different from one another, everything from the actors' salaries to set construction, from technical equipment to editing rooms, from distribution to publicity – all those hundreds of completely disparate things. The way money unites everything is of interest to me as regards one point in particular, which is that there is no cinematic purity. In a famous article on the cinema[3] Malraux explained the essence of the image; he also explained why Charlie Chaplin's films were shown in Africa, and he compared cinema to the other arts. But the last sentence of the text was this: "In any case, the cinema is an industry." But is it really a question of "in any case"? In actual fact, the cinema is *first and foremost* an industry. And it is an industry even as concerns the great artists of cinema. The vast majority of them worked in the industrial system of the cinema. And so money, the industry, implies something about cinema itself, not just about the social conditions of cinema. This means: cinema begins with an impure infinity. Art's task is to make a few fragments of purity emerge from that impurity, a purity wrested, as it were, from a fundamental impurity. So I would say that cinema is about purification: it is a work of purification. With only slight exaggeration cinema could be compared to the treatment of waste. You start out with a bunch of different things, a sort of indiscriminate industrial material. And the artist makes selections, works on this material. He'll condense it, he'll eliminate some things, but he'll also gather things together, put different things together, in the hope of producing moments of purity. This is a very important point, because in the other arts, in music or painting, or even in dance or writing, you begin with purity. As Mallarmé said, "You begin with the purity of the blank page." With those other arts, the aim is to preserve purity in the production itself, to keep the silence in speech, to keep the blank page in the writing, to keep the invisible in the visible, to keep the silence in the sound. Being faithful to that original purity is the great problem of art.

Cinema works the other way around. The artist starts out from disorder, from accumulation, from the impure, and he tries to create purity. It is extremely difficult. Where the other arts are concerned, the artist doesn't have *enough* things; he has to create out of nothing, out of absence, out of the void. Where cinema is concerned, there are too *many* things, absolutely and always too many. Even if I just wanted to film a bottle, there are way too many things about this bottle – its contents, its label, its background, the quality of its glass . . . It all gets out of hand: the label is too much, the color of the cork is too much, the shape is too much! What will I film? How can I create the *idea* of the bottle on the basis of a bottle? I've got to purify, to simplify. This is an essential point: cinema is a negative art because it proceeds from too many things to a sort of reconstituted simplicity. And the problems are even greater today because the technical resources have increased the resources of the "too much."

When cinema first began, the artist, or rather the cameraman-craftsman, was in a studio, with constructed sets. No color, no sound. Cinema was still very akin to a primitive art form, and what a piece of luck that was for the artist! He could control the visible much more easily. The set wasn't the infinity of nature; it was an artifice. The artist was a lot closer to his artistic creation. Then came sound, color, exterior filming, digital techniques, and so on. You can produce anything at all now with an image and a movie camera – it's terrifying, terrifying for art. How can this sensible infinity be dominated, how can it be mastered?

My own hypothesis is that it has become impossible to master that sensible infinity. This impossibility is the real of cinema, which is a struggle with the infinite, a struggle to purify the infinite. In its very essence, the cinema is this hand-to-hand combat with the infinite, with the infinity of the visible, the infinity of the sensible, the infinity of the other arts, the infinity of musics, the infinity of available texts. It is an art of simplification, whereas all the other arts are arts of complexity. Ideally, cinema involves creating nothing out of complexity, since the ideal of cinema is, at bottom, the purity of the visible, a visible that is transparent, a human body that is like an essential body, a horizon that is a pure horizon, a story that is an exemplary story. To attain that ideal, cinema must pass through impure material, must use everything there is, and must above all find the path to simplicity.

Let's take a few examples. First, the question of sound. The contemporary world is the world of a confused jumble of sounds; that is one of its major features. Terrible noises, different kinds of music that you can't even hear anymore, engine noises, disparate conversations, loud-speakers, and so on. What is cinema's relationship with this sonic chaos? Either it reproduces the sonic chaos (but in that case it is not a creation) or else it cuts through it in order to rediscover, to give birth to a new simplicity of sound. This is once again a synthesis. For the idea is not to deny the sonic chaos – if you deny it, you give up talking about the world as it is – but to recreate a pure sound out of this sonic chaos, out of today's terrible musics, out of that sort of typical loud beat. The best example of this work on sound can be found in Godard. In a Godard film, you come up against the sonic chaos: for example, several people all speaking at once (and, what's more, you can't really understand what they're saying). You've got bits of music, you've got cars going by . . . But the chaos is gradually organized, as if there were a hierarchy of noises in Godard's work. Godard transforms the sonic chaos into a murmur, like a sort of new silence made from the noises of the world. It is the invention of a silence contemporary with the sonic chaos, as if we could then hear a secret the world were confiding.

A second example is the use of cars. The use of cars is one of cinema's, or even television's, big clichés. I think that two out of every three films or four out of every five TV shows open with a car driving away or arriving somewhere. It is the most clichéd image there is. So, we might think: a great artist will get rid of all the cars. But, just as with the sonic chaos, if you get rid of these stupid shots of cars, you deprive yourself of an opportunity for a synthesis with the contemporary world.

That is why the great artists, our contemporaries, have come up with another use of the car. Let me give you two examples. In Kiarostami's films, the car becomes a place of speech. Instead of being an image of action, as with gangsters' or police cars, it becomes the closed place of speech about the world; it becomes a subject's destiny. The impurity of the image of the car creates a new purity here, which is basically that of contemporary speech. What can we say to one another within this absurd world of the car? There are similar operations in Manoel de Oliveira's films, where the car also becomes a place for self-exploration, a sort of movement back toward origins. The banality of the car isn't eliminated; it is, as it were, purified.

My third example is sexual activity. The image of sex is a staple in the cinema: naked bodies, embraces, even sexual organs have

228

become a commonplace of the screen, as uninteresting as cars. This is what the audience has always hoped to see, but it has never, even today, seen anything ... except disappointing things. This disappointment can actually be called "pornography." And the pornographic image is a staple, like noise, like cars, like gunshots. What can be done with such material? Does a great filmmaker have to be prudish? Does he or she have to eliminate bodies? Eliminate sexuality? Clearly, that's not the real way. Rather, it is a matter of accepting pornographic imagery but transforming it from within. I think there are three ways of transforming the pornographic image. The first is to change it into an image of love, where the light of love is internal to the sexual figure. The second way is to stylize it, to make it almost abstract, to transform the bodies into a sort of ideal beauty without, however, giving up the sexual representation. Some remarkable scenes in this vein could be mentioned, in Antonioni's films, for example. The third way amounts to being even more pornographic than pornography: this could be called "super-pornography," a kind of meta-pornography. It can be found in some of Godard's scenes: for example, in the big daisy chain scene in *Sauve qui peut (la vie)* (*Every Man For Himself*). Once again, the artist starts with the impurity of the image, its banal and obscene nature, and reworks it from within, gearing it toward a new simplicity.

Now for my fourth and last example: shoot-outs, gunshots, gunfights. In this case, too, it is hard to find anything more conventional and clichéd. The number of gunshots fired in the cinema is truly extraordinary. A Martian watching our films would think that human activity boiled down to using guns. Will the great artist give up guns? Of course not. There are shoot-outs in some very great films. But, once again, the artist reworks things differently. In *The Lady from Shanghai* the gunshots are also images that explode, and in John Woo's and Takeshi Kitano's films the gun battles turn into a kind of dance, a very visual choreography. They, too, accepted the rule of the gangster film and took the material with all its triviality but transformed it through a unique stylization.

The most important feature of cinema, in my opinion, is precisely this acceptance of the material of the images – contemporary imagery – and its reworking. Cars, pornography, gangsters, shoot-outs, the urban legend, different kinds of music, noises, explosions, fires, corruption, everything that basically makes up the modern social imaginary. Cinema accepts this infinite complexity, assimilates it, and produces purity with it. And so it is true that cinema treats contemporary waste products: it is an absolutely impure art and that is also why it is an art of money. The artistic endeavor involves transforming this material from within in order to produce movement-images or time-images through this traversal of impurity.

That, in a nutshell, is the issue of the status of violence in cinema. Cinema can very easily be violent and obscene; that is one of its obvious features. Even in the works of great artists there is sometimes unbearable violence, manifest obscenity. But these artists – David Lynch, for example – are interesting precisely because they have the ambition to take what is worst in the contemporary world as their material and to show how, even with such material, an artistic synthesis of great purity can be created. These artists constantly show the struggle with their own material. In Kitano's gangster films, we are often confronted with images that are unbearable owing to the violence of the relationships, to the dark, sinister nature of the stories. And yet, something luminous occurs, something that is not the negation of the material but, quite mysteriously, its transmutation, in the sense of alchemy, as though something terrible and terrifying were changing into pure, undreamt-of simplicity.

I think that if you accept this hypothesis you'll understand why cinema is a mass art. We come back to our original synthesis here, namely that cinema is a mass art because it shares the social imaginary with the masses. Cinema's starting point isn't its history but the impurity of its material. This is why cinema is a shared art form: everyone recognizes contemporary imagery in a film. The material is common to all films, so everyone can go see it, everyone will recognize themselves in it. Cinema can reproduce the world's noise; it can also invent a new silence. It can reproduce our restlessness; it can invent new forms of stillness. It can accept the powerlessness of our speech; it can invent a new conversation. But, at the beginning, the materials are the same, and that is why millions of people can consider a great film as being contemporary with their own lives, whereas they can only do the same for the other arts if they have been educated for a long time.

We may know why cinema is a mass art, but we must nonetheless ask ourselves what the price to be paid for it is, because there is indeed a price to be paid. The impurity is so extensive, the materials so infinite, the question of money so important, that it is impossible for cinema to attain the same degree of purity as the other arts. There is always a remnant of impurity that remains. In any film, there are whole bits of it that are banal, images that are pointless, lines that could disappear, over-done colors, bad actors, rampant pornography, and so on. At bottom, when we see a film we are seeing a fight: the struggle against the material's impurity. We don't see only the result, only the time-images or the movement-images; we see the battle, that artistic battle against impurity. And the battle is won at times and lost at others, even in the same film. A great film is one in which there are a lot of victories, only a few defeats for a lot of victories. That is why a great film always has something heroic about it. It is also why the relationship with cinema isn't one of contemplation but of par-ticipation, solidarity, admiration, or even jealousy, irritation, or hatred. Cinema's hand-to-hand combat amazes us. We take part in it; we assess the victories; we assess the defeats; we admire the cre-ation of a few moments of purity. Those victorious moments are so extraordinary that they account for cinema's emotional power. There is an emotion of combat: all of a sudden the purity of an image seizes us and, similarly, so does the outcome of a battle. That is also why cinema is an art that makes you cry. You cry from joy; you cry from love, from fear, from rage; you cry on account of the victories and sometimes on account of the defeats. Something almost miraculous happens when cinema manages to extract a little bit of purity from all that is worst in the world.

So we can now return to the question of the relationship between cinema and philosophy. What they have in common is the fact that they both begin with the contemporary real: thanks to them, that real is no longer missing from thought. The other arts start with the purity of their own histories; science starts with its own axioms, with its own mathematical transparency. Cinema and philosophy start with impurity: the opinions, images, practices, and events of human exis-tence. And they both choose to believe that an idea can be created out of this contemporary material, that an idea doesn't always come from an idea, that it can come from its opposite, from ruptures in existence, and that an image is made from the imagery of the world, from its infinite impurity. In both cases, the work is a cross between a struggle and a sharing. The work of philosophy involves creating conceptual syntheses where there is rupture; the work of cinema involves creating purity out of the most trivial conflicts in the world. That is the real connection between cinema and philosophy; that is what they share.

What's more, cinema is a real piece of luck for us philosophers because it shows the power of purification, the power of synthesis, the possibility that something can happen even though the worst may prevail. Basically, cinema teaches philosophy a lesson of hope. Cinema tells philosophers "All is not lost," precisely because it deals with the greatest abjection: violence, betrayal, obscenity. It tells us that it is not because such things exist that thought is done for; thought can triumph even in a milieu like that. It won't always triumph, it won't triumph everywhere, but victories do exist.

The idea of potential victory strikes me as being a very important issue today. For a long time, with the idea of revolution there was the hope of a great potential victory, a definitive, irreversible victory. And then the idea of revolution disappeared. We are the orphans of the idea of revolution. As a result, we often think that no victory is possible anymore, that the world has lost its illusions, and we eventually become resigned. Cinema, however, says in its own way: "There are victories even in the worst of worlds." Naturally *the* victory probably doesn't exist any longer, but there are individual victories. To be faithful to these individual victories already means a lot for thought. So let's watch films philosophically, not just because they create new figures of the image but because they tell us something about the world, something as simple as can be: "The worst of worlds shouldn't cause despair." We should not despair. That is what cinema tells us, I think, and that is why we should love it. It can keep us from despair if we know how to look at it, to look at it as a struggle against the impure world, to look at it as a collection of precious victories.

Text unpublished in French, transcribed from the
"*Penser le cinéma*" seminar,
Buenos Aires, Alliance Française, September 24 and 25, 2003

—28—

ON CINEMA AS A DEMOCRATIC
EMBLEM

There is philosophy only insofar as there are paradoxical relation-ships, relationships that don't, or shouldn't, connect things. When all the connections are naturally legitimate, philosophy is impossible or of no use.

Philosophy is the violence done by thought to impossible relationships.

Today – "after Deleuze," we might say – there is a clear requisition-ing of philosophy by cinema – or of cinema by philosophy. It is therefore certain that cinema offers us paradoxical relationships, altogether improbable connections.

Which ones?

The prefabricated philosophical response amounts to saying that cinema is an untenable relationship between total artifice and total reality. Cinema simultaneously offers the possibility of a copy of reality and the entirely artificial dimension of that copy. With con-temporary technologies, cinema can produce the real artifice of the copy of a false copy of the real, or the false real copy of a false real. And other variations. This is tantamount to saying that cinema has become the immediate (or "technical") form of an ancient paradox, that of the relations between being and appearance (which are far more fundamental than the ubiquitously displayed relations between the virtual and the actual). Consequently, cinema will be declared to be an ontological art. Many critics, André Bazin in particular, have been saying as much for a long time now.

I'd like to enter into the question in an infinitely simpler, more empirical way, and one that is at a greater remove from any philo-sophical prefabrication. I'd like to start with the elucidation of a fact: cinema is a "mass art."

The phrase "mass art" can be given an elementary definition: an art is a "mass art" if the masterpieces, the artistic productions that the educated (or dominant, it doesn't matter) culture declares to be indisputable, are seen and loved by millions of people from every social group at the very time they were created.

Adding "at the very time they were created" is especially important, because we know we are under the sway of a melancholy historicism, so there is a pure effect of pastness. Millions of people from every social group (except, no doubt, the lowest stratum of the proletariat) can to go to museums, because they love the icons of the past as treasures, and because the modern passion for tourism extends to a kind of tourism of treasures. It is not this sort of tourism that I am speaking about, but rather about the millions of people who love an exceptional work of art at the very time that it appears. In the short history of cinema we have indisputable examples of such love, examples that can probably only be compared to the public triumph of the great Greek tragedies – Chaplin's great films, for example. They were seen all over the world, even by the Eskimos, or were projected on tents in the desert. Everyone immediately understood that these films spoke in a profound and crucial way about what I have suggested calling (with regard to Beckett's writings) "generic humanity," or humanity subtracted from its differences. The character of Charlie, perfectly situated in a recognizable context and filmed from close up and frontally, is no less a representative of generic "popular" humanity for an African, a Japanese or an Eskimo.

But we shouldn't think that this kind of example is limited to the comic or slapstick genre, which has always captured the vital energy of the people, the force and cunning of survival in society. An extraordinarily condensed film of staggering formal invention, doubtless one of the greatest cinematic poems that has ever existed, could also be mentioned: Murnau's *Sunrise*. This sheer masterpiece was a phenomenal hit in the United States. It was a sort of *Titanic*, relatively speaking, given the conditions of the industry back then.

There is no question that cinema is capable of being a mass art on a scale that brooks no comparison with any other art. Of course there were writers of the masses, poets of the masses in the nineteenth century: Victor Hugo in France, for example, or Pushkin in Russia. They had, and still have, millions of readers. However, the scale – at the time their works were created – can't be compared to that of cinema's greatest hits.

So the point is this: "mass art" defines a paradoxical relationship. Why? Because "mass" is a political category, or more precisely a category of activist democracy, of communism. The Russian revolutionaries were able to define their action as being that of the era when "the masses mounted the stage of History." And nowadays we oppose "mass democracy" to representative and constitutional democracy. "Mass" is a fundamental political category. Mao said that "the masses, the masses alone, make universal history."

However, the other half of the phrase "mass art," namely "art," is, and can only be, an aristocratic category.

To say that "art" is an aristocratic category is not a case of being judgmental. You are simply noting that "art" includes the idea of formal creation, of visible novelty in the history of forms, and therefore requires the means for understanding creation as such, necessitates a differential education, a minimal proximity to the history of the art concerned and to the vicissitudes of its grammar. A long and often thankless apprenticeship. A technological broadening of the mind. Pleasures, of course, but sophisticated, developed, acquired pleasures.

In "mass art" there is the paradoxical relationship between a pure democratic element (in terms of eruption and evental energy) and an aristocratic element (in terms of individual education and differential registers of taste).

During the twentieth century all the arts were avant-garde arts. Painting was an avant-garde art and only stops being one at that always somewhat gloomy moment when it enters museums. Music was an avant-garde art, and, from Schoenberg's day until our own, has continued to be one (unless we also call the moaning of popular music "music"). Poetry exists today only as an avant-garde art. The twentieth century can be said to be the century of avant-gardes. But it can also be said to be the century of the greatest mass art that has ever existed.

The basic form of the paradoxical relationship: the first great art that is mass *in its essence* appears and develops in an era that is the era of the avant-gardes. The derived forms: cinema's imposition of impossible relationships, between aristocracy and democracy, between invention and familiarity, between novelty and general taste.

That is why philosophy is concerned with cinema: because it imposes a vast and obscure complex of paradoxical relationships.

"To think cinema" comes down to forcing the relationship, to arranging the concepts that, under the constraint of real films, displace the established rules of the connection.

I think that there have been five major attempts at such a displacement. Or rather, five different ways of entering into the problem, i.e., "to think cinema as a mass art." The first of these starts with the paradox of the image. This is a classic entry point, the one I mentioned at the beginning: the ontological art. The second deals with the paradoxes of time, with the filmic visibility of time. The third examines cinema's difference, its strange connection to the established system of the fine arts, or, if you prefer: the paradox of the seventh art. The fourth locates cinema at the border of art and non-art; its paradox is that of artistic impurity. The fifth proposes an ethical paradox: cinema as a reservoir of figures of conscience, as a popular phenomenology of every situation in which a choice has to be made.

Let me say a word about these five attempts.

1. About the image. It could be said that cinema is a "mass art" because it is the height of the old art of the image, and because the image, as far back as we go in the history of mankind, has always been ruthlessly fascinating. Cinema is the high point of the visual as semblance. And since there can be no identification that is not based on semblance, cinema can be said to be the final mastery of the metaphysical cycle of identification. Movie theaters, dining rooms, bedrooms, even the streets amaze the masses owing to a seductive network of disparate identifications, inasmuch as the technique of semblance renders the religious fable obsolete and distributes the small change of the miracle to one and all. Cinema's masses are basically *pious* masses. This is the first explanation.

2. Time. This approach is fundamental for Deleuze and many other critics as well. It is tempting to think that cinema is a mass art *because it transforms time into perception.* With cinema we have the most powerful visible becoming of time. Cinema creates a temporal feeling that is distinct from lived time. More precisely, it transforms "the intimate sense of time" into representation. It is this representative gap that enables cinema to be addressed to the immense audience of those who want to suspend time in space in order to avoid fate.

    This hypothesis brings cinema closer to music, which, in its lowest forms, is also a mass production. But music – and "great" music much more so than popular music – is also a distanced organization of time. It could be said very simply that music makes time audible while cinema makes time visible. And of course, cinema makes time audible as well, since music is incorporated into cinema. However, the hallmark of cinema, which was silent for a long time, is indeed its ability to make time

236

visible. The production of that visibility delights everyone. This is the second explanation.

3.   The series of the arts. It is clear that cinema retains from the other arts everything that is popular about them, everything that, once isolated, filtered, separated from those arts' aristocratic requirements, *might* enable them to be addressed to the masses. The seventh art borrows from the other six what is most explicitly addressed to generic humanity in them.

For example, what does cinema retain from painting? The pure possibility of changing the sensory beauty of the world into a reproducible image. It does not retain the intellectual technique of painting. It does not retain the complicated modes of representation and formalization. It retains a well-regulated, sensory relationship with the outside world. In this sense, cinema is a painting without painting. A world painted without paint.

What does cinema retain from music? Not the extraordinary difficulties of musical composition, not the subtle arrangement of harmonic verticality and thematic horizontality, not even the chemistry of tones. What matters for cinema is that music, or its rhythmic ghost, should accompany the vicissitudes of the visible. What it imposes everywhere – nowadays even in everyday life – is a certain dialectic of the visible and the audible. To stuff all representable existence with a musical filling is cinema's enormous task. We regularly give in to the emotion aroused by a strange blend of existence and music, a musicalized subjectivation, a melodious accompaniment of the drama, an orchestral punctuation of the cataclysm . . . All of that injects into representation a music without music, a music freed from musical problems, a music borrowed and returned to its subjective or narrative pretext.

What does cinema retain from the novel? Not the complexities of subjective development, or the infinite resources of literary fabrication, or the unique, gradual restoration of the *flavor* of an era. No, what cinema has an obsessive, insatiable need of, and for the sake of which it constantly plunders world literature, is the story, the narrative, which *it* calls "the screenplay." Cinema's imperative – which is artistic *and* commercial indivisibly, inasmuch as it is a mass art – is to tell great stories, to tell stories that can be understood by all of humanity.

What does cinema retain from theater? The actor, the actress, the charm, the *aura* of the actor and the actress. By separating

237

this aura from the literary text's powers, a basic requirement of theater, cinema transformed actors and actresses into *stars*. This is one possible definition of cinema: a device for transforming the actor into a star.

It is absolutely true that cinema takes something from each of the other arts. But the way it goes about this appropriation is complex, because it involves separating a common, accessible element from its sophisticated artistic conditions. Cinema *opens up* all the arts; it weakens their aristocratic, complex, and composite dimension. It delivers this simplified opening over to images of unanimous existence. As painting without painting, music without music, the novel without subjects, the theater reduced to the charm of the actors, cinema ensures the *popularization* of all the arts. This is why it has a universal calling. This is the third hypothesis: the seventh art is a mass art because it is the democratization in actuality of the other six.

4.   Impurity. Let's now examine the relationship between art and non-art in cinema. We will then be able to affirm that it is a mass art because it is always at the edge of non-art. Cinema is an art particularly *laden with* non-art. An art that is always full of trite forms. Owing to a large number of its ingredients, cinema is always *beneath* art. Even its most obvious artistic successes include an immanent infinity of shoddy ingredients, of blatant bits of non-art. It could be argued that, at every stage of its brief existence, cinema has explored the border between art and what is not art. It is located on this border. It incorporates the new forms of existence, be they art or non-art, and it makes a certain selection among them, albeit never a complete one. And so, in any film, even a pure masterpiece, you can find a great number of banal images, trite materials, stereotypes, images seen a hundred times elsewhere, completely trivial things.

Bresson was particularly annoyed by the resistance put up by artistic non-being. He wanted pure art and called such purity "cinematic writing." But it was to no avail. In Bresson's work, too, the worst of the visible, the inconceivable invasion by the sensory base things of the times has to be endured. As fundamental as it is involuntary, this impurity does not prevent a number of Bresson's films from being artistic masterpieces. But it does shed light on how this art can be a mass art. For you can enter into the art of cinema from what – always present in it in abundance – *is not art*, whereas for the other arts it is the opposite

238

case. You must enter their non-artistic part, their flaws, from art, from the grandeur of art. You could say that with cinema *you have the possibility of rising*. You can start with your most common ideas, your most nauseating sentimentality, your vulgarity, even your cowardice. You can be an absolutely ordinary film viewer. You can have bad taste in your access, in your entry, in your initial attitude. But that doesn't prevent the film's allowing you to rise. You may arrive at powerful, refined things. But the opposite approach isn't required of you, whereas with the other arts you always have a fear of falling. That is the great democratic advantage of the art of cinema: you can go there on a Saturday evening, to relax, and suddenly, unexpectedly rise. Aristotle said that if we do good, pleasure will come "as a bonus." When we see a film, it is often the other way around: we feel an immediate pleasure, often suspect (owing to the omnipresence of non-art), and the Good (of art) comes as a bonus.

At the cinema, we get to the pure from the impure. This is not the case with the other arts. Could you deliberately go and see bad painting? Bad painting is bad painting; there is little hope that it will turn into good painting. You won't rise. Just by being there, lost in bad painting, you have already come down, you are a fallen aristocrat, whereas at the cinema you are always more or less a democrat on the rise. Therein lies the paradoxical relationship, the paradoxical relationship between aristocracy and democracy, which is ultimately an internal relationship between art and non-art. And this is also what accounts for cinema's political significance: cinema achieves a cross between ordinary opinions and the work of thought. A subtle cross, which you won't find in the same guise elsewhere.

This, then, is the fourth hypothesis: cinema is a mass art because it democratizes the process whereby art uproots itself from non-art by turning that process into a border, by turning impurity into the thing itself.

5. Ethical figures. Cinema is an art of figures. Not only figures of visible space and active places. It is first and foremost an art of the great figures of humanity in action. It proposes a kind of universal stage of action and its confrontation with common values. At bottom, cinema is the last place still inhabited by heroes. Our world is so commercial, so family oriented, so unheroic . . . However, even today no one could imagine cinema without its great moral figures, without the great American battle

between Good and Evil. Even the gangsters in films stand for nothing but moral dilemmas, redemptive decisions, the elimination of inner Badness. The most sordid cruelty is a kind of cunning of reason intended for didactic enlightenment. The same goes for the cops. Angelic police captains, often women nowadays, keep watch among them. The ridiculousness of these stories, their dogmatic impurity, their disgusting hypocrisy, in no way prevents there being something admirable about them, as admirable as were the Greek tragedies, the cinema of Antiquity, about which we have the noblest yet falsest idea as can be, since the countless turkeys performed in the amphitheaters were not passed down to us. All we have are a few dozen masterpieces, something like three Murnaus, one Lang, two Eisensteins, four Griffiths and six Chaplins. And so we can no longer see the impurity and overwhelming banality of those spectacles. Nevertheless, we can trace their common purpose: to present the typical and excessive figures of all the great conflicts of human life to an immense audience. To speak of war, of passion, of justice and injustice, of truth, using as ordinary material all the cock-and-bull stories of old criminals, female poisoners, and mad kings. Cinema, too, speaks to us of courage, of justice, of passion, of betrayal. And the great genres of cinema, the most coded kinds, such as the melodrama, the western, and the "space opera," are in fact ethical genres, that is to say, genres that address humanity in order to offer it a moral mythology.

We know that philosophy began as a vast discussion with tragedy, with the theater, with the impurity of the visible and the performing arts. Plato's key interlocutors were on the stage, including in this broader rhetorical visibility the public stage, the democratic assembly, and the performance of the sophists. So we shouldn't be surprised that philosophy today, as regards an increasing part of its activity, is a vast discussion with cinema, because cinema and its derivatives, including television, represent, on a human scale, the third historical attempt, after Tragedy and Religion, at a spiritual subjugation of the visible that would be available to everyone, without exception or reserve. Democratic politicians and their sophist advisors, rebranded "communications consultants," are involved in this, too. The screen has become their supreme challenge.

The question has changed only in terms of its focus. It is now expressed as: "If there is such a thing as a sovereign technique of semblance, and if this technique, when it is cinema, is also capable of producing a mass art, what torsion, what transformation does this art impose on that which philosophy is based on, which is called 'truth'?"

Plato sought the answer in a transcendent mimesis. To figurative semblance he opposed the participation of everything that exposes itself to the Idea, which does not expose itself. This gesture required the support of that which is in itself subtracted from semblance: the mathematics of finite perfection, numbers and figures. We are instead seeking that which in the visible itself exceeds its own visibility, linking semblance to the immanent, yet eternal, register of its infinite form. Mathematics, this time the mathematics of infinite perfection, is also needed: sets, topologies, sheaves.

So, just as Plato dominated semblance with allegory, saving the image in the very place of Truth with his immortal "myths," we can similarly hope that cinema will be defeated by cinema itself.

After the philosophy of cinema must come – is already coming – philosophy *as* cinema, which consequently has a chance of being a philosophy of the masses.

Critique, special issue *Cinéphilosophie*, January–February 2005

—29—

THE END OF A BEGINNING

Notes on *Tout Va Bien* (*Everything's All Right*)
by Jean-Luc Godard and Jean-Pierre Gorin[1]

Let me suggest the following proposition: *Tout va bien* is an allegory of *gauchisme* on the wane. It is a film devoted to what took place between 1968 and 1972, but it is only able and willing to be devoted to an overview of those events under the implicit (unconscious?) assumption of an end.

Or more precisely: of the end of a beginning. It is this ambiguous quality of beginnings (does their end usher in the "real" beginning, or the (re)beginning of what there was before the beginning?) that accounts for the film's being both rosy and gloomy, just as it is both red and blue in its deliberate mix of colors.

We could also say: it is part of a virtual genre, the *political assessment*.

Additionally, it is a return to cinema, after the long years of experimentation, from '68 on, during which Godard completely subordinated the collective production of images to militant aims. A return to cinema, since it is a film, a "real" film, with movie stars (Montand and Fonda), a plot, a development . . . And perhaps it is also an opportunity given Gorin, Godard's companion during the "red" years, the difficult years, to become involved in "real" cinema.

But it is a return wholly conditioned by a subject that is especially resistant to cinematic fictionalization: live current events, the fluctuating situation of the country. An almost impossible film, by virtue of its being a film from this country, by virtue of its being a *French* film, *Tout va bien* is particularly unreal in that it is about France's real. The "*gauchiste*" real of France as it might be revealed by a cinematic spectrogram through the colossal density of a French reality (Pompidou and so on) that couldn't be any less *gauchiste*.

Let's examine the three terms of the proposition one by one: *gauchisme;* on the wane; allegory.

242

– *I* –

Gauchisme

Let's agree (this suffices for understanding the film) to call "*gauch-isme*" a form of revolutionary political consciousness that, on the one hand, preserves and even revives the major categories of Marxism, and, on the other, strenuously opposes the interpretation and use of these same categories by the official organizations that the French Communist Party and its labor union lackey, the CGT [General Confederation of Labor], have become.

The film creates a stage on which both parts of this definition can be heard.

First of all, it is about typical incidents in class struggle. At the heart of the film is the portrayal of a strike at a food industry plant, complete with occupation of the premises and sequestration of the boss. (The incident was inspired by a number of *gauchiste* maneuvers carried out in a sordid factory in the Paris suburbs where the Olida brand ham was produced.) The end of the film depicts a wildcat action by a militant (Maoist, needless to say) group in a provincial supermarket that leads (forces?) the customers to bypass the checkout lines without paying. This is an allusion to the big demonstration inside the BHV department store that was organized by the UCFML [Union of Marxist-Leninist Communists of France] (another Maoist group, to which I belonged). The two petit-bourgeois "witnesses" (Montand, a filmmaker, and Fonda, a reporter) become involved in these incidents somewhat by chance.

Next, the leitmotif is the working class. The film introduces us to a whole gamut of workers – men and women, old and young, black and white, strikers and workers afraid to strike, organized (the Maoists, needless to say) and unorganized, pro- and anti-union, and so forth. At the height of the strike (which is presented honestly as a minority action, at least as concerns its most militant dimension), the occupiers all sing to the boss: "*Keep on like this and the working class will kick your ass.*"

The legitimacy of mass violence is shown. There are plenty of fights, with management, with the union bigshots, in the factory as well as in the supermarket. They won't let the boss go to the bathroom, so he runs down the halls with everyone jeering at him. A young woman worker recites a sort of hymn to the struggle . . .

All this is integrated into the sense of the historical movement. The fictional story is in fact supplemented by a sort of reportage recreated from real events, in particular the CRS [riot police] repression, out in the countryside, of an expedition led by the Gauche prolétarienne (the rowdiest Maoist organization of the period) to the Renault plant in Flins in 1969. An expedition during which Gilles Tautin, a young militant, died.

So much for the fidelity to Marxism. As for the second issue (the bitter conflict with the PCF [French Communist Party] and the CGT), aside from the scuffles in the stairwells of the factory administration building, what is especially worthy of note is the very long speech given by the union bureaucrat, which corresponds exactly to the boss's speech and is in fact based on the same reference: economic objectivity. Formally, this slow-paced speech, delivered with great difficulty, at once gloomy and threatening, is an accomplished portrayal of what the unions represented for the whole Maoist movement at the time. Statistics, judicious caution, calling for elections, denouncing "provocateurs": all this was radically opposed to *gauchisme* (the word was incidentally the PCF's), which gave priority to the subjective force of the moment, to the local desire for rupture and innovation, to the creative resources that any real confrontation brings to light. *Gauchisme* is shown here as the intrinsically worthy reign of pure subjective possibility, as opposed to that of the tactical and overly procedural handling of the objective masses.

In the *gauchistes'* eyes, this opposition made it possible for a local struggle, even an isolated one, to serve as a useful example. Throughout Godard/Gorin's film, which does not embellish the situation, we feel the force, but also the anxiety, of that sort of lonely exemplarity. It must be said that these features are magnified owing to the fact that the political referent, which remains nameless (there is only an indiscriminate mention of "Maos"), was the Gauche prolétarienne organization, which, at the time and shortly before they self-dissolved, exaggerated the themes of violence, exemplarity, the cult of the present, and the imminent revolution in a particularly hyperbolic way. The result was an overly fraught vision of the overall situation, a terrible gap (which would later be responsible for many of that adventurist organization's leaders becoming renegades and aligning themselves with parliamentary "democracy") between what was said or announced and the overall situation of the country.

We will nevertheless see that Godard's artistic and "moral" aim is ultimately well served by this hyperbolic political context. It will in fact serve as a source of energy for him for the only thing that ultimately concerns him: changing people's consciousness.

That said, the film plays the same game as all the Maoist groups – the GP as well as the UCFML and VLR [*Vive la Révolution*] – that intervened actively (not in a merely institutional or routine way) in the factories: an outright hostility to unionism, to which they opposed the direct unity, evidenced politically in the developing situations, of the working-class masses (in actual fact: of a concrete avant-garde connected with the anonymous majority and filtered through the real episodes of the strike, the occupation, the sequestration, and so on).

– *II* –

On the wane

Tout va bien is an ambiguous title, a sort of declaration that is deliberately in excess not only of the situation in France in 1972 but of what the film shows of that situation. Informed readers know that this is the style of the Chinese revolutionaries, first during the "difficult" years of the Cultural Revolution (mainly between 1966 and 1968) but ultimately during the whole period of the influence of the "Gang of Four" (Jiang Qing, Yao Wenyuan, Wang Hongwen, and Zhang Chunqiao), between 1966 and 1976. Back then, when the risks were building up and the political problems were becoming intractable, it was customary to write long articles entitled "The situation is excellent." This can only be understood in the light of one of Mao's statements, "Unrest is an excellent thing," which is proof that the Gang of Four was really the Gang of Five.

In any case, Godard/Gorin are part of that culture when they cinematically proclaim, not without humor (but Mao's declarations were humorous, too), that "everything's all right."

It is important to remember the pivotal position of the year 1972, after all. Without the slightest doubt, it was the year that marked the beginning of the ebbing of the wave of mass revolts that the phrase "May '68" came to denote but that culminated, in terms of their political originality, sometime between 1969 and 1971. This was the case at least as regards the high school and university youth, the intellectuals and the connection they were trying to establish with the common people, because, as regards the workers, the new political movements could be discerned until much later (probably at least up until the big strike at the Sonacotra workers' hostels, between 1976 and 1979). Nevertheless, it is undeniable that, as regards the masses of young militants, a great *weariness* could be felt right from the beginning of 1972. Due to the realization that nothing essential had changed at the level of the country as a whole and that the hypothesis of "taking power," whatever the form, was quixotic, many groups began to break up or to consider disbanding. Meanwhile, an increasing number of young people – having become less young, it's true, over the course of five years of frenzied activism – slunk back to their studies and to the homes of their parents or spouses. Waiting in the wings was the Common Program between the Communists and the Socialists, Mitterrand's long march to power. In the early 1980s the vast majority of youthful rebels and Maoists from the 1968–72 period – often having become little old men hungry for whatever scraps of power they could lay their hands on – would align themselves with the official left, after many of them, around 1976–7, had been involved in the anti-Maoist, counterrevolutionary farce that was dubbed with the strange name of "the New Philosophy."

It took time for this sort of Restoration to become established, of course, but it is nevertheless certain that it began subjectively, as regards a great number of militants, in 1972.

This was also the year that the young Maoist Pierre Overney was killed by a security guard named Tramoni outside the Renault factory in Billancourt. The protest of mourning, which united all the different *gauchiste* factions, would result in the largest street demonstration of the whole period. But, as often happens, it was to be the last one on that scale, for its very size had exposed the political vacuum behind the united front it displayed. Returning to experimentation, to restricted action, to minority thinking, to organization divorced from any media hype, to the counter-current, would now be necessary – in short, returning to everything that was the cause of the general weariness. Only the most resilient people would emerge victorious from the ordeal, only those who were able to change their thinking in the mature continuation of their dissidence. A very small number.

Should we say that Godard/Gorin's film anticipates all this? It would be an exaggeration to claim that it explicitly includes such a prediction. But its ultimately melancholy tone shows that the question of the end of the beginning is an integral part of what it is about. There are three things that indicate this. First, the overall plot of the film is not driven by the meaning of the revolts or political conflicts. The main theme is in fact the fate of the couple comprised of a Frenchman (a filmmaker, played by Montand) and an American woman (a reporter, played by Jane Fonda). So it is a matter of the subjective effects of collective praxis (an indirect method) and not of the (directly assessed) future of that praxis. The real question is: What does this (historical) beginning, which is probably over, allow every-one to begin (psychologically) for their own sake? Second, the film provides many details that prove that the situation in the occupied factory is a limited, fragile, minority, isolated one, even if these fea-tures are part of its educational virtue (for Montand and Fonda, at any rate, who have never seen anything like it). Third, the value of the scenes of revolt and fighting is not related to any political *con-struction*, only to ideology (the rampant ideologism that was more-over characteristic of the era in general and of the Gauche prolétari-enne in particular). The film ends with the need to understand the fundamental historicity of all things, the divided nature of all that is, and therefore the practical possibilities of every experience, in par-ticular the experience of the couple. But in no way does it pronounce a verdict on the political future of revolts. That is why it is as much a film about the end as it is a film about the beginning. Pushing things a bit, we could say that it grafts the possibility of a personal (re) beginning onto a collective end. Whereby Godard – if not Gorin – goes back to being what he has always been: an existentialist.

– III –

Allegory

The film's formal organization is very abstract. It is structured com-pletely artificially on the basis of politically filtered real references, which are the canonical forms of *gauchisme* of the Maoist variety: the strike, complete with occupation and sequestration; the "political commando"-style interventions; the expression of grievances by the common people; and the savage caricature of enemies (management and the unions).

What I am struck by is the extent to which this film is inspired by Brecht's theater. It actually involves a series of extremely well-honed and distanciated didactic operations, seven of which I'll now mention:

(1)   The reduction of the factory to a sort of vertical cutaway and the supermarket to a horizontal cutaway where several actions can be perceived in both breadth (different rooms or floors are visible simultaneously in the cutaway) and depth (in the super-market, the check-out counters are in the foreground and the scuffle between the Maoists and the security guards goes on in the background). As in the theater, only a small number of actors and extras are used, on what is very obviously a film set,

even to represent the crowd, or "the masses." We could thus say that the style is a *figural minimalism*.

(2) Consequently, the collective situations are expressed by means of a few typical gestures: grouping together, running, fighting, waiting, and speaking. This set of stereotypical gestures often evokes, as with Brecht, the techniques of slapstick comedy.

(3) The film is punctuated by long monologues addressed to the camera, with the "speaker" usually remaining almost motionless and intently focused on what he or she is saying, which is preferably slow and shot through with silences. This technique, which was used by Godard right from his very first films (and was in some respects invented by him), formalizes the importance, for a Puritan like him, of introspection, of soul-searching. In *Tout va bien*, it naturally fulfills that function in Montand's and Fonda's speeches. (Montand is particularly delightful, stuck in his role as a petit-bourgeois media type, a fellow traveler of the PCF, who has been prodded by *gauchisme* into having a little more artistic ambition.) The technique meanwhile allows Godard to subvert the whole movie star system and take it down a peg or two. But its use is expanded to include the allegorical figures of the revolt scene: the boss, the union bigwig, the fierce young woman worker, the old worker who has rallied to the cause, and the Maoist *établi* (an intellectual working in the factory for political reasons) who, in keeping with the Gauche prolétarienne's instructions, doesn't reveal who he really is but "blends in with everyone else" (although the sly Godard/Gorin have him dressed differently from the other workers: he wears a suspicious sweater).

(4) Snippets of documentary footage, whether real or recreated (the memorial ceremony for Gilles Tautin in Flins, the various clashes with the CRS, the TV shows, and so forth) are inserted into the fictional story in order for a didactic interplay to be set up between partisan stylization and the complex magnitude of History.

(5) Like so many "signposts" that have descended onto the stage, allegorical exteriors designate the blurriness of the overall situation: big misty landscapes, long pans over brick factory walls, and so on.

(6) I've already mentioned the symbolism of individual colors: the red of revolt, the blue of the old world, the white of ambiguity. But, in addition, all of them together symbolize the colors of

France, this country that we are told right from the start is the setting for the film, a country filled with "farmers farming and workers working," a country in which "everything's all right," a phrase that is expressed with two different meanings. For the reactionaries, everything is calm, ultimately; everything is continuing in line with "advanced capitalism." For the revolutionaries, "everything's all right" in a more complex way: something new and fragile can be tried out.

(7) Since contradiction, or dialectics, constitutes the essence of everything, the film makes systematic use of major symmetries (the strike and work, the boss's office and sequestration, the factory and the filming of a Dim pantyhose commercial, and so on), with the understanding that the most vital, real contradiction for Godard/Gorin is the one having to do with the future of cinema, the fate of a filmmaker: either selling out (here symbolized by the yellow and blue prancing of the Dim dancers in their hiked-up skirts) or serving the people (telling the story of the strike). As we know, Godard would only escape from this "either/or" situation – still rudimentary in *Tout va bien* and the last incarnation of which is *Passion* (1982) – by gradually turning cinema in on itself, on a meditation on the powers and powerlessness of the image.

All these techniques serve to maintain the film in a sort of fruitful middle ground between the urgency of ideological conviction and the slowness of time, between the discontinuity of scenes and the continuity of problems, as though the film's didactic were conveying the message: "It is right to rebel. That is the principle of all creation. But, even so, let's not think that the world's inflexibility, to which the ruses of the mind have always adapted, will simply disappear."

– IV –

The new, on what conditions?

The film tells the story of a re-education, a theme that also comes from Maoism (the re-education of the intellectuals through their political relationship with the broad masses of workers and peasants). The re-education of a petit-bourgeois artist (Godard?) and of a young woman, who is moreover quicker than her partner is to take advantage of the opportunity offered by the revolts. The direct, militant form of this re-education is not adopted (neither of them become "Maos"), only its indirect form is: their creative life (cinema and investigative journalism), their love life (the couple, their habits, the dialectic between their private life and their action on the world) will – perhaps – be altered by the experience of the popular struggles that has been imposed on them.

So we might say that it is not *organizations* here that have the power to impose the new on subjects but *situations*. Situations teach what it means to really *say* something. To say the thing that matters. To have the courage to say. What the Maoists of the UCFML called, and what the militants of the Organisation Politique[2] still call, a declaration. Politics begins with a declaration and continues with the consequences of that declaration. Jane Fonda is really the heroine of Godard's film because it is she, not Montand, who understands that what the workers did during the occupation of the factory was absolutely new for *themselves*. And from this she draws the conclusion, itself a declarative one, that the new is possible in love, too.

The underlying issue is obviously that of a new cinema. Not just of a new (militant) use of cinema like that to which Godard dedicated himself between 1968 and 1972, but of a new fiction cinema, addressed to the widest possible audience and reviving (subverting?) what the credits of *Tout va bien* ironically, against a background of checks being signed with much fanfare, list as the indispensable ingredients for success: stars, technicians of all sorts, equipment, and, above all, a story, preferably a love story, a man, a woman . . .

Such is the burden of the beginning and the end. Under the conditions of the political revolts of the period that was beginning to end in 1972, what was beginning where cinema was concerned, what was ending? From cinema, from the money that necessarily circulates in it, from the ancient symbols of which it is woven, can I *in any case* make something new (as Malraux, in the exact opposite way, said that "*in any case, the cinema is an industry*")? If so, then everything's all right. If not, everything's all right, too. But in another sense.

The film sparks a debate about the different possible meanings of "everything's all right." The debate is by no means over. In our self-satisfied "democracies," is "everything all right"? And what about in cinema? Is everything all right? Everything's all right, thanks. Precisely to the extent that you are able to declare such a thing and assume the consequences when there's obviously no proof to support it.

Such, in its strange, timeless beauty, is the declaration of Godard's film. "Everything's all right" is a statement whose creative force can be gauged by the fact that, in real life, it seems clear that everything is going to hell in a handbasket. "Everything's all right" is the attitude of those who organize themselves freely and are answerable to no one but themselves.

L'Art du cinéma, Spring 2005

—30—

THE DIMENSIONS OF ART

Udi Aloni, *Forgiveness*

This film, like any other, presents visible two-dimensional images and successions of sounds: voices, musics, and noises. That is the obvious material of which it is composed.

I would nevertheless like to examine a somewhat different idea, namely that this film is a four-dimensional universe. As a sensory object, as you see and hear it, the film has three dimensions, two in the visible world and one in the audible. But to the extent that it constructs an artistic idea, to the extent that it is capable of transforming its spectator, or viewer, or of changing our thinking – yours or mine – it actually has four dimensions.

I call these four dimensions the historical dimension, the narrative dimension, the psychoanalytic dimension, and the cultural dimension. The aim of the film, as artistic work, is to make these four dimensions hold together. The artistic dimension is thus like a fifth dimension, achieved through the knotting together of the other four.

I will now analyze these four dimensions one by one.

The historical dimension in *Forgiveness* is obviously a meditation on Israel and Palestine. Udi Aloni's basic idea is that "Palestine" is the name of what prevents Israel, as it is, from being able to embody Jewish universality in the eyes of the world. But his idea is also that "Israel," considered as a hateful word of separation, or as the object of senseless violence, is what prevents Palestine from being able to embody Arab universality in the eyes of the world. Udi Aloni doesn't inscribe his films in a prefabricated, abstract vision of the division or conflict between Israelis and Palestinians. The issue of war or of the division of the territories is not a problem of primary concern to him, because my friend Udi thinks that Palestine and the Palestinians are part of Israel's very essence. The powerful image conveying this

252

notion is that dead Palestinians, their things, their vestiges, make up the substratum of the mental hospital that was built on the ruins of a village destroyed during the 1947 war. What this means is that, right from the start, what has been disturbing and perturbing Israel like a ghost, like a thought, is precisely the fact that the subterranean, fundamental presence of the absolute wrong done to the Palestinians cannot be uprooted from Israel's existence. So it is impossible to think Israel's future, any more than Palestine's, incidentally, in terms of separation, entrenchment, walls. Quite on the contrary, the final scene of the film, which involves the curing of the spiritual malady that Israel, as it is, introduces into Jewish identity, is a scene of descent into the underground world, a scene of purification through the confession of origins, a scene in which another history can begin, because there is no longer any need for separation and war. It was said, declared, that the eternal land could be shared, had to be shared right from the start, and so there was no reasonable reason for the bond of everyday life capable of uniting Palestinians and Israelis to be endlessly cut.

I want to stress the following point: what the film tells us, its own particular Idea, is in no way a political thesis in the current sense of the term. The truth is inscribed in art here. It is an effect of art. In the same shots, the film shows what is, what might have been, and what must come to be. What is: separation, war, obstruction, and violence. What might have been: a shared love for the place as a powerful new universality, combining heterogeneous elements in a music without precedent. (Music and dance in Udi Aloni's films express, from within what is, that which testifies to what might have been.) And, finally, what must be: a new declaration that would allow for a new beginning, which the film's title, *Forgiveness*, encapsulates. Once expressed in the movement of what exists, the original sin loses its age-old power. The separation created by deceit no longer needs to be repeated. Once their effects are combined, in an undivided land, Jewish and Arab universality will have the soothing, creative effect in the world of what Mao called "a spiritual atomic bomb."

Let's turn to the narrative dimension now. The film does indeed tell a story, that of a young Jew, the son of a German Jew living in the United States. Outraged by his father's stony silence, he enlists in the Israeli army in order to finally confront real enemies, not just historical phantoms, head on. He will kill the child of a woman he loves. He will go insane and become catatonic, a virtual criminal, or suicidal, in the form of the potential repetition of his act upon the child of another woman he loves. The women, always, come from somewhere else, from the other visible world, from the Arab world. The film reveals the terrifying logic of the repetition of what has not been expressed. But it also rejects that logic, by engaging the process that I already mentioned of purification through an acknowledgment of origins. The story lets in ordinary materials, in their ordinary order: revolt, violence, and war; love, crime, and madness; the temptation of suicide and ultimate salvation. We have everything we need here for a melodrama. And, in fact, we do have such a melodrama. However, this second dimension, this melodrama, carries the first dimension with it, since each of its terms is also a term of one of the stages of the subject's (the young hero's) inscription within the historical problem in which he is at once situated and transformed. In this way, Udi Aloni connects back up with the old tradition of the *bildungsroman*. And, as usual in that type of novel, individual decisions are also symbols of historical and political choices. Such is the case with the two possible endings that the film so masterfully presents. Either the young man, a symbol of Israel, agrees to remember that he was a murderer, in which case the peace of reconciliation is possible, or else he shuts himself up in silence, forgetting, and repetition, and in that case he will commit suicide, which also means: for Israel, continuing to pursue its current policy represents a real death threat, a historical suicide.

The third dimension, the psychoanalytic one, casts the connection between the first two dimensions in metaphor. Just as the historical substratum of the Jewish spiritual malady is the buried Palestine, the secret of the son's insanity lies in the father's obscurities. One of the main themes of the film is that the contemporary problem no doubt lies in sons' acknowledgment of their fathers, but even more so in fathers' acknowledgment of their sons.

In this respect, the film's defining scene may be the confrontation between the hero's two possible fathers, both of whom are survivors of deportation and extermination, as the tattooed numbers on their arms prove. On the one hand, there is the real father, the German musician, in America, who wants to forget the historical fate of the Jews. And, on the other hand, there is the true father, the old lunatic of the asylum, the guardian of the bowels of the earth ("Well burrowed, old mole!" says this Marxist-turned-prophet), who knows that denying the existence of the dead Palestinians also prevents there being any active, peace-bringing memory of the camps and extermination. Having to choose to obey one or the other of these fathers leads to the son's all-important decision, a decision that also means: continuing on the path of separation, of war, of the wrong done to the Palestinians is tantamount to grimly ensuring that the millions of Jewish dead really and forever died for no reason, whatever the monuments dedicated to them. In reality, the only thing that can be dedicated to these dead is the living monument of a reconciled Palestine.

Udi Aloni does not shy away from allusive complexity. That is the difficult charm of his works. Here, we have both Oedipus, who must kill his father to fulfill his destiny, and Freud, with his famous dream of the son burning right before the helpless eyes of the father, who is incapable of really understanding what the son means when he says: "Father, can't you see that I am burning?" And isn't it true that all over the world today our sons are burning right before our eyes, in general incomprehension? But we also have Oedipus at Colonus, whom the dead Palestinian girl, a new Antigone, both haunts, as an embodiment of his crime, and gently leads toward purification at the end. However, the film is also an altogether contemporary defense of the subjective processes of psychoanalysis against the objective, memory-less doctrine of chemical therapy. To cure the young soldier, the old Jewish doctor, played with astonishing naturalness by a great Palestinian actor, opposes, as best he can, his desire to understand and be close to the patient to the official regulations mandating a big syringe of total-forgetfulness serum. He gives in from weakness, on account of a power struggle with the state (a power struggle symbolized here by a trivial sex scene with a female staff member). There is an obvious connection here with the first dimension of the film: in this blood-soaked land, forgetting the original wrong, using chemicals against thought, amounts to paving the way for the endless repetition of separationist violence. What will impel fate toward salvation is neither the father's new-found love for his son nor the doctor's inadequate sympathy, but the voice of the unconscious itself, both individual and historical, the voice of the lunatic, or of the prophet, who knows that you have to go down beneath the hospital, into the depths of the earth, to put an end to the fatal destiny of separation and restore the chance for love.

The fourth dimension, which I call "cultural," is immediately more polyphonic. It involves filling the story with artistic or cultural implants of sorts from at least four different worlds, and in this way making us see or hear that the way to salvation is through this multiplicity itself, as a figure of both the place and the world, and not at all through warmongering talk about the clash of civilizations. It is not a matter of some bland principle of tolerance or respect for differences. It is a matter of expressly asserting that contemporary universality is no longer the province of any one particular tradition. Rather, it is like a braid with knots of varying tightness. And it is precisely because Israel and Palestine are the names of an exemplary knot, in which different traditions can all be involved together, that it is there that a wholly new universal homeland can and must come into being.

The four cultural worlds referred to in Udi's film are: the old world of European artistic creativity; the Arab world's subtle, quasi-timeless civility and love of life; American modernity; and irreplaceable Jewish spirituality. Some extraordinary scenes show the interpenetration, the collision, the simultaneous birth of these worlds that have all been swept up in the Israeli-Palestinian maelstrom. Among these scenes are, for example, the Palestinian woman's song, which stops and enthralls the dancers at an Israeli nightclub, or the soldiers dancing in the synagogue, as if they, the boorish oppressors, were all drunk with love for the whole world. Let me also mention the scene that really gets to me, the one in which the hero, accompanying himself at the piano, sings a Schumann *lied* about the idea of forgiveness in love as tears stream down his face. Because, at this juncture, the essential questions of the film – the father, Germany, the extermination of the Jews, Israel, Palestine, the universality of art and the difficulty of love – all merge together in a whole so complex that a lone, defenseless subject can't endure it without going to pieces.

You can see how intricate Udi Aloni's film is, how each of the elements of its construction is grafted onto others in such a way that the fictional story is at one and the same time an artistic allegory, a psychoanalytic interrogation, a historical meditation, and a spiritual proposition. And that the emotional elements nevertheless circulate freely, since each of the viewers, rather than separating out the ingredients of the film's composition as I have done here, is expected to feel the impact of a situation that is depicted by a film, by a gripping melodrama, and that is thus subject to both the sharing and the indivisibility of something self-evident.

I would like to conclude by saying, in addition, that this film is essentially optimistic. However repetitive and desperate a situation may be, there exists within it, within its own entanglement, the possibility of a glimmer of hope. It is this conviction that the film conveys. In this sense, it is an instance of what I have called, in the hopes of making it a watchword, if possible, for the art of the future, affirmationism, namely the doctrine that the ideas generated by art make a judgment about the world only to the extent that they indicate the point from which the world can be transfigured. The filmic figures of Israel and Palestine that Udi offers are affirmationist in that sense. They indicate the point at which separation can be overcome; they announce the power of Palestisrael, or of Israpalestine, as a transfiguration immanent to the disaster itself.

Thank you, dear Udi.

Unpublished text, 2006

—31—

THE PERFECTION OF THE WORLD, IMPROBABLE YET POSSIBLE

Clint Eastwood, *A Perfect World*

"A perfect world"? What does that mean? We know right off the bat that the film's title is ironic. No, the world that Clint Eastwood presents us with, full of sound and fury, ending with a death whose injustice horrifies us, is certainly not a world in the image of its Creator's supposed perfection. And yet, inasmuch as we are tipped off right from the title that the theme of perfection is lurking in it, if only in its negative guise, the film's secret lesson must be about what perfection in this world might be.

The plot is basically very simple and the formal structure a conventional one (the "road movie"). A man escapes from prison. On the run from the authorities, he takes a child hostage. The subject matter of the film is the twists and turns of the manhunt. We learn that the fugitive (Kevin Costner) is both sensitive and capable of terrible violence. We learn that the police, rattling around in a trailer, are a motley bunch. In contrast to the typical cop, who finally shoots the escaped convict under a tree out in the middle of the countryside, there are the brusque, thoughtful cop – the melancholy Eastwood – who gradually comes to gain a subtle understanding of the man he is hunting down, and the well-educated yet naïve female psychological profiler, whose presence is required in the situation by the fate of the child hostage.

What is the world's imperfection in all of this? It is, first of all, the fact that every judgment covers over, cancels out a more essential judgment, so that truth remains impotent. Thus, the fugitive, regarded on all sides as a potential child killer (justifiably, as we are shown, since it is clear that he is capable of being a murderer), has not only saved this child's life and is enraged by anyone who disrespects or mistreats him (because he, the criminal, was once a threatened or neglected child himself) but, as time goes on, has become something

258

like the child's adoptive father over the course of their forced companionship. Similarly, his predetermined death at the hands of the
pack of cops, with all the crude certainty of societal imperatives, is
filmed – from a distance, in the peace of the world, near a tree that
looks as if it could have been the one under which Saint Louis rendered justice – as the true horrifying murder for which the world
could never provide the slightest justification, thus abdicating any
perfection it may be assumed to have.

But the imperfection lies also and above all in the fact that those
who, right from within their difference, turn out to be the potential
components of a world finally restored to its perfection are separated,
split up. In this regard, there is a sort of symmetry between the forced-
together, "illegal" couple made up of the escapee and the child, on
the one hand, and, on the other, the bureaucratically forced-together
couple made up of the old cynical yet sensitive male cop and the
young, fresh-out-of-school female psychologist. In defiance of everything required by appearances, these "couples," mere products of
chance, create a sort of completely new kind of love. That love,
according to Eastwood and as we see in practically all of his films,
is the only thing that can provide the world with a bit of truth. And
the radical imperfection of the world as it is consists in preventing,
insidiously and, when necessary, with violence, these true loves from
becoming publicly the truth that they are.

With the deceptive simplicity of a story that rambles through sleepy
backwater towns, the film tells us that if the world were perfect our
motto would have to be: "Birds not of a feather flock together wonderfully." The imperfect world is the world that disassembles unlikely
assemblages whose truth is nevertheless glaring. The child everyone
wants to save has actually found his potential savior in the violent
escaped convict who will be shot down out in the middle of the
countryside. The temperamental incompatibility between the old
cop's pragmatism and the psychologist's "politically correct"-type
sophistication is in fact what enables them to agree, on a deep level,
about what saving the child means "in truth."

But we have seen all this before in Eastwood's work. The "impossible" love between the old man and the young girl, so that life might
be perfect. The relationship woven between the black drag queen and
the Southern gentleman, so that Savannah might bring its latent perfection to life. The real shock experienced by the blasé, secretive film
director and the black elephant-loving guide in Africa, which would
allow Africa to be something other than colonial. The improbable
adultery, among the bridges of Madison County, which will be the

perfect secret of an ordinary life. Mandela's inflexible will to bridge the gap between Whites and Blacks through rugby, so that a country might exist in the perfection of its differences . . . But, every time, imperfection returns, or threatens to do so.

If the scene of the convict's killing by the cops is so terrible, if it is almost unbearable in its criminal tenderness and fatality, it is because something irremediable happens to the world as a result of this murder: the massacre of a local possibility of perfection, which all the vicissitudes of the construction of the relationship between the escapee and the child had foregrounded, like the flip side of the dark, hopeless order represented by the pursuers and their law-and-order backers.

This is what Eastwood's films are basically all about, with a sort of neo-classical light that serves to illuminate today's problems: the ruthless struggle – often, but not always, a losing one – for those, full of true love, who are separated by the order of an imperfect world, to be finally connected. Yes, as usual, but here in a very obvious way, art, as Conrad says, has no purpose other than to "introduce a little justice into the visible universe." That is truly what Eastwood's own kind of perfection – the sort of integrity that does not allow itself any risky formal inventiveness, that calmly and consistently uses the resources at its disposal – wants to convey to us, namely that life-saving encounters do happen in the world, that they are always unlikely and endangered, and that our only duty is to protect their future as best we can. Because then, at least, we would know what "a perfect world" might be.

L'Art du cinéma, Spring–Summer 2010

NOTES

1 July 7, 2010.
2 As the founder of the Cinémathèque française, Henri Langlois (1914–77) was singlehandedly responsible for preserving thousands of films. A whole generation of cinephiles, many of whom would later become directors, attended the daily screenings and in this way owed their education to Langlois. – *trans.*

1 Émile Chartier (1868–1951), commonly known as Alain, was an influential French philosopher who taught in secondary schools and contributed numerous short essays to newspapers over the course of his career. This quotation comes from his article "La musique mécanique" (June 3, 1923), collected in *Préliminaires à l'esthétique* (1939). – *trans.*
2 That is why the naïve expression "the film is as good as the novel" should be defended. Its artlessness encapsulates the problem as well as the choice we have to make.
3 A French filmmaker (in the years 1914 to 1920) who mainly transposed boulevard comedies to the screen.
4 A French filmmaker (d. 1952) who had the dubious honor of making the first in the long series of *Count of Monte Cristo* films.
5 An example of this is the scene in Alexandre Astruc's *Les Mauvaises Rencontres* (*Bad Liaisons*) where Jean-Claude Pascal picks Anouk Aimée up in his arms and carries her into the bedroom.

261

NOTES TO PP. 22–25

6 The last three films of each of these directors were, respectively, *Le Rouge et le Noir* (*The Red and the Black*), *Marguerite de la nuit* (*Marguerite of the Night*), and *La Traversée de Paris* (*Four Bags Full*); *Le Salaire de la peur* (*The Wages of Fear*), *Les Diaboliques* (*Diabolique*), and *Le Mystère Picasso* (*The Mystery of Picasso*); *Jeux Interdits* (*Forbidden Games*), *Monsieur Ripois* (*Knave of Hearts*/US title *Lovers, Happy Lovers!*), and *Gervaise*.

7 A theoretician and director whose principle was "to attain psychological precision" and whose techniques were technical innovation and the "monologue."

8 A proponent of intellectual cinema, featuring a complicated, outmoded style. His one "great work," *El Dorado* (*Eldorado*), has become unwatchable.

9 A very original film made by the Austrian director Friedrich Feher. There is an excellent analysis of this little-known work in Claude Mauriac's *L'Amour du cinéma*, published by Albin Michel.

10 A French poet and dramatist (1868–1918) best known for his play *Cyrano de Bergerac*. – *trans.*

11 A Canadian novelist and playwright (1879–1961) whose series of sentimental novels were best-sellers. – *trans.*

12 A terrible film by Léo Joannon, starring Pierre Fresnay.

13 René Clair's latest film (1955).

14 By borrowing a certain number of ideas from *À nous la liberté* (*Freedom for Us*) to make *Modern Times*, Chaplin testified to his admiration for René Clair much more surely even than Renoir did his for Stroheim when he said he had seen *Foolish Wives* ten times before he made *Nana*.

15 Between 1919 and 1928 Erich Von Stroheim gave the cinema several of his masterpieces: *Foolish Wives* (1921), *Greed* (1924), *The Wedding March* (1928), and the never-completed *Queen Kelly* (1928). His directorial career was destroyed by the Hollywood production system.

16 Abel Gance, another director destroyed by the production system, gave us, among others, *La Roue* (*The Wheel*, 1923) and the tremendous *Napoleon* (1927).

17 A minor film by Jean Vigo (1930).

18 A young Spanish director whose three films, *Muerte de un ciclista* (*Death of a Cyclist*), *Cómicos* (*Comedians*), and *Calle Mayor*, admittedly contrast with Spanish cinema's current lackluster state.

19 A new trend in American animation that replaces Walt Disney's insipid imagery with "two-dimensional" forms borrowed from caricature.

20 Badiou is referring to Gaston Bachelard's book *Water and Dreams* (1942). – *trans.*

3 REVISIONIST CINEMA

1 In no particular order: *The Night Porter, Lacombe Lucien, Le Chagrin et la pitié* (*The Sorrow and The Pity*), *Français, si vous saviez* (*French People, If You Only Knew*) . . .

2 The pernicious, vile *Barry Lyndon.*

3 The coalition, originally agreed upon in 1972, between the French Communist Party and the Socialist Party. – *trans.*

4 They will be put into practice, and corrected, in the future, by examining specific works, by political intervention, by struggle. I am just setting out a few principles here, which are the result of a preliminary assessment.

5 An annual open-air festival organized by the PCF's newspaper, *L'Humanité.* – *trans.*

6 In fact, like all bourgeois, the revisionists are based on the political division of the people. At the heart of this arrangement is the labor union dictatorship of the worker aristocracy over the productive masses of semi-skilled workers, youth, immigrants, and women.

4 ART AND ITS CRITICISM

1 It will be objected: that doesn't work where music is concerned. Be patient, though! I have a few ideas about progressivism in music, although they are still too sketchy. I will nevertheless venture the following remark. Notwithstanding the apparent primacy of formal questions, the principles of progressivism in music are no different. The difficulty lies in the fact that the subject of a musical work entertains a relationship of proximity with form that is without parallel, even in painting. This was something that had already been seen by Plato, who classified musical modes according to ethical criteria, exactly like Jdanov, who said that serial music was hysterical. But this is not an insurmountable obstacle, as far as I am concerned.

6 A MAN WHO NEVER GIVES IN

1 Cited from the text of *In girum imus nocte et consumimur igni*. [For some of the citations from Debord's text below I have used, with modifications, the English translation by Ken Knabb (http://www.bopsecrets.org/SI/debord.films/ingirum.htm) – *trans.*]
2 Ibid.
3 Cited from another of Debord's films: *Refutation of All the Judgements, Pro or Con, Thus Far Rendered on the Film* The Society of the Spectacle.

7 IS THE ORIENT AN OBJECT FOR THE WESTERN CONSCIENCE?

1 While the film was released in the US as *Circle of Deceit*, its title has also been translated more literally as *False Witness*. – *trans.*

8 REFERENCE POINTS FOR CINEMA'S SECOND MODERNITY

1 Co-authored with Philippe Noyel.
2 Badiou's first play, a *romanopéra*, published in 1979 and staged in 1984 by Antoine Vitez, with music by Georges Aperghis. – *trans.*
3 Richard Dindo, a Swiss documentary director, whose film *Max Frisch, Journal I-III* (1981) Badiou mentions below. – *trans.*

9 THE DEMY AFFAIR

1 Although Demy's film, a sort of "popular opera," was unanimously acclaimed by the critics, it was a box office flop. The same week it came out, in October 1982, another film, Gérard Oury's *L'As des as* (*Ace of Aces*), starring Jean-Paul Belmondo, became an instant hit, going on to become the second highest grossing film of the year in France. A spirited polemic arose around *Une Chambre en ville* as critics, reacting to the extensive advertising campaign for *L'As des as*, published articles and petitions in support of Demy's film in *Libération*, *Le Monde*, *Télérama*, etc. and called on the public to boycott *L'As des as*. – *trans.*

2   May 10 was the day the Socialist candidate François Mitterrand won the presidential election in 1981. – *trans.*

3   The French Section of the Workers International. – *trans.*

4   Small and medium-sized enterprises and industries. – *trans.*

5   General Confederation of Labor, the largest of the five national confederations of trade unions and, at the time of this article's writing, closely linked with the French Communist Party. – *trans.*

6   Pascal Bonitzer, an actor and screenwriter turned director, also wrote several books on cinema, including *Le Regard et la Voix* (1976). – *trans.*

11   INTERRUPTED NOTES ON THE FRENCH COMEDY FILM

1   In French farce, "*Ciel! Mon mari!*" is the typical outcry of the unfaithful wife in bed with her lover when her husband returns home unexpectedly. – *trans.*

2   A prolific author, Eugène Marin Labiche (1815–88) transformed French comic vaudeville into the bourgeois farce, a genre in which he was matched only by Feydeau. One of his most popular plays, *Un Chapeau de paille d'Italie* (*The Italian Straw Hat*, 1851), was adapted into a film by René Clair in 1928. – *trans.*

3   "Enlisted soldier," i.e., "barracks humor" films, of which, at the time of the writing of this article, at least nine had appeared, with such titles as: *Les Bidasses en folie* (*Rookies Run Amok*), *Les Bidasses s'en vont en guerre* (*Sadsacks Go To War*), *Arrête ton char . . . bidasse!* (*Gimme a Break, Rookie!*), etc. – *trans.*

4   Author (1858–1929) of numerous comical and satiric novels, sketches, and plays in which bourgeois attitudes and institutions are skewered. *Fun in Barracks* is the English title of the 1932 film adapted by Maurice Tourneur from *Les Gaîtés de l'escadron*. – *trans.*

5   Written by Louis Pergaud and published in 1912. – *trans.*

6   This phrase, no doubt alluding here to Fernandel's horse-like teeth, is from French poet Saint-John Perse's *Exile* (*Saint-John Perse, Collected Poems*. Trans. Denis Devlin. Princeton: Princeton University Press, 1971, p. 149) – *trans.*

7   The gentleman thief Arsène Lupin first appeared in what was to become a series of crime fiction novels written first by Maurice Leblanc and later by the mystery-writing team of Boileau-Narcejac. – *trans.*

8   In the 1970s, Gérard Jugnot was one of the founders of the comedy troupe Le Splendid (see below), which adapted a number of its hits for the cinema. Well known in France for the roles he played in *Les Bronzés* (*French Fried Vacation*, 1978), *Les Bronzés font du ski* (*French Fried Vacation 2*, 1979), and *Le Père Noël est une ordure* (*Santa Claus Is A Stinker*, 1982), he eventually achieved international fame in the role of the music teacher in *Les Choristes* (*The Chorus*) (2004). – *trans.*

9   These were comedy troupes founded by a collection of writers and actors in the 1970s who went on to become some of the most significant actors and directors in French cinema from the 1980s on. – *trans.*

10 Bazaine and Trochu were generals responsible for France's defeat in the Franco-Prussian War of 1870–1. In World War II General Weygand surrendered to and collaborated with the Germans as part of the Vichy regime, headed by Marshal Pétain. – *trans.*

12   *Y A TELLEMENT DE PAYS POUR ALLER*

1   Text co-authored with Natacha Michel.

2   The eponymous, Chaplinesque hero of Jacques Tourneur's 1933 film starring Albert Préjean. – *trans.*

3   This is a play on words involving the river mouths in the South of France (*les bouches du Sud*) and the "mouths from the South" – i.e., the way of speaking of the characters who come from the south, from Tunisia. – *trans.*

4   La Goulette is the port of Tunis. – *trans.*

5   André Schwartz-Bart's prize-winning novel about the Holocaust, *Le Dernier des Justes* (*The Last of the Just*), was published in 1959. – *trans.*

6   Traditional Tunisian dress, a wide coat covering the whole body. – *trans.*

7   Triangular-shaped pastry traditionally stuffed with tuna, herbs, and an egg and fried in oil. – *trans.*

8   Tunisian fig brandy. – *trans.*

13   RESTORING MEANING TO DEATH AND CHANCE

1   Paul Nizan (1905–40), a close friend of Jean-Paul Sartre, was the author of three novels, *Antoine Bloye*, *Le Cheval de Troie*,

and *La Conspiration*, and several essays, which reflected his Communist political convictions. – *trans*.

14 A PRIVATE INDUSTRY, CINEMA IS ALSO A PRIVATE SPECTACLE

1 A film directed by Louis Malle (1974).
2 *Il Portiere di Notte* (1974), a film by Italian director Liliana Cavani.

18 "THINKING THE EMERGENCE OF THE EVENT"

1 Interview with Emmanuel Burdeau and François Ramone.
2 On August 23, 1996 the French riot police raided the Saint-Bernard-de-la-Chapelle Church in Paris, which had been occupied since June by several hundred *sans papiers* (undocumented workers), arresting and evicting them. Some were eventually deported. Thousands of Parisians later marched to protest the brutality of the police. The Saint-Bernard occupation became a *cause célèbre*, with commemorative marches for many years thereafter. – *trans*.
3 See n. 6 in ch. 9, this volume.
4 Before making *Du Jour au lendemain* (1997), which was based on an opera by Arnold Schoenberg, Straub and Huillet had directed two other films also dealing with Schoenberg's works: *Introduction to Arnold Schoenberg's Accompaniment to a Cinematic Scene* (1973) and *Moses and Aaron* (1975). – *trans*.

20 SURPLUS SEEING

1 The nineteenth-century French historian Jules Michelet claimed that history was "a complete resurrection of the past." – *trans*.
2 In French, the adjective "*nouvelle*" can be placed before or after the noun "*vague*." Thus, "*la Nouvelle Vague*," or "New Wave," refers to the renowned film movement of the late 1950s–early 1960s, while "*une vague nouvelle*" can mean "a new (or different) wave."– *trans*.
3 The play on words here is based on the homophony between "*m'abuse*" in "*Si je ne m'abuse*" ("*If I'm not mistaken*") and

Mabuse, the surname of the doctor protagonist in three films by Fritz Lang. – *trans.*

4 *La Monnaie de l'absolu* (*The Coin of the Absolute*), published in 1949, was the third volume of Malraux's art history series *La Psychologie de l'art*, later expanded and issued as *Les Voix du silence* (*The Voices of Silence*). – *trans.*

5 See n.1 in ch. 2, this volume.

6 The French – "*il ne faut pas faire tant d'histoire(s)*" – plays on the expression "*faire des histoires*," "to make a fuss or a big deal about," by simultaneously alluding to the "*histoire(s)*" of the film's title. – *trans.*

21 CONSIDERATIONS ON THE CURRENT STATE OF CINEMA AND ON THE WAYS OF THINKING THIS STATE WITHOUT HAVING TO CONCLUDE THAT CINEMA IS DEAD OR DYING

1 L'Organisation Politique is the activist group of which Badiou was a founding member. – *trans.*

22 THE CINEMATIC CAPTURE OF THE SEXES

1 Diafoirus and Trissotin are two ridiculous pedants in Molière's *Le Malade imaginaire* and *Les Femmes savantes*, respectively. – *trans.*

25 "SAY YES TO LOVE, OR ELSE BE LONELY"

1 Alain Badiou interviewed by Élisabeth Boyer, Daniel Fischer, Slim Ben Cheikh, Denis Lévy, Annick Fiolet, Emmanuel Dreux, and Anaïs Le Gaufey on June 5, 2002.

2 The French word for "threads," "*fils*," is written in the same way as the word for "son" or "sons," and Badiou is playing on the homology here. – *trans.*

3 Alain Badiou, "Esquisse pour un premier manifeste de l'affirmationisme," *Utopia 3, La question de l'art au IIIème millénaire* (Actes du colloque international Université Paris-VIII-Université de Venise, Éditions Ciro Giordano Bruno), GERMS [Groupe d'Étude et de recherche des médias symboliques] 2002.

26 DIALECTICS OF THE FABLE

1 This text derives from a paper delivered in March 2000 in the context of a day-long workshop on "Cinema and Philosophy," organized by the Philosophy master's program at the Université de Paris-VIII.
2 Arles: *Actes Sud*, 1988.

27 CINEMA AS PHILOSOPHICAL EXPERIMENTATION

1 In English in the text.
2 In fact, the slightly different quotation is from the Preface to *Cinema 1: The Movement-Image*. Trans. Hugh Tomlinson and Barbara Habberjam. (Minneapolis: University of Minnesota Press, 1986), p. xiv.
3 "Esquisse d'une psychologie du cinéma," *Verve*, vol. II, no. 8 (1940), p. 33.

29 THE END OF A BEGINNING

1 Text of a lecture delivered in Nantes on February 14, 2003 at the invitation of the Association La vie est à nous, as part of the "*Jean-Luc Godard: années politiques*" retrospective.
2 A "post-party" militant organization founded by Alain Badiou, Natacha Michel, and Sylvain Lazarus. From 1985 to 2007 it dealt with housing, immigration, and labor issues, among others, and was particularly active in support of undocumented migrant workers (*sans papiers*). – *trans.*